CULPEPER COUNTY

VIRGINIA

Will Books B and C
Court Suits
Loose Papers
Inscriptions

Compiled and Published
by
Dorothy Ford Wulfeck

1965

This volume was reproduced from
An 1965 edition located in the
Publisher's private library,
Greenville, South Carolina

All rights reserved. No part of this publication
may be reproduced, stored in a retrieval system,
transmitted in any form, posted on to the web
in any form or by any means without the
prior written permission of the publisher.

Please direct all correspondence and orders to:

www.southernhistoricalpress.com
or
SOUTHERN HISTORICAL PRESS, Inc.
PO BOX 1267
375 West Broad Street
Greenville, SC   29601
southernhistoricalpress@gmail.com

Originally published: Naugatuck, CT. 1965
Reprinted by:
Southern Historical Press, Inc.
Greenville, SC
ISBN #0-89308-791-2
All rights Reserved.
Printed in the United States of America

CONTENTS

Will Book B (1770-1783)	1
Will Book C (1783-1791)	47
Will Book G (1813-1817) Index	85
Old Miscellaneous Papers	
Package No. 1	90
Package No. 2	97
Package No. 3	105
Package No. 4	110
Package No. 5	110
Package No. 6	113
Package 1880-1900	114
Court Suits	116
Tombstone Inscriptions	136
Index	157

CULPEPER COUNTY, VIRGINIA

Will Book B (1770-1783)

IN MEMORIAM

HELEN STEWART LEWIS

A Descendant of the Kay, Waggoner and Garnett
Families of Culpeper County, Virginia

Restored by her Daughter
Mrs. Samuel W. (Ida Lewis) Pinkerton
St. Paul, Minnesota
1940

Will of John Floyd of St. Mark's Parish of Culpeper Co., being aged and in very sick and low condition of Health.
Dated 21 March, 1770. Proven 18 July, 1770.
I lend to my beloved wife, Jane Floyd, my land whereon I now live and all my personal estate. After decease of my said wife land to be held by Nathaniel Pendleton until my son or heir-at-law do appear and legally claim the same.
Executrix: Wife.
Wit.: Philip Clayton, N. Pendleton, Thomas Morris.
Inventory taken 18 July, 1770 and returned by Jane Floyd, Extrx.

Will of Joseph Belfield of Culpeper Co.
Dated 9 Aug., 176_. Proven 1 July, 1770.
Legatees: Brother William Glass and nephew Belfield Cave, slaves divided equally with survivor to have all. If both die, then to brother-in-law Benjamin Cave and sister Elizabeth Cave.
Also mentioned cash, furniture, etc., in same manner.
Executor: Brother-in-law Benjamin Cave.
Wit.: Lucy (L) Sharman, Ann Sharman, Robt. Sharman.

Inventory of Estate of William Bledsoe, dec'd., by his admr. (not named). Appraisers: William (X) Clark, William (X) Sparks, Thomas Piner. 17 May, 1770.

Inventory of Estate of Adam Bumgardner, dec'd. Appraisers: Robt. Terrell, Joh_ ____. 7 ____, 1770.

Will of William Child of Culpeper Co.
Dated 24 June, 1769. Proven 15 Oct., 1770.
Legatees: Wife Miner, during her widowhood. Sons: William Child, James Child. Daus.: Ann, Elizabeth, Isable. "My five children."
Executors: David Partlow, William ____ and wife.
Wit.: James Crass, Joshua Hinnins, Frankay (X) Jennens.

Will of Courtney Norman of Brumphill Parish, Culpeper Co.
Dated 14 March, 1770. Proven 20 Aug., 1770.
Legatees: Wife Mary Norman. Sons: John Norman, Courtney Norman,

Reuben Norman, Benjamin Norman, Ezckiel Norman, William Norman. Dau. Amey Murphey. "rest of estate equally amongst five youngest children."
    Executors: Thomas Jorden, Sebasten Hatter(?), Edwin Hickman.
    Wit.: Edwin Hickman, James Hickman, Joseph Boggess.

Account of Betty Rogers by her guardian, William Rogers. Recorded 20 Aug., 1770.

Account of Martha Sims, guardian of the orphans of William Sims, dec'd. 20 Aug., 1770.

Will of Thomas Curtis.
Dated 31 July, 1770. Proven 20 Aug., 1770.
Includes list of debts and amounts due him for "schooling" children.
Legatee: Mrs. Sarah Hughes.
Wit.: John Lowen, Mary Rosekranse. Some additions witnessed by N. Pendleton and John Butler.

Estate sett. Robert Tureman, dec'd. 19 April, 1770.
List of debts paid. Estate legacies to George Tureman, Robert Tureman.
Credits 306℔ 3s 3½d 1766-1770 from renting out slaves.
Signed: Joseph Wood, Thomas Scott, Robert Throckmorton.

Acct. of est. of Kalem Price, dec'd., made by Alexander Burk. 15 Oct., 1770.

Will of William Green of St. Mark's Parish, Culpeper Co.
Dated 24 Aug., 1763. Proven 15 Oct., 1770.
His ancestors had entailed a great part of his estate.
Legatees: Wife, 6000℔ annually and other items. Sons: William Green, a minor, legacy and pay 300℔ to each of other children when arrives at age 21. Entailed by uncle, William Duff, so that if son William died without leaving a male issue lawfully begotten, property descends to brother, Duff Green. Dau. to be educated. Sister-in-law, Miss Elizabeth Coleman, a mourning ring.
    Executors: Bros. Robert Green, Duff Green and John Green.
    Wit.: Mary Wood, Elizabeth Wood, William Lightfoot, William Field, Thomas Triplett, George Slaughter.

Will of Richard Pollard of St. Mark's Parish, Culpeper Co.
Dated 11 Oct., 1769. Proven 19 Nov., 1770.
Legatees: Wife Elizabeth. Sons: Richard Coleman Pollard, Robert Pollard. Daus.: Elizabeth Pollard, Sarah Pollard, Milley Pollard.
    Executors: William Williams, Samuel Clayton, Jr., Edward Watkins.
    Wit.: John Pollard, Zachary Taylor, Ann Pollard, Samuel Clayton.

Inventory of Estate of Joseph Latham, dec'd., by N. Pendleton, Samuel Clayton, Jr., P. Pendleton. 21 Jan., 1771.

Inventory of Estate of Col. William Green by Henry Field, Jr., Wm. Ball and John Gray. 21 Jan., 1771.

Will of Finley McAlester of Brumfield Parish, Culpeper Co.
Dated 28 Sept., 1776. Proven 21 Jan., 1771
Legatees: Wife Elizabeth McAlester. Sons: John McAlester, James McAlester, Robert McAlester, William McAlester. Daus: Elizabeth Henson, Catherine Henson, Mary McAlester, Ann McAlester, Sarah McAlester.
Mentions boundary lines of Charles Henson, Maj. Roote and John Frogg.
Executrix: Wife Elizabeth McAlester.
Wit.: John Kelly, Manoah Corley, James Rush.

Inventory of Estate of Joseph Towles, dec'd., 18 March, 1771.
Appraisers: Ambrose Powel, Thomas Graves, Russell Hill, Thos. Porter.

Inventory of Estate of Mary Slaughter, dec'd. Appraisers: James Green, Thomas Triplett, William Field. Recorded 15 April, 1771.

Will of William Crosthwait of Bromfield Parish, Culpeper Co.
Dated 10 July, 1770. Proven 15 April, 1771.
Legatees: Wife. Sons: Jacob Crosthwaite, William Crosthwaite. Mentions "Youngest son or dau."
Executors: Joseph Early, Maj. James Barbour, John Terril and wife, Milley Crosthwaite.
Wit.: Reuben Terrill, Jonathan (X) Cowherd, William (X) Bates.

Inventory of Estate of Finley McAlester, dec'd. Recorded 15 April, 1771. Appraisers: Elias Campbell, John Yowell, George Row.

Inventory of Estate of Richard Pollard, dec'd. Recorded 20 May, 1771. Appraisers: Philip Pendleton, Joseph James and Samuel Clayton.
Division of slaves and personal estate of Richard Pollard, dec'd.
Legacies: 1/3 of slaves to widow, Mrs. Elizabeth Pollard.
    Thomas Camp who intermarried with Elizabeth Pollard. Value: 105₤ 10s 2½d.
        To Robert Pollard - same amount.
        To Sarah Pollard - same amount.
        To Milley Pollard - same amount.
        To Richard Coleman Pollard - same amount.
Date: 20 May, 1771. Report made by Philip Pendleton, Joseph James and Samuel Clayton.

Will of James Lear of Culpeper Co.
Dated 28 Feb., 1771. Proven 15 July, 1771.
Legatees: Wife Hannah Lear. Sons: William Lear, eldest. Mentions "all my children."
Executors: Wife Hannah Lear, Bushrod Dogget.
Wit.: James Pendleton, Henry Pendleton, Henry Stringfellow.

Inventory of Estate of James Lear, dec'd. Recorded 19 Aug., 1771.
Appraisers: Henry Stringfellow, William Hawkins, Mayson Colvin.

Inventory of Estate of Courtney Norman, dec'd. Recorded 19 Aug., 1771.
Appraisers: John Frogg, John Roberts, John Corbin.

Will of Robert Adams.
Dated 29 July, 1771. Proven 20 Aug., 1771.
Legatee: Peter Russell Asher, son of Jeremiah Asher.
Wit.: John Morgan, William (X) Gregory.
Adm. granted by Court to Jeremiah Asher.

Account redered by William Rogers, extr. Recorded 19 Aug., 1771.

Will of William Robinson of Brumfield Parish, Culpeper Co.
Dated 16 June, 1771. Proven 21 June, 1771.
Legatee: Wife Mary Robinson.
Executrix: Wife Mary Robinson.
Wit.: George Wetherall, Jas. (X) Henson, Charles (C) Henson.

Will of William Peyton of St. Mark's Parish, Culpeper Co.
Dated 27 July, 1771. Proven 21 Oct., 1771.
Legatees: Sons: William Payton, Charles Payton, Benjamin Payton, John Payton. Daus.: Ann Stone, Mary Smith, Judith Allen, Susannah Perfect, dau. Hannah and her eldest son.
Executor: Benjamin Roberts
Wit.: John Stone, Bryan Stone.

Account of Sale of Estate of Courtney Norman, dec'd. to 5 Nov., 1771.
Purchasers: Reuben Norman, Ezekiel Norman, Cornelius Mitchell, John Norman, Caleb Browning, John Corbin, Richard Murffie, Samuel Poe, William Murffie, Jonathan Poe, William Norman, Miles Murffie, Alexander Baxter, William Reding, Jessey Thompson, Thurmon Crim, William Daniell, Jacob Weekley, Thomas Conn, William Corbin, John Weekley, Jeramiah Corbin, James Attwood, James Browning, William Grimsley, William Day, Miles Murphey, Amry Day, John Norman, Isaac Reding, William Atwood, John Bradford, Joseph Boggess, Courtney Norman, John Norman, Mary Norman.

Will of William Golding of Culpeper, schoolmaster.
Dated 7 Sept., 1771. Proven 21 Oct., 1771.
Legatees: Godson Hiram Rousau for schooling, to be paid out at the discretion of Robert Garnett. Mrs. Crittenden, a ring; her dau. a ring; Mrs. Sarah Rousau, a ring; Henrietta Hudson, a ring; Elizabeth Clark, a ring; Sarah Garnett, dau. of Anthony, a ring. Remainder of Estate to Anthony Garnett. Lend books to John Garnett until Hiram Rousau can use them.
Executor: Robert Garnet.
Wit.: Samuel (X) Dogan, Daniel White.

Will of William Morris.
Dated _____. Proven 18 Nov., 1771
Legatee: Son Thomas Morris. Mentions boundary line where John Levell did live.
Wit.: Timothy Hodway, John (X) Floyd, Jane Floyd.
Brought to Court by widow, Mary Morriss, who was appointed admx.

Inventory and appraisal of Estate of John Jett. 29 Nov., 1771.
Appraisers: Henry Pendleton, James Spilman, George Passons. Recorded

16 Dec., 1771.

Will of John Jett, Planter, of Culpeper Co.
Dated 6 May, 1763. Proven 18 Nov., 1771.
Legatees: Wife Ann Jett. Sons: Stephen Jett, James Jett, William Jett, John Jett. Daus.: Elizabeth Roach, Margret Butler, Mary Tapp.
Executors: Wife Ann Jett, John Jett, James Jett.
Wit.: James Prilman, David (X) Corbin, Ellender (X) Cornaggey, Jacob (J) Clinch.

Will of Richard Tutt.
Dated 10 April, 1771. Proven 18 Nov., 1771.
Legatees: Wife Million Tutt. Sons: James Tutt, Archebald Tutt, Richard Tutt. Dau.: Betty Tutt.
Executors: Wife, William Newton, Edward Watkins, William Williams.
Wit.: Weatt Coleman, Mary Tutt, Richard Tutt, younger, David Darnold.

Inventory of Estate of Richard Tutt, dec'd. Recorded 16 Dec., 1771. Appraisers: Henry Pendleton, Richard Yancey, Lewis Yancey.

Inventory of Estate of Robert Adams, dec'd. Recorded 16 March, 1772. Appraisers: John Gray, William Underwood, Frederick Zimmerman.

Will of John Ryan.
Dated 6 Dec., 1769. Proven 16 March, 1772.
Legatees: Wife Elizabeth Ryan. Dau. Martha Simms. Grandson John Simms.
Executors: David Hening and Samuel Clayton.
Wit.: Samuel Clayton, Abraham Gregory, William (X) Barran.

Inventory of Estate of William Robinson, dec'd. Recorded 16 March, 1772. Appraisers: Richard (X) Maze, Reginal Burdine, Joseph King.

Will of Betty Hill of Culpeper Co.
Dated 1 Aug., 1771. Proven 16 March, 1772.
Legatees: Daus.: Caty Price, Ann Hill. Sons: George Hill, LeRoy Hill, Charles Hill, Joseph Hill.
Executors: Sons Charles Hill and LeRoy Hill.
Wit.: Abbott White, Presly White.

Account of Administration of Estate of John Daniel Jecoby. Recorded 18 March, 1772. Expenses of Francis Jecoby to Germany to recover an estate for use of the children and expenses of farm and children, 20 April, 1768 to Jan., 1772. Purchasers or debtors from whom money was received: William Lospike, Thomas Baker, John Hopper, John Crim, John Burk, William Roberts, Richard Brooks, Joseph Coons, James Williams, John Wallace, Frederick Burditt, Robert Collins, Francis Slaughter, Adam Barler, John Manifee, Anthony Strother, Jacob Woodford, John Elilagle.

Will of William Marshall of Brumfield Parish, Culpeper Co.
Dated 5 Aug., 1771. Proven 20 March, 1772.

Legatee: Friend Jean Lawrence and her heirs.
Executrix: Jean Lawrence.
Wit.: George Wetherall, John McKenzie.
Note: Name given as William Mershall at beginning of will and so entered by clerk when proven.

Inventory and Appraisal of Estate of Betty Nash, dec'd., made 25 Oct., 1766 by Reuben Long, John Leavel, Samuel Stigler.
Estate Division: equal shares to William Nash, Robert Sanders and wife, Elizabeth Nash, John Nash, Leanna Nash, Elijah Nash, Mary Nash. Division dated 17 July, 1767. Presented by Edward Watkins and Samuel Clayton, Jr. Recorded 20 April, 1772 (Inv. and division).

Inventory of Estate of William Morriss, dec'd., by N. Pendleton, Edward Watkins, Joseph Janes. Recorded 20 April, 1772.

Inventory and Appraisal of Estate of William Peyton, dec'd., by Robert Green, Daniel Field, George Roberts. Recorded 10 May, 1772.

Inventory and Appraisal of Estate of Daniel Brown, dec'd., made by John Gray, William Underwood and Richard Hackley. Recorded 18 May, 1772.

Inventory and Appraisal of Estate of Betty Hill, dec'd., by Richard Gaines, Ambrose Jones and James White. Recorded 10 May, 1772.

Will of Samuel Fargeson of Culpeper Co.
Dated 15 Feb., 1772. Proven 18 May, 1772.
Legatees: "Lands and slaves in the possession of Elizabeth Fargeson, widow of my son Francis Fargeson, dec'd., be disposed of in the manner he directed by his will." Wife: Ann Fargeson. Sons: Samuel Fargeson. Daus.: Elizabeth Fargeson, Susanna Daniel, Ann wife of Francis Strother, Lucy wife of John Graves. Grandson: Benjamin Fargeson, son of my son Francis Fargeson. Granddau.: Elizabeth Daniel. Grandsons: Samuel Clayton, George Clayton and Philip Clayton, sons of a deceased dau. Granddau.: Elizabeth Pendleton. Granddaus.: Ann Fargeson and Susanna Fargeson, daus. of son Francis Fargeson, dec'd. Grandson: Samuel Fargeson, son of my son Samuel Fargeson.
Executors: Wife Ann Fargeson, son Samuel Fargeson.
Wit.: Henry Pendleton, James Pendleton.

Will of John Kilby of Brumfield Parish, Culpeper Co.
Dated 8 Dec., 1770. Proven 18 May, 1772.
Legatees: Wife Elizabeth Kilby. Sons: Henry Kilby, Michael Kilby, William Kilby, John Kilby, Adam Kilby, James Kilby. Daus.: Ann Catherine Kilby, Elizabeth Kilby, Nancey Kilby and Susannah Kilby.
Executors: Sons William Kilby and James Kilby
Wit.: Thomas Sparks, Thomas Porter, Robert Floyd.

Inventory and Appraisal of Estate of John Kilby, dec'd. Does not state by whom taken nor presented. Recorded 15 June, 1772.

Will of Leonard Ziglar
Dated 26 April, 1772. Proven 20 July, 1772.
Legatee: Ann Zigler during widowhood and then divided equally among children.
Executrix: Wife Ann Zigler.
Wit.: Christopher Ziglar, Joshaway (X) Tillery.

Will of John Hoofman of Brumfield Parish, Culpeper Co.
Dated 30 Dec., 1762. Proven 17 Aug., 1772.
Legatees: Wife Mary Hoofman. Sons: (Ten) Frederick Hoofman, John Hoofman, Nicholas Hoofman, Michael Hoofman, Jacob Hoofman, Paul Hoofman, William Hoofman, George Hoofman, Henry Hoofman, Dilman Hoofman. Daus.: Catharine Spilman, Elizabeth Hoofman, Margaret Hoofman, Mary Hoofman.
Refers to boundary line of George Utz, of William Hoofman, of Matthias Wilhoite, of Nicholas Hoofman, George Long, John Carpenter.
"I give my two Great Bibles amongst my nine sons as I have by my last wife Mary which is now present; the two eldest to take them the first year and then deliver them to the two next 'till they have had them round and beginning again with the two eldest and so continue as long as the Bibles shall last.
Executors: Sons John Hoofman, Nicholas Hoofman and Michael Hoofman.
Wit.: Dan Smith, Christopher Blankenbaker, John Railsback.

Inventory and Appraisal of Crosthwait's Estate presented by William Kirtley, Thomas Kirtley and John Blake. Recorded 17 Aug., 1772.

Inventory and Appraisal of Estate of John Ryan, dec'd. Presented by Samuel Hening, Francis Gaines and David Hening. Recorded 17 Aug., 1772.

Account of Administration of Estate of George Strother, dec'd. Presented by John Strother. Recorded 22 Aug., 1772. Begins with 21 May, 1767.

Inventory and Appraisal of Estate of William Latham, dec'd. By William Knox, John Read and James Spilman. Recorded 21 Sept., 1772.

Will of Walter Butler
Dated 31 Aug., 1772. Proven 21 Sept., 1772.
Legatees: Son Peter Butler. Estate sold and divided "among all my children or their survivors."
Executor: Henry Pendleton.
Wit.: Philip Pendleton, Edward Sims.

Inventory and Appraisal of Estate of John Hufman, dec'd. Presented by Henry Hill, William Hill and Adam Wiland. Recorded 21 Sept., 1772.

Inventory and Appraisal of Estate of John Hufman, dec'd. Presented by James Spilman, Frederick Fishback and John Young. Recorded 18 Nov., 1772.
(Note: Both inventories state for John Hufman's estate but were presented by different appraisers on different dates and do not contain duplicate items.)

Will of John Thompson, Clerk of the Parish of St. Mark in County of Culpeper.
Dated 5 Feb., 1771. Proven 16 Nov., 1772.
Legatees: Son: William Thompson (John Ashley's deed of land, Samuel Ferguson's deed of land, Capt. Robert Green's deed of land, etc.)
Son: John Thompson (Francis Thornton's deed of land, Anthony Strother's deed and other assets.)
Son: Philip Roots Thompson (John Roberts' deed of land, etc.)
Son-in-law: Francis Thornton and my daughter Ann ("a tract of land contiguous to Rev. John Dixon's tract formerly Col. Russell's")
Sister: Ann Nielson
Wife: (mansion house and plantation containing 390 a. also Thomas Yates' deed adjoining Quarles' tract, etc.)
Dau.: Mildred Thompson (money due me from the Estate of the late Col. John Spotswood. He had money due from the Estate of the late Alexander Spotswood, Esq., grandfather of the present Alexander Spotswood.)
Executors: Wife, Col. Fielding Lewis, Joseph Jones; Francis Thornton and William Thornton.
Wit.: Benjamin Johnston, Thomas Walker, John Thornton.

Division of Estate of Betty Nash by James Nash, Admr.
Dated 19 Oct., 1772.
Legatees: James Nash, William Nash, Robert Saunders and wife Ann, James Saunders and wife Elizabeth, Bryant Thornhill and wife Leanna, John Nash, Elijah Nash, Nathaniel Robertson and wife Mary.
Recorded 16 Nov., 1772.

Will of Judith Hackley of Culpeper Co.
Dated 19 Oct., 1771. Proven 16 Nov., 1773.
Legatees: Son-in-law Richard Hackley. 5s to each of other children.
Executor: Richard Hackley.
Wit.: Charles Bruce, Margaret Barrow.

Appraisal and Division of Estate of John Hackley. Recorded 16 Nov., 1772.
Legatees: James Hackley, Samuel Hackley, John Hackley, Judith Hackley - 4 equal parts. Made by Benjamin Roberts, Wm. Ball and John Gray.

Appraisal and Division of Estate of Capt. Thomas Stubblefield. Recorded 16 Nov., 1772.
Legatees: Mrs. Elonder Underwood, relict of Capt. Thomas Stubblefield, dec'd., James Stubblefield, Elizabeth Long wife of Gabriel Long, Miss Mary Stubblefield. Made by Benjamin Roberts, Lawrence Slaughter and John Gray.

Inventory and Appraisal of slaves and personal property of the late Reverend John Thompson. Recorded 15 March, 1773. Made by Nathaniel Pendleton, Reuben Long and William Ball.

Appraisal of Estate of Sharper Atkins, dec'd. Recorded 15 March, 1773. Made by James Graves, John Nalle and John Parks.

Appraisal of Estate of James Tutt, Jr., dec'd. Recorded 15 March, 1773. Made by Martin Nalle, John Nalle and Richard Parker.

Sale of Estate of Sharper Atkins, dec'd. Purchasers: Martin Davenport, William Dulany, John Parks, Francis Nalle, Thomas Coleman, William Dulany, John Duncan, Martin Nalle, Ann Atkins, William Jones, Job Popham, Thomas Garriott. Reported by Martin Nalle, admr. Recorded 15 March, 1773.

Inventory and Appraisal of Estate of Richard Breeding alias Cross, dec'd. Made by Jonathan Cowherd, John Delany and John Pemberton. Recorded 15 March, 1773. Proven 15 March, 1773.

Will of Charles Blunt of Culpeper Co.
Dated 2 Oct., 1769.
Legatees: Wife Mary Blunt and at her death equally to youngest daus. Sarah, Betty and Eloner. Sons: Francis Blunt, Charles Blunt.
Executors: Sons Francis Blunt, Charles Blunt.
Wit.: James Barbour, Jr., Robert Throckmorton, Jr., Adam Nelson.
Codicil: Executors: Sons Francis Blunt and Charles Blunt.

Case of Richard Vernon vs Merryman Marshall.
Lists debits from Jan., 1771 through Nov., 1772. Recorded 15 March, 1773. Names appearing in the accounts: Anthony Deering, Mr. Mitchell, Mr. Hackley, Mr. Johnston, John Zachary, Samuel French, ____ Miller, Francis Bushop, Mr. Roebuck, William Walker, Wood and Powell, Mrs. Mildred Crosthwait, Mr. Lewis, Thomas Clifton, Mr. Bullitt, Mr. Buchanan, Mr. Towles, Capt. John Scott, Benjamin Johnston, Richard Easten, Isaac Smith, Capt. John Strother. Reported by Richard Vernon.

Will of Lewis Fisher of Culpeper Co.
Dated 4 Feb., 1773. Proven 19 July, 1773.
Legatees: Wife Barbara Fisher. Sons: Barnett Fisher, Adam Fisher (already had his), Steven Fisher. He had estate in Germany.
Executors: Sons Steven Fisher and Adam Fisher.
Wit.: John Tompkins, Jacob Wilhoit, Mark Finks.

Will of Lot Underwood.
Dated 3 Oct., 1772. Proven 19 July, 1773.
Legatees: Wife Mary Underwood. Children: William Underwood, Francis Underwood, Elizabeth Underwood, Jaley Underwood, Mary Underwood.
Executrix: Wife Mary Underwood.
Wit.: Charles Bruce, William Underwood.

Inventory and Appraisal of Estate of Lott Underwood, dec'd. Made by William Ball, John Gray, William Hawkins and Richard Hackley. Recorded 16 Aug., 1773.

Mr. Sallis Hansford in Account with Nicholas Porter. Recorded 26 Aug., 1773. Mentioned: Robert Johnson, Rev. James Marye, Mr. Willis, Dr. Mercer, Henry James, Mr. Fox (rent), Mr. John Green, Sheriff, Roger Dixon, Joseph James, Dr. Campbell, William Knox, Francis Hackley, Robert Jackson, extrs.,

Nathaniel Pendleton, Thomas Wright, James Jameson, Thomas Carter, Frederick Zimmerman, Brumfield Long, Lynn Banks, Richard Reynolds, Goodrich Lightfoot, Allen Wiley, Alexander Frazier, James Hackley. Also: John Lankford, John Craig. Mrs. Lucy Hansford, William Allen, Richard Been. This account covers Oct., 1758 thru 1772.

Inventory and Appraisal of Estate of John Shelton, dec'd., by William Walker, John Buford, Ephraim Rucker. Recorded 16 Aug., 1773.

Inventory and Appraisal of Estate of Theophilus Read. Made by John Green, Henry Pendleton, James Pendleton. Recorded 16 Aug., 1773.

Account of John Read, admr. of Dr. Theophilus Read's Estate. Recorded 16 Aug., 1773. Mentioned: William Dillard, Edward Sims, Major Dillard, Henry Stringfellow, Patterson Fletcher, Henry Huffman, John Sear, Gavin Samson, Hugh Freeman, William Fargison, William Knox, George Parson.
"To Winifred Reid's share."
Credits: James Robison, James Pendleton, Harris Freeman, David Elkins, Henry Pendleton, James Robinson.
Report made by James Pendleton, John Green, Henry Pendleton.

Inventory and Appraisal of Estate of Charles Blunt. Made by William Rogers, Joseph Rogers, Thomas Quinn. Recorded 20 Sept., 1773.

Estate Settlement of Courtney Norman, Dec'd., by William Eastham, Owen Minor, R. Eastham, Jr. Recorded 20 Sept., 1773.
Legatees: Ezekiel Norman, William Norman, Mary Norman, Milley Norman, Elizabeth Norman.

Will of John McKenny of Bromfield Parish, Culpeper Co.
Dated 21 May, 1770. Proven 15 Nov., 1773.
Legatees: Wife Mary Ann McKenny. John McKenny, son of my daughter Margaret. "my daughter the wife of Thomas Williamson" already provided for.
Executors: John Strother and John Slaughter.
Wit.: Richard Gaines, Benjamin Gaines, William Johnson, George (X) Christial.

Inventory and Appraisal of Estate of Lewis Fisher, dec'd. Made by William Chapman, Adam Wayland, Zachariah Blankenbeekar. Recorded 15 Nov., 1773.

Inventory and Appraisal of Estate of Honorias Powell, Jr., dec'd. (He had one saddle and one coat.). Made by William Walker, Peter Rucker, James Collins. Recorded 16 Nov., 1773.

Will of Zacharias Gibbs of Culpeper Co.
Dated 5 Aug., 1773. Proven 16 Nov., 1773
Legatees: Wife Mary Gibbs. Sons: John Gibbs, Francis Gibbs, Zacharias Gibbs. Daus.: Sarah Gibbs, and four married daughters but names

not given. (Note: Zacharias was only son who was not married.)
   Executors: Wife and 3 sons.
   Wit.: Richard Vernon, William Roebuck, Anthony Deering, Norman Ballard.

Inventory and Appraisal of Estate of John McKenny, dec'd. Made by Benjamin Gaines, Anthony Hughes, William Johnson. Recorded 20 Dec., 1773.

Account of Sale of Estate of ___ Mildrum. Recorded 20 Dec., 1773. Purchasers: Samuel Hening, Samuel Clayton, Jr., Gabriel Jones, Alexander Tulley, William Thompson, James Slaughter, Charles Henson, Francis Hackley, George Bourn, William Hill, Timothy Holdway, Richard Chism, John Smith, George Bourn, Thomas Camp, Nathaniel Brown, William Bradley, William Lodspike, Thomas Graves, Jr., John Williams, Abraham Grigory, Thomas Graves, Leonard Smith, Matthias Wilhite, Leonard Barnhyth(?-hyple), John James, Joseph James, Jr., John Strother, Robert Coleman, John Robbins, Thomas Graves, Jr., Robert Blackburn, Henry Frilas, Jr., John Seales, John Williams, John Holdaway, Henry Hill, Samuel Fargeson, Mordicai Baughan, William Dulaney, John Harbison, James Griffith, Job Popham, William Williams, Joshua Pilcher, Mrs. Mildrum, John Williams, Martin Nalle, William Hill, Ambrose Powell, Benjamin Roberts, Henry Pendleton, Gabriel Jones, Robert Throckmorton, Charles Henson, John Smith, John Brown, Francis Strother, John Turner, Benjamin Gaines.

Will of Joel Bumgarner of Brumfield Parish, Culpeper Co.
Dated 3 Oct., 1773. Proven 20 Dec., 1773.
Legatee: Mother, Catron Deer. Brother, Frederick Bumgarner.
Wit.: Benjamin Pulliam, William Jones, David (X) Davis, Jr.

Inventory and Appraisal of Estate of James Wood, dec'd. Made by John Williams, Martin Nalle, Thomas Griffin, John Tutt. Recorded 17 Jan., 1774.

Inventory of Estate of Zachariah Gibbs, dec'd., submitted by Walker. Recorded 21 Feb., 1774.

Will of Thomas Williamson of Brumfield Parish, Culpeper Co.
Dated 9 June, 1773. Proven 21 Feb., 1774.
Legatees: Wife Margreat Williamson. Sons: William Williamson, Thomas Williamson. "all my children" - others not named.
Executors: Wife and Thomas McClanahan.
Wit.: John Norman, *Sinboysion Sattler(?), Suanah (X) Peck.
*When proven, the clerk listed him as Sebastian Hatler.

Will of Philemon Conner of the Parish of St. Mark, Culpeper Co.
Dated 24 Jan., 1774. Proven 21 Feb., 1774.
Legatees: Wife Rachel Conner. Children (all minors): Mary, John, Elizabeth, Philemon and the child my wife is now pregnant with.
Executors: Wife Rachel Conner, brother John Conner, friends William Cave and John Craig.
Wit.: Nicholas Arnold, Margaret Arnold, John Butler.

Inventory and Appraisal of Estate of Walter Butler, dec'd. Made by Bushrode Doggett, Samuel Fargeson, Edward Sims. Recorded 21 March, 1774.

Inventory and Appraisal of Estate of Matthew Harbison, dec'd. Made by Thomas Griffin, John Nalle, John Tutt. Recorded 21 March, 1774.

Inventory and Appraisal of Estate of Philemon Conner, dec'd. Made by Nicholas Arnold, John Dillard, John Butler. Recorded 21 March, 1774.

Inventory and Appraisal of Estate of Thomas Williamson, dec'd. Made by Francis Lucus Jecobi, John Norman, Thomas McClanahan. Recorded 22 March, 1774.

Will of Balthasar Blankinbeeker of Bromfield Parish, Culpeper Co.
Dated 7 Jan., 1762. Proven April, 1774.
Legatees: Wife Anne Margaret Blankenbeeker. Dau. Elizabeth married to Adam Wayland. Dau. Anne Barbara married to Lewis Fisher.
Executors: George Utz and Christopher Blankenbeeker.
Wit.: Samuel Klugg, ____ ____ (cannot read it but clerk has will proven by Christopher Blankinbeeker.), ____ Utz.

Will of Robert Sharman of Bromfield Parish.
Dated 21 June, 1773. Proven 18 April, 1774.
Legatees: Wife Lucy, dau. Ann Sharman, "grandson Elisha Sharman, illegitimate son of Ann Sharman."
Executors: Benjamin Head "friend and son-in-law," Ann Sharman.
Wit.: Richard Quinn, Francis Quinn.

Inventory and Appraisal of Estate of Joel Bumgarner, dec'd. Made by Benjamin Pulliam, William Jones, John Dillard. Recorded 18 April, 1774.

Account of Sale of Estate of Thomas Williamson, dec'd. Made by John Strother. Recorded 18 April, 1774. Purchasers: Margaret Williamson, Susanna Peach, William Hopper, John Minor, Robert Eastham, William Roberts, Edmond Browning, James Hickman, Ann McKinny, John Strother.

Inventory and Appraisal of Estate of Robert Sharman, dec'd. Made by John Cave, Benjamin Cave, William Walls. Recorded 16 May, 1774.

Will of John Pilcher of Culpeper Co.
Dated 25 Sept., 1773. Proven 16 May, 1774.
Legatees: Son: John Pilcher. Daus.: Mary Pilcher, Sary Pilcher, Elizabeth Pilcher (a minor), Rachel Pilcher (a minor).
Executors: Wife Frances Pilcher, Robert Smith.
Wit.: Thomas Bryan, Benjamin Roberts, Jr.

Will of William Underwood of Culpeper Co.
Dated 2 Aug., 1773. Proven 18 April, 1774.
Legatees: Wife Ellen Underwood. Dau. Jael Underwood.
Contingent Legatees: If wife and dau. leave no heirs, then to George Stubblefield and James Stubblefield.

Owned land in Culpeper and Orange Counties. Mentions Anne Brown, wife of Hezekiah Brown and her dau. Nelly Brown, Sarah Underwood Zigler as contingent legatees.

Also children of his brothers Lott Underwood and Zachariah Underwood and children of his sister, Sarah Schooler. Two of Lott Underwood's children were William Underwood and Jail Underwood.

Executors: Wife Ellen Underwood, Charles Bruce.

Wit.: William Hawkins, Anne Stubblefield, Mary Stubblefield.

Inventory and Appraisal of Estate of Joseph Belfield, dec'd. Made by Thomas Scott, William Watts, John Gibbs, William Rogers. Recorded 20 June, 1774.

Administrator's Account on Estate of Richard Pollard. Oct. 17, 1770 through Dec., 1773. Recorded 6 June, 1774. Made by French Strother. Recorded 6 June, 1774.

Payments made to Francis Gaines, Dr. Archibald Campbell, Thomas Bryant, George Bourn, James Brooks, Thomas Clifton, John Saunders, William Gaines, Robert Stuart, Jr., Frederick Zimmerman, extrs. of Dr. Wallace, William Robertson, William Gaines, Brooks Jones, Henry Stringfellow, Matthias Rinehart, Benjamin Pendleton, Leonard Smith, Jacob Rigour, Miss Elizabeth Fargeson, James Read, Thomas Marshall, John Edwards, Isaac Smith, Jr., William Ried, Nathaniel Pendleton, William Sparks, William Long, Robert Coleman, Samuel Clayton, Sr., Thomas Slaughter, Francis Strother, James Duncason, John Glassell, James Gildart, William Hansford.

Received from: Roderick Perry, William Reid, John Yeaman, John Hanie, Zachary Petty, James Slaughter, P. Pendleton, Timothy Holdway.

Appraisal and Estate Division of Joseph Bellfield, dec'd. 6 June, 1774. By Thomas Scott, William Watts, John Gibbs, William Rogers. Recorded 20 June, 1774. Legatees: Belfield Cave and William Glass.

Account of Estate of Richard Pollard, dec'd. 6 June, 1774 by William Williams, Samuel Clayton, Jr.

Inventory and Appraisal of Estate of Jacob Vaughan, dec'd. 2 June, 1774 by William Ball, Richard Hackley, William Strother.

Inventory and Appraisal of Estate of John Bourn, dec'd. 22 Nov., 1774 by John Grigsby, John Fushee, Peter Gatewood.

Account of Estate of Elizabeth Clore, dec'd. 17 Aug., 1774. Made by Benjamin Roberts, William Ball, John Gray, Lawrence Slaughter.

Inventory of Estate of John Pilcher, dec'd. 19 Sept., 1774 by James Sims, Joseph Sleneard(?), William Delany.

Will of William Prichett.
Dated 25 July, 1770. Proven 15 Aug., 1774
Legatees: Wife Jane. Land to John Craigg at wife's death. Wife to dispose of personal property.

Executor: John Craig.
Wit.: John ____ (?Jarvin ?Lorvin), Isbell Camble, John Hill.

Inventory of Estate of Pritchett. 17 Oct., 1774.

Account of Sales of Benjamin Powell from Feb., 1769. Recorded 21 Nov., 1774.

Inventory of Estate of Benjamin Long, dec'd. By William Robertson and Richard Parker. Recorded 21 Nov., 1774.

Administrator's Settlement of Estate of John Powell, dec'd. Payments made to James Powell, his part, William Powell, his part, Honorous Powell, his part, Ambrose Powell, his part, John Stowers, his part, John Shiflet, Stephen Shiflet, Benjamin Powell, Francis Powell, John Powell. 25 Aug., 1766 by the amounts of your Father's Estate as Settled by Col. James Barbour, Robert Throgmorton and Ephraim Rucker.
Final report by EE William Walker. Recorded 21 Nov., 1774.

Account Report of Estate of Ambrose Booton, dec'd. 20 Feb., 1775. Made by Ephraim Rucker.

Inventory and Appraisal of Estate of Ambrose Booton, dec'd. Made by William Kirtley, Jonathan Cowherd, Thomas Kirtley.

Inventory and Appraisal of Estate of William Underwood, dec'd. 17 July, 1775. Made by William Ball, John Gray, Richard Hackley.

Will of James Barbour of Culpeper Co.
Dated 23 Feb., 1775. Proven 17 April, 1775.
Legatees: Sons: Richard Barbour, James Barbour, Thomas Barbour, Philip Barbour, Ambrose Barbour. Daus.: Mary Barbour, Betty Barbour. Grsons.: James Boyd, James Barbour, Richard Barbour son to Thomas Barbour. Grdau.: Frances Smith.
Executors: Wife ____, son Richard Barbour, son James Barbour, son Thomas Barbour.
Wit.: William Rogers, Joseph Rogers, George Scott, John Deering.

Will of John Field of St. Mark's Parish, Culpeper Co.
Dated 21 Aug., 1774. Proven 15 May, 1775.
Legatees: Wife Anna. Son Larkin Field (a minor) "land I purchased of my bro. Daniel and my nephew Abram Field as well as Maddox' Tract." (?Haddocks in will later). Dau. Elisabeth Slaughter and her husband Laurance Slaughter, among other possessions he gave them land in the mountains known as "Joy Bottom" or "Stanton's Encampment." Dau. Mary Slaughter and son-in-law George Slaughter. Dau. Anna Field. Grson. John Field Slaughter. Grson. Robert Slaughter. Grdau. Milly Slaughter. Son Ezekiel Field "is unhappily missing."
Executors: Wife Anna Field, Lawrence Slaughter, John Field.
Wit.: William Ball, Joseph Minor, John Gray, William Field.

Division of Estate of William Peyton, dec'd. Extr. Benjamin Roberts is also guardian to the orphan. Signed: Robert Green, John Hume, Henry Field. Recorded 15 May, 1775.

Will of Edward Bush of Bromfield Parish, Culpeper Co.
Dated 13 Feb., 1775. Proven 20 Feb., 1775.
Legatees: Richard Strother of South Carolina. Nephew: Enoch Bush, son of my brother Maximilian Bush. Dau.: Margaret Bush (a minor). If she dies without heirs, entire estate equally to nephews, William Bush and Enoch Bush, sons of my brother, Maximilian Bush.
Executors: friends Henry Fields, Jun., and James Nash.
Wit.: Adam N. Barlow(?), John Marcos, Robert Floyd.

Will of George Roberts of St. Mark's Parish, Culpeper Co.
Dated __ Sept., 1774. Proven 17 April, 1775.
Legatees: Son John Roberts, son Joseph Roberts, son Benjamin Roberts, son William Roberts "land whereon Frances Clifton now lives." Wife. None to son George Roberts and Charles Cliffton as they have had their part.
Executors: Wife, son George Roberts.
Wit.: Benjamin Roberts, Roger Abbett.

Mrs. Moadley, lately Mrs. Klug, in account with Estate of Rev. George Samuel Klugg, dec'd. Recorded 18 Sept., 1775. Made by James Barbour, Jr., A. Powell, Henry Field, Jr.

Division of Estate of Rev. George Samuel Klugg. Widow's third - and remainder divided among 9 children. None named except where payments were made to the following men who had "intermarried with daughters of the dec'd.": Godfrey Yeager, Michael Broile, Matthias Broile, William Lutspick.

Account of Estate of James Powell, dec'd. Recorded 21 Nov., 1774. Made by James Wood, Benjamin Roberts, Jr., James Steward, Thomas Porter.

Will of Abraham Field of St. Mark's Parish, Culpeper Co.
Dated 2 July 1774. Proven 18 Sept., 1775.
Legatees: Wife Elianah Field. Sons: John Field, Daniel Field, Henry Field, William Field, Abraham Field, Reuben Field, Abner Field (a minor). Daus.: Judith Yancey, dec'd., former wife of Capt. Richard Yancey, Elizabeth Alford, Ellenor Greenwood, Jenny Field. Grsons.: John Greenwood, Abraham Field.
Wit.: Robert Green, John Hume, Mary Green, Armistead Green, Robert Wright.

Will of Richard Young of Culpeper Co.
Dated 23 Jan., 1775. Proven 18 Sept., 1775.
Legatees: Wife Mary Young. At her death to John Wigington. "my former wife's two brothers, my godson, Thomas Green, and his brother, Caleb Green. Grson.: Richard Young Wigington, son of the above John Wigington. Schools for poor children.

Executors: Capt. Henry Field, Jr., John Green and John Wigington.
Wit.: William Collins, John Buller, James Nash.

Inventory and Appraisal of Estate of James Barbour. Recorded 26 April, 1775. Made by William Watts, John Cave, Ben Cave.

Will of John Smith of Culpeper Co.
Dated 4 Jan., 1776. Proven 16 April, 1776.
Legatees: Wife Anne Smith. Sons: William Smith, Daniel Smith. Daus.: Mary Smith, Patty Smith. All children were minors.
Executors: Capt. Edward Wadkins, Thomas Wright.
Wit.: Ambrose Coleman, Richard Parkes, Nanny (X) Habler(?Kabler).

Will of John Walker of St. Mark's Parish, Culpeper Co.
Dated 27 Dec., 1775. Proven 16 April, 1776.
Legatees: Wife Isabel Walker. Sons: Benjamin Walker, John Walker (youngest). Daus.: Janet Gore, Elizabeth Walker, Elisabeth Walker, Mary Walker.
Wit.: Teasly(?) Oliver Clark, Reuben (X) Washburn, Mary (X) Clark.

Inventory and Appraisal of Estate of John Smith, dec'd. Recorded 17 June, 1776. Made by W. Robertson, N. Robertson, Thomas Sims, Jr., William Camp.

Inventory and Appraisal of Estate of Shadrach Shavue, dec'd. Recorded 17 June, 1776. Made by James Pendleton, Lewis Yancey, Mason Colvin.

Inventory and Appraisal of Estate of Abraham Field, dec'd. Recorded 15 July, 1776. Made by Edward Doss, William Ball, John Gray, James Green.

Inventory and Appraisal of Estate of Richard Young, dec'd. Recorded 15 July, 1776. Made by William Williams, George Bowen, Francis Gains.

Inventory and Appraisal of Estate of Richard Tutt, dec'd. Recorded 15 July, 1776. Made by James Tutt, John Saunders, John Williams.

Will of Francis Gaines of St. Mark's Parish, Culpeper Co.
Legatees: Wife Dorothy Gaines. Son: James Gaines. Daus.: Lucy Gaines, Salley Gaines, Betty Gaines, Dorothy Gaines, Susanna Gaines. Isabella Gaines, dau. of my nephew, Henry Gaines.
Executors: Son James, friends Edward Watkins and Samuel Clayton, Jr.
Wit.: William Williams, John Williams, Henry Stringfellow.

Richard Pollard in Account with Elisabeth Pollard.
Sarah Pollard in Account with Elizabeth Pollard.
Milley Pollard in Account with Elizabeth Pollard.
Guardianship Account of Elizabeth Pollard for orphans of Richard Pollard. Audited by James Slaughter, Burkett Davenport, N. Pendleton. Recorded 15 July, 1776.

Inventory and Appraisal of Estate of Massey Thomas, dec'd. Recorded 19 Aug., 1776. Made by Geo. Wetherall, John Sampson, Michael Jijdger(?).

Will of James Murry of Culpeper Co.
Dated 5 May, 1776. Proven 19 May, 1776.
Legatees: Bro. Prettyman Murry, Nephew Prettyman Murry son to Thomas Murry, Sis. Ann Walker, Sis. Mary Murry.
Executors: Bro. Prettyman Murry and William Walker.
Wit.: Merry Walker, Elizabeth Walker, James Walker.

Will of Edward Walker of Culpeper Co.
Dated 18 March, 1775. Proven 19 Aug., 1776.
Legatees: Wife, at her death equally "to all my children."
Executors: Sons James Walker, William Walker and John Walker.
Wit.: Elliott Rucker, Robert (R) Warran, Merry (X) Walker.

Will of Benjamin Taylor of St. Mark's Parish, Culpeper Co.
Dated 11 Feb., 1775. Proven 19 Aug., 1776.
Legatees: Son: Thomas Taylor. Daus.: Elizabeth Miles and Mary Buller. Grandsons: Charles Taylor, Benjamin Taylor and James Taylor for schooling.
Executors: Son Thomas Taylor and son-in-law Charles Miles.
Wit.: James Brooks, William Green, Charles Yancey, John Morgan.

Inventory of Estate of Henry Threldkill. Recorded 10 Aug., 1776. Made by Thomas McClanahan, Thomas Jordan and Thomas Magruder.

Sales of Estate of Henry Threldkill. 3 Nov., 1775.
Purchasers: William Wright, Owen Minor, Edward Riley, Walter Wright, William Strother, William Pinnell, Jason Isbell, Benjamin Turner, William Grimsley, Jacob Browning, Jno. Glandening, John Picket, John Duncan, John Fincham, Elmore George, Edward Wilson, John Threldkell, Miss Sarah Threldkeld, Natly Maddox, Zachariah Compton, Christian Vought, Philip Cox, Mary Threldkeld, Joseph Wright, Ezekiel Norman, Frederick Sutherland, Henry Putman, James Carder, Benjamin Smoot, William Crawford, Traves Sutherland, John Jett, Joseph Steers, Philip Cox, Courtney Norman, William Pannill, Rice Duncan, Martin Fugate, Ellick Makfercen. Made by John Threldkeld, Admr.

Will of John Marsh of Culpeper Co.
Dated 7 Sept., 1776. Proven 21 Oct., 1776.
Legatees: Wife Mary Marsh. Sons: William Marsh, Joshua Marsh, John Marsh, Jonathan Marsh. Dau.: Margaret Underwood.
Executors: Son William Marsh and William Roberts.
Wit.: John Strother, John Roberts, William Hughs.

Will of Thebolt Christler of Culpeper Co.
Dated 20 Feb., 1776. Proven 18 Nov., 1776.
Legatees: Wife Rosanna Christler. Sons: Henry Christler, George Christler, Adam Christler, Michael Christler, Leonard Christler, David Christler. Daus.: Dortha Broyles, Mary Carpenter, Elisabeth Wilhoit, Margaret Clore, Catharine Christler.
Executors: Henry Christler and George Christler.
Wit.: Michael Souther, Jacob Souther, Adam Goar.

Inventory and Appraisal of Estate of Edward Bush, dec'd. Recorded 18 Nov., 1776.

Inventory of Estate of John Wilhoit, dec'd. Recorded 18 Nov., 1776.

Will of John Simpson of Culpeper Co.
Dated 22 July, 1776. Proven 16 Dec., 1776.
Legatees: Wife Elizabeth Simpson. Daus.: Elenor Booton, Mary Burk, Elizabeth Berry, Anne Simpson, Jane Simpson. Sons: William Simpson, James Simpson, Alexander Simpson, John Simpson.
Executors: Col. James Barbour, William Simpson, James Simpson, Alexander Simpson and John Simpson.
Wit.: Richard Vawter(?), Charles (X) Neal, Micajah (X) Neal.

Inventory and Appraisal of Estate of Francis Gains, dec'd. Recorded 16 Dec., 1776. Made by James Slaughter, Samuel Clayton, Sr., David Henning.

Inventory and Appraisal of Estate of William Hopper, dec'd. Recorded 16 Dec., 1776. Made by Bryan McGrath, Cornelius Mitchell, Sebastine Hatler.

Inventory and Appraisal of Estate of Theobolt Christler, dec'd. Recorded 20 Jan., 1777. Made by John Wayland, Nicholas Wilhoit, Michael Gaar.

Inventory and Appraisal of Estate of Charles Miles, dec'd. Recorded 20 Jan., 1777. Made by Francis Slaughter, Cadwallader Slaughter, John Williams.

Division of Estate of John Weatherall, dec'd. Divisees: John Weatherall, John Marshall, James Long. Recorded 17 Feb., 1777. Made 29 Nov., 1776 by Edward Watkins, N. Pendleton, Thomas Camp.

Will of James Stubblefield of Culpeper Co.
Dated 24 Oct., 1775. Proven 17 Feb., 1777.
Legatees: Wife Ann Stubblefield. Son: Thomas Stubblefield (a minor). If son dies without heirs then, at decease of wife, all to be divided among children of sister Ann Brown.
Wit.: Robert Pollard, Phil Slaughter, Robert Yancey, James Hackley.

Inventory and Appraisal of Estate of William Bragg. Recorded 17 Feb., 1777. Made by Christopher Zimmerman, Joseph Thornhill, William Kabler.

Inventory and Appraisal of Estate of Benjamin Allen, dec'd. Recorded 17 Feb., 1777. Made by Daniel Grinnan, Christopher Sutton, Francis Bowin.

Inventory and Appraisal of Estate of Edward Walker, dec'd. Recorded 17 Feb., 1777. Made by Thomas Scott, Jno. Scotwood, John Scott, Robert Alcock.

Inventory and Appraisal of Estate of Isaac Norman, dec'd. Recorded 17 Feb., 1777. Made by Ephraim Hart, Robert Coleman, Lawrance Catlett.

Account report of Elisabeth Ryan, Admr. of Estate of John Ryan, dec'd. Recorded 17 March, 1777.

Inventory and Appraisal of Estate of John Marsh, dec'd. Recorded 17 March, 1777. Made by William Duncan, younger, John Lawlor, James Duncan.

Inventory and Appraisal of Estate of William Hensley, dec'd. Recorded 17 March, 1777. Made by Joseph King, Michael Kluge, John Thomas.

Inventory and Appraisal of Estate of Daniel Brown, dec'd. Dated 22 April, 1777. Made by Jonathan Underwood, William Rucker, James Alexander.

Inventory and Appraisal of Estate of William Dulaney, dec'd. Recorded 22 April, 1777. Made by James Sims, James Murrey, William Hill.

Inventory and Appraisal of Estate of William Hammet, dec'd. Recorded 19 May, 1777. Made by John Read, ____ Read, Jessee Parsons.

Will of Margaret Ward of St. Mark's Parish, Culpeper Co.
Dated 17 April, 1778. Proven 19 May, 1777. (Error in dates ?)
Legatees: Dau.: Leucey Ward (a minor). Nephews(?): Elisabeth Ward, dau. of Richard Ward; Caty Ward, dau. of Richard Ward. Thomas Newman to bring up my dau. until she comes of age.
Executor: Cornelius Mershon.
Wit.: James Jett, David (X) Corbin, William Corbin.

Division of Estate of Winifred Read, dec'd. ½ to Francis Morgan who intermarried with the widow of Theofelus Read, dec'd. Recorded 17 May, 1777. Made by Henry Pendleton, Philip Pendleton, John Wigington.

Will of Jacob Clinch of Culpeper Co.
Dated 15 Jan., 1777. Proven 16 June, 1777.
Legatees: Wife Gean Clinch. Children: Rachel Clinch, Mary Clinch, Barbary Clinch, Jacob Clinch and Ledia Clinch.
Executor: James Freeman.
Wit.: Cornelius Mershon, John (X) McDanold.

Will of James Newman of Culpeper Co.
Dated 7 March, 1776. Proven 16 June, 1777.
Legatee: Bro. Joseph Newman. Includes his own inventory of household items at brother Reuben Newman's in Orange. Crop of tobacco made at my bro. Alexander Newman's and wheat "if I do not return from the wars."
Executor: Bro. George Newman.
Wit.: Thomas Newman, Abner Newman.

Will of Susannah Edgar.
Dated 24 March, 1777. Proven 16 June, 1777.
Legatees: William Corbin, son of David Corbin; John McDanold; Lucy Ward, dau. of Margaret Ward; Elizabeth Corbin, wife of David Corbin; Elizabeth Jones, relict. of Joshua Jones, dec'd.; Mildred Jett, dau. of

William Jett; Susanna McDanold, wife of John McDanold; Sarah Ward, wife of Richard Ward; Susanna Jett, wife of William Jett.
    Executor: Thomas Newman.
    Wit.: James Jett, Cornelius Mershon, Andrew Mershon.

Inventory and Appraisal of Estate of John Simpson, dec'd. Recorded 16 June, 1777. Made by William Kirtley, Joseph Earley, James Archer.

Inventory and Appraisal of Estate of Joshua Jones, dec'd. Recorded 16 June, 1777. Made by James Jett, Thomas Newman, Cornelius Mershon.

Estate Settlement of James Lear, dec'd. One third to Shadrach Chavieu who had married the widow of James Lear. Chavieu had died and bonds were delivered to Capt. Richard Yancey, admr. of Chavieu. Recorded 16 June, 1777. Made by James Pendleton, Samuel Clayton, Jr.

Administrator's Account of Estate of Samuel Henning, dec'd. Recorded 16 June, 1777.

Will of Michel Russell of Culpeper Co.
    Dated (none). Proven 16 June, 1777.
    Legatees: Wife Mary Russell. Sons: Elijah Russell, John Russell, William Russell. Daus.: Hannah Rice, Elisabeth Russell, Frances Lakey, Milly Russell (the youngest). Grandson: Benjamin Rice, son to Benajer Rice and Hannah, his wife.
    Administrator appointed was George Passons.
    Wit.: George Hume, Michael Delp, George (X) Reason.

Inventory and Appraisal of Estate of Michael Russell, dec'd. Recorded 21 July, 1777. Made by Adam Wayland, Andrew Carpenter, John Weaver.

Inventory and Appraisal of Estate of James Newman, dec'd. Recorded 21 July, 1777. Made by John McDanold, James Jett.

Inventory and Appraisal of Estate of Susanna Edgar, dec'd. Recorded 21 July, 1777. Made by John Wiginton, John McDanold, James Jett.

Inventory and Appraisal of Estate of Margaret Ward, dec'd. Recorded 21 July, 1777. Made by James Jett, John McDanold, John Wiginton.

Inventory and Appraisal of Estate of Jacob Clinch, dec'd. Recorded 21 July, 1777. Made by James Jett, John Wiginton, John McDanold.

Will of Thomas Pinar.
    Dated 17 April, 1776. Proven 18 Aug., 1777.
    Legatees: Wife Margot Pinar. Sons: Thomas Pinar (a minor), John Pinar. Dau.: Ruth Pinar (a minor).
    Executors: Henry Field, Jr., William Walker and son, John Pinar.
    Wit.: John Walker, W. Robertson, William (X) Jett.

Will of Ambrose Scott.
Dated 23 Feb., 1776. Proven 18 Aug., 1777.
Legatees: Bro. James Scott, father Thomas Scott.
Executors: Same as legatees.
Wit.: George Scott, John Stockdell, Jr., John Stockdell.

Will of Jacob Mitchell of Culpeper Co.
Dated 24 Jan., 1777. Proven 18 Aug., 1777.
Legatees: Wife Leah Mitchell, all my children including the unborn one. Children: Caty Allen, Benjamin Mitchell, Fisher Mitchell, William Mitchell, Peggy Mitchell.
Executors: Thomas Allen, James Thomas.
Wit.: Vincent Allen, John Hill, Weeden Maddox.

Will of William Sims of Culpeper Co.
Dated 17 July, 1777. Proven 15 Sept., 1777.
Legatees: Wife Ruth Sims; grandson, Isaac Smitty, Jr.; dau. Susanner Roberts.
Executors: William Sims, Jr. and Ruth Sims.
Wit.: Hugh Roberts, Winnie (X) Shorter.

Will of John Williams of Culpeper Co.
Dated 27 Feb., 1777. Proven 15 Sept., 1777.
Legatees: Wife Susannah Williams, Dau. Sarah Williams.
Executrix: Wife Susannah Williams.
Wit.: Ambrose Coleman, Thomas Wright, Jane Floayd.

Account of Estate of Richard Y. Wigington, dec'd. Recorded 15 Sept., 1777. Made by John Wiginton.

Inventory and Appraisal of Estate of Edward Bush, dec'd. Recorded 29 Aug., 1777. Made by Henry Field, Jr.

Account of Estate of Edward Bush, dec'd. Recorded 29 Aug., 1777. Made by James Nash.

Will of Gabriel Jones of Culpeper Co.
Dated 3 Sept., 1776. Proven 20 Oct., 1777.
Legatees: Dau. Ann Jones, grdau. of Mrs. Ann Waller. Wife Martha Jones. Children: Robert Jones, Gabriel Jones, Frances Slaughter, Mary Jones. If no issue of his children, then to his sisters Lucy(?) Poindexter, Betty Green, Jane Gray, Dorothy Johnston. Held some lands on the waters of the Ohio.
Executors: Friends James Green and John Gray.
Wit.: B. Johnston, William Hawkins, Jr. Ruth Gaines.

Inventory and Appraisal of Estate of Bartholomew Vawter, dec'd. Recorded 20 Oct., 1777. Made by Michael Garr, Lewis Gaar, James Archer.

Account of Estate of Ambrose Camp, dec'd., for years 1769 through 1774. Recorded 17 March, 1777. Made by Birkett Davenport, Ambrose Coleman.

Will of Robert Deatherage of Culpeper Co.
Dated 26 Jan., 1775. Proven 20 Oct., 1777.
Legatees: Wife Mary Deatherage. Children: Philemon Deatherage, George Deatherage, William Deatherage, Thomas Deatherage, Susanna Deatherage - all minors.
Executors: Wife Mary Deatherage, friends John Strother, Robert Strother and Joseph Strother.
Wit.: Robert Eastham, Jr., Philip Eastham, George Eastham.

Division of Estate of Courtney Norman, dec'd. Equally to Mary Norman, Milly Norman, Elizabeth Norman, Ezekiel Norman, William Norman.

Will of Francis Strother of Culpeper Co.
Dated 22 Aug., 1777. Proven 20 Oct., 1777.
Legatees: Son, John Strother; wife, Ann Strother. Sons: Francis Strother, Samuel Strother, George Strother (all minors).
Executors: Bro. John Strother, friends James Pendleton, William Pendleton.
Wit.: Bushrode Doggett, Henry Pendleton, William Hawkins.

Administrator's Account of Estate of Christopher Yowell, dec'd. Recorded 15 Dec., 1777. Made by William Thornton, John Lillard, Ambrose Barbour.

Inventory and Appraisal of Estate of James Yowell, dec'd. Recorded 26 July, 1777. Made by William Chapman, Henry Lewis, Sr., Robert Shotwell.

Division of Estate of John Butler, dec'd. 10 Jan., 1778. Equal parts to Thomas Taylor, James Butler, William Collins, Thomas Butler, John Butler, Edward Jones; and report of Estate Account of Susanna Butler. Made by James Nash, Charles Davenport, Samuel Stigler.

Inventory and Appraisal of Estate of John Williams, dec'd. Recorded 30 Dec., 1777. Made by Ambrose Coleman, Thomas Wright, James Long, Thomas Morriss.

Will of Henry James.
Dated (none). Proven 19 Jan., 1778.
Legatee: Daniel James, son of Joseph James and his wife, Mary. If he die without heirs then to Joseph James, bro. of Daniel James.
Executor: Henry Field, Jr.
Wit.: None
Proven in Court by James Campbell, George James and Joseph Steward. Henry Field, Jr., refused to act as executor and the Court appointed Joseph James.

Inventory and Appraisal of Estate of Charles Tutt, dec'd. Recorded 16 Feb., 1778. Made by Henry Pendleton, Bushrod Doggett, James Duvall.

Inventory and Appraisal of Estate of James Stubblefield, dec'd. Recorded 16 Feb., 1778. Made by Richard Gaines, James Graves, Benjamin Gaines.

Inventory of Estate of John Jones, dec'd. Recorded 16 Feb., 1778. Made by Benjamin Pulliam, Benjamin Gaines, Richard Gaines.

Inventory of Estate of Henry James, dec'd. Recorded 16 Feb., 1778. Made by John Long, William Gaines, James Gaines.

Inventory of Estate of Samuel Hening, dec'd. Recorded 16 March, 1778.

Will of William Williams.
Dated 27 April, 1775. Proven 20 April, 1778.
Legatees: Wife Lucy Williams. Sons: John Williams, James Williams, Clayton Williams, Philip Williams, William Williams, Samuel Williams. Mentions bro. John Williams and land given to them by their father at Stonehouse Mountain in Town of Fairfax. "education of rest of my children." Daus.: Ann Williams, Lucy Williams, Susanna Williams, Mary Williams.
Executors: Wife Lucy Williams, son John Williams, bro. John Williams, bro.-in-law Samuel Clayton and James Slaughter.
Wit.: John Banks, Henry Banks, James Bruce.

Will of Henry Field of St. Mark's Parish, Culpeper Co.
Dated 19 Nov., 1777. Proven 16 March, 1778.
Legatees: Daus.: Elizabeth Field, Judith Field, Sarah Ranolds. If daus. die before they come of age, then "equally divided between my sister Greenwood's children."
Executor: Robert Coleman, Jr.
Wit.: Benjamin Roberts, William Field, Hannah Tryplett.

Will of Charles Neale of Culpeper Co.
Dated 28 July, 1776. Proven 20 April, 1778.
Legatees: Wife Esther Neale. Children: Micajah Neale, John Neale, Fielding Neale, Charles Neale, Mary Neale, John Neale, Lucy Neale, Sally Neale.
Executors: Wife Esther Neale, son John Neale, son Micajah Neale.
Wit.: Joshua (X) Jack, Charles Cock, John Neall.

Inventory and Appraisal of Estate of William Sims, dec'd. Recorded 20 April, 1778. Made by Elijah Kirtley, Joseph Dulany, John Dulany.

Will of Thomas Triplett.
Dated 6 Sept., 1777. Proven 20 April, 1778.
Legatees: Wife Hanah Triplett. Sons: George Triplett, Peter Triplett, Thomas Triplett. Daus.: Milley Triplett, Jean Triplett, Frances Triplett.
Wit.: John Triplett, John Johnston, William Hall, William (X) Asher.

Inventory and Appraisal of Estate of William Williams, dec'd. Recorded 18 May, 1778. Made by Robert Slaughter, Sr., James Slaughter, Jr., Robert Coleman, Jr.

Will of George Bourn.
Dated 23 March, 1776. Proven 18 May, 1778.
Legatees: Wife. Daus.: Betsey Bourn, Salley Bourn, Lucey Bourn (all minors).
Executors: Wife, bro. John Bourn, uncle Robert Gaines, Capt. James Pendleton.
Wit.: Richard Yancey, David Hening.

Division of Estate of Michael Russell, dec'd. Surveyor's plat on this page. Recorded 16 June, 1778. Made by Ambrose Powell, Robert Terrell, John Graves. Devisees: Widow, Hanah Rice, Elizabeth Russell.

Will of Goodrich Lightfoot of St. Mark's Parish, Culpeper Co.
Dated 24 April, 1778. Proven 15 June, 1778.
Legatees: Wife Susanna Lightfoot. Daus.: Elizabeth James, Ann Grasty, Mary Hubbard, Fanny Hackley, Susanna Brooks, Priscilla Lightfoot, Martha Lightfoot. Sons: John Lightfoot, Philip Lightfoot (a minor), Goodrich Lightfoot, Jr., (a minor).
Executor: Son John Lightfoot.
Wit.: Daniel Grinnan, John Grinnan, Jane J. Grinnan.

Inventory and Appraisal of Estate of Thomas Piner, dec'd. Recorded 15 June, 1778. Made by John Flynt, Robert Terrill, Ambrose Powell.

Will of John Sampson of Bromfield Parish, Culpeper Co.
Dated 18 June, 1778. Proven 20 July, 1778.
Legatees: Wife Mary Sampson. Daus.: Elizabeth Rend, wife of Lewis; Bathsheba Clerk, wife of Reuben; Ann Burdine, wife of Reginal; Delilah Dicken, wife of William; Lucey Berry, wife of Aaron; Franky Berry, wife of Elisha, have already had their part. Sons: William Sampson, Joseph Sampson, Thomas Sampson. Dau.: Rhoda Sampson. Sons-in-law: John Hughs, William Hughs.
Executors: Wife Mary Sampson, Reuben Clark, Reginal Burdine, Henry Lewis.
Wit.: George Witherall, Michael (X) Yeager, Joseph (X) Campbell.

Will of Bromfill Long of St. Mark's Parish, Culpeper Co.
Dated 21 Jan., 1778. Proven 20 July, 1778.
Legatees: Wife Sarah Long. Sons: John Long, Bromfield Long, Reuben Long, Gabriel Long, Thomas Long. Daus.: Nancy Chisham, Betty Long, Milly Long. My son Benjamin Long's son, Benjamin Long.
Executors: Son John Long, son Bromfield Long.
Wit.: Robert Pollard, William Gaines, Joseph (X) Hitt.

Will of Conwright Kabler of St. Mark's Parish, Culpeper Co.
Dated 20 Nov., 1777. Proven 20 July, 1778.
Legatees: Wife (not named but was "last wife"). Sons: Frederick Kabler, William Kabler. Daus.: Barbary Sackett(?), "my four youngest daughters."
Executors: Son William Kabler, William Collins.
Wit.: Samuel Stigler, Rachel Jewell, William Collins.

Inventory and Appraisal of Estate of Henry Field, dec'd. Recorded 20 July, 1778. Made by Lawrence Catlett, Peter Abell, Harry Taliaferro.

Memorandum of Estate of Jacob Mitchell, dec'd. Recorded 17 Aug., 1778. Made by Daniel Grinnan, William Carty, Peter Gatewood.

Inventory and Appraisal of Estate of Conwright Kabler, dec'd. Recorded 8 Aug., 1778. Made by Reuben Long, Samuel Stigler, James Nash.

Inventory and Appraisal of Estate of John Freeman, dec'd. Recorded 21 Sept., 1778. Made by Anthony Thornton, John Strother, Thomas Jordan.

Division of Estate of Courtney Norman, dec'd. Devisees: Mary Norman, Milley Norman, Elisabeth Norman, Ezekiel Norman, William Norman. Recorded 21 Sept., 1778. Made by R. Eastham, Jr., Owen Minor, John Minor.

Guardian Account of Richard Young Wiginton. Recorded 21 Sept., 1778.

Inventory and Appraisal of Estate of Goodrich Lightfoot, dec'd. Recorded 21 Sept., 1778. Made by James Slaughter, James Thomas and Daniel Grinnan.

Will of Christopher Dicken.
Dated 21 Aug., 1778. Proven 21 Sept., 1778.
Legatees: Son Christopher Dicken (a minor), son Richard Dicken, son Benjamin Dicken, son William Dicken; Agness Rice, aunt to my dau. Sarah Dicken, act as guardian to her; Betty Burdine, sis. to my dau. Winnefred Dicken, act as her guardian; dau. Susanna Render. Divide rest of estate "amongst all my other fifteen children."
Executors: Richard Dicken, Benjamin Dicken, sons, and Henry Lewis.
Wit.: George Witherall, Benjamin Haynes, William Sampson, Joseph Sampson.

Inventory and Appraisal of Estate of John Sampson, dec'd. Recorded 19 Oct., 1778. Made by John Hume, William Chapman, Richard Dicken.

Inventory and Appraisal of Estate of William Favers, dec'd. Recorded 19 Oct., 1778. Made by B. Slaughter, Robert Coleman.

Will of John Scott Wood of Culpeper Co.
Dated 31 July, 1778. Proven 16 Nov., 1778.
Legatees: Wife Mary Wood. Son James Wood, and Grandson James Wood, Jr. Daus. Judith Wood, Betty Wood.
Executors: Wife, father Joseph Wood, Ambrose Barbour, Robert Alcock.
Wit.: Archibald Campbell, Eliza Wood, Joseph Wood, Jr.

Inventory and Appraisal of Estate of Henry Threlkeld, dec'd. Recorded 16 Nov., 1778.

Inventory and Appraisal of Estate of George Bourn, dec'd. Recorded 19 Oct., 1778. Made by John Long, William Gaines, Francis Hackley.

Division of Estate of Richard Pollard, dec'd. Recorded 22 Nov., 1778. Made by Edward Stevens, Charles Davenport, Edward Watkins. Devisees: Thomas Camp, Robert Pollard, John Camp, Milley Pollard - equal shares.

Inventory and Appraisal of Estate of Elisabeth Estes, dec'd. Recorded 18 Jan., 1779. Made by Edward Stevens, Charles Davenport, Edward Watkins.

Executors' Account of Estate of Margaret Ward, dec'd. Recorded 15 Feb., 1779.

Inventory and Appraisal of Estate of William Shackelford, dec'd. Recorded 15 Feb., 1779. Made by Bushrod Doggett, Oliver Clark, John Read.

Will of John Washburn of St. Mark's Parish, Culpeper Co.
Dated 3 Sept., 1778. Proven 15 Feb., 1779.
Legatees: Wife Susannah Washburn. Son Lewis Washburn. Other children not named.
Executors: Wife Susanna Washburn, son Eley Washburn.
Wit.: N. Pendleton, Ankay (X) Carder.

Will of Cornelius Mitchell of Bromfield Parish, Culpeper Co.
Dated 27 Nov., 1778. Proven 15 March, 1779.
Legatees: Wife Jane Mitchell, dau. Mary Frogg, grandson Mitchell Burk, dau. Fanny Mitchell (a minor).
Executors: Wife Jane Mitchell, William Roberts.
Wit.: John Jett, Robert Nixon, William Allen.

Will of William Mallory of Culpeper Co.
Dated 9 Feb., 1779. Proven March, 1779, Wilkes Co., No. Carolina.
Recorded 15 March, 1779, Culpeper Co.
Legatees: Daus.: Ann Mallory, Dorothy Mallory, Elisabeth Mallory, Mary Mallory (all minors).
Executors: Roger Mallory, Nathan Mallory, Henry Baker, David Baker.
Wit.: Wm. Gambill, Martin Deavenport, Thomas Gambill.

Will of Elizabeth Marshall of Culpeper Co.
Dated 17 April, 1779. Proven 17 May, 1779.
Legatees: Granddau. Elizabeth Marshall, dau. to my son, Thomas Marshall; grandson Lewis Marshall, son to my son, William Marshall; grandson George Marshall; grandson Thomas Marshall, son of John Marshall; grandson Thomas Smith; grandson William Lovell; dau. Mary McClanahan; son Markham Marshall; dau. Margaret Snelling; granddau. Elizabeth Snelling.
Executors: Sons William Marshall and Markham Marshall.
Wit.: Samuel Stallard, Peter Wood, George Hammett.

Will of Joseph Minor of Culpeper Co.
Dated 17 April, 1779. Proven 17 May, 1779.
Legatee: Grandson Eliott Minor, son of Armistead Minor.
Executor: Joseph Earley.
Wit.: Ephraim Rucker, Reuben Underwood, Joseph Earley, Jr.

Inventory and Appraisal of Estate of Brumfill Long, dec'd. Recorded 18 May, 1779. Made by John Gray, Richard Gaines, William Hawkins.

Inventory and Appraisal of Estate of William Mallory, dec'd. Recorded 18 May, 1779. Made by Thomas McClanahan, Mordecai Redd, George Calvert, Jr.

Estate Settlement of William Shackleford, dec'd. Devisee: His bro. James Shackleford. Recorded 17 May, 1779. Made by Henry Pendleton, Samuel Fargeson, Philip Pendleton.

Inventory and Appraisal of Estate of William Gaines, dec'd. Recorded 17 May, 1779. Made by John Crittenden, Thomas Garnett, John Garnett.

Will of Samuel Hening of St. Mark's Parish, Culpeper Co.
Dated 13 Nov., 1770. Proven 18 July, 1774(?1779).
Legatees: Sons: Samuel Hening, James Hening, David Hening. Daus.: Mary Stephens, wife of Lewis Stephens, Jr., of Frederick Co., Joanna Hening, Nancy Hening, Elenor Hening, Sally Hening.
Executors: Wife Elenor Hening, son David Hening, son Samuel Hening, son James Hening (when of age).
Wit.: Mary Meldrum, Briskett Davenport, William Meldrum.

Inventory and Appraisal of Estate of John Barracle(?). Recorded 21 June, 1779. Made by John Bradford, William Hughes, James Humphrey.

Will of Ann Abbott of Culpeper Co.
Dated 18 March, 1774. Proven 21 June, 1779.
Legatees: Dau. Margret and Armistead White and Presley White, my grandsons.
Executors: Grandson Armistead White, grandson Presley White.
Wit.: Isaac Campbell, Charles Clifton, Mary Elling (X) Campbell.

Inventory and Appraisal of Estate of Cornelius Mitchell. Recorded 8 April, 1779. Made by John Minor, James Browning, Benjamin Settle.

Will of John Foshee of St. Mark's Parish, Culpeper Co.
Dated 15 April, 1777. Proven 21 June, 1779.
Legatees: Wife Aphia Foshee. Sons: John Foshee, Benjamin Foshee, Thornton Foshee, George Foshee, Charles Foshee, Joseph Foshee, William Foshee, Elijah Foshee, Daniel Foshee. Daus.: Nancy Turgeman, Jemimah Foshee, Hannah Foshee, Elizabeth Foshee.
Executors: Wife Abphia Foshee, John Foshee, Benjamin Foshee.
Wit.: Luke Thornton, Peter Gatewood.

Inventory and Appraisal of Estate of James Mason, dec'd. Recorded 21 June, 1779. Made by Jacob Fishback, John Read, Hank Read.

Inventory and Appraisal of Estate of Mary Wash, dec'd. Recorded 21 June, 1779. Made by John Strother, Jr., James Browning, Robert Burk.

Inventory and Appraisal of Estate of John Lowen, dec'd. Recorded 19 July, 1779. Made by Richard Waugh, William Johnston, John Wharton.

Inventory and Appraisal of Estate of John Foshee, dec'd. Recorded 19 July, 1779. Made by James Thomas, Daniel Grinnan, Francis Lowen.

Will of John Berry of Bromfield Parish, Culpeper Co.
Dated 14 May, 1777 or 1779. Proven 19 July, 1779.
Legatees: Wife Jemima Berry. Children: Malchia Berry, Ann Whiten, John Berry, Jeriah Yeager, Anthony Berry, Jerusha Stinett, Acary, Elijah, Elisha and Aaron Berry, deceased dau. Betty Sutton's children one-eleventh of estate.
Executors: Son Malechiah Berry, son Aaron Berry, George Witherall.
Wit.: Elizabeth Towles, Ann Witherall, Mary Witherall, John Wetherall.

Will of William Greenless.
Dated 24 May, 1779. Proven 16 Aug., 1779.
Legatees: James Greenless, son of dec'd. bro. Simoh Greenless; Mary Greenless, sis. of James; the eldest son of bro. Peter Greenless; Jemima Greenless, Elisabeth Greenless.
Executor: James Cross.
Wit.: William Green, Joseph James, Nicholas Green.

Will of James Barker of Bromfield Parish, Culpeper Co.
Dated 31 Jan., 1770. Proven 15 March, 1779.
Legatee: Henry Hickman.
Executor: James Hickman.
Wit.: Edwin Hickman, David Hickman.

Administrator's Account of Estate of Shadrach Chavue. Recorded 16 Aug., 1779. Made by Henry Pendleton, James Pendleton, P. Pendleton.

Division of Estate of John Lowen, dec'd. Recorded 16 Aug., 1779. Made by Richard Waugh, William Johnston, John Wharton. Devisees: Widow, Margaret Lowen; Benjamin Lowen, Francis Lowen, Sarah Sisson, wife of William Sisson, Mary Thomas, wife of James Thomas, Ann Lowen.

Guardian's Account: The Estate of Richard Y. Wigginton to John Wigginton. Recorded 16 Aug., 1779.

Account of Guardian of ____ Ward, a girl. (Name can be Lewry, Lenory, etc.).

Inventory and Appraisal of Estate of Thomas Smith, dec'd. Recorded 16 Aug., 1779. Made by James Jett, Cornelius Mershon, John Freeman.

Lot and Houses of Thomas Smith, dec'd., divided. Recorded 16 Aug., 1779. Made by N. Pendleton, Edward Watkins, James Slaughter.

Account of Guardian of Winifred Dicken. Recorded 16 Aug., 1779.

Inventory and Appraisal of Estate of John Berry, dec'd. Recorded 20 Sept., 1779. Made by Joseph James, Jr., Ambrose Barbour, Michael Klugge.

Inventory and Appraisal of Estate of John Washburn, dec'd. Recorded 20 Sept., 1779. Made by Samuel Fargeson, James Hackley, William Dulany.

Inventory and Appraisal of Estate of Alexander Gaines, dec'd. Recorded 20 Sept., 1779. Made by John Gray, Richard Gaines.

Will of Hugh Crutcher of St. Mark's Parish, Culpeper Co.
Dated 17 Jan., 1778. Proven 20 Sept., 1779.
Legatees: Wife. Sons: Coleman Crutcher, William Crutcher, Robert Crutcher. At wife's death, divided among all of his children.
Executors: Wife, Edward Watkins, French Strother, Samuel Clayton.
Wit.: James Slaughter, Charles Davenport.

Executor's Account of Estate of Mrs. Elizabeth Estes, made by Robert Pollard. Estate Division gave one-sixth part to Robert Pollard, Thomas Camp, John Camp, Milley Pollard, Richard Coleman Pollard, Coleman Estes. Recorded 20 Sept., 1779.

Inventory and Appraisal of Estate of Elisabeth Marshall. Recorded 20 Sept., 1779. Made by John Hudnall, Thomas Henderson, Walter Stallard.

Inventory and Appraisal of Estate of Hugh Crutcher, dec'd. Recorded 18 Oct., 1779. Made by James Gaines, Zachary Petty, James Branham.

Will of Humphrey Gaines of Culpeper Co.
Dated 3 July, 1778. Proven 18 Oct., 1779.
Legatees: Wife Sarah Gaines. Son: William Gaines. Daus.: Frances Watts, Sarah Gaines, Esther Gaines, Hannah Gaines, Molley Gaines, Elizabeth Ann Gaines, Catharine Gaines.
Executrix: Wife Sarah Gaines.
Wit.: Ignatius Freeman, Charles Brooking.

Inventory and Appraisal of Estate of James Pollard, dec'd. Recorded 18 Oct., 1779. Made by Lawrence Slaughter, William Ball, George Slaughter.

Inventory and Appraisal of Estate of James Barker, dec'd. Recorded 18 Oct., 1779. Made by John Calvert, John C. Cocke, James Browning.

Inventory and Appraisal of Estate of Thomas Triplett, dec'd. Recorded 18 Oct., 1779. Made by Lawrence Slaughter, Edward Voss, John Field.

Account Report of Benjamin Dicken, guardian of Isaac Dicken and Daniel Dicken. Recorded 15 Nov., 1779, and Charles Dicken's Account.

Will of Esther Rucker of Bromfield Parish, Culpeper Co.
Dated 12 June, 1779. Proven 15 Nov., 1779.
Legatee: Sister Frances Rucker

Executors: Bro. William Rucker, Joseph Rucker.
Wit.: William Rucker, Elizabeth Rucker, Joseph Rucker.

Will of William Crawford of St. Mark's Parish, Culpeper Co.
Dated 2 Sept., 1777. Proven 15 Nov., 1779.
Legatees: Wife Sarah Crawford. Sons: John Crawford, William Crawford, Reuben Crawford, Charles Crawford, David Strother Crawford, Peter Crawford, Moses Crawford. Daus.: Jean Corbin, Ursley Crim(?). My several young children: Rosanna Crawford, Maryann Crawford, Lucey Crawford, Aaron Crawford, Betsey Crawford, Daniel Crawford, Nancey Crawford, George Crawford, Hannah Crawford.
Executor: Cornelius Mershon.
Wit.: Charles (X) Dores, Elizabeth (X) Dores.

Inventory and Appraisal of Estate of William Greenless, dec'd. Recorded 15 Nov., 1779. Made by William Champe, William Thornton, John Thornton.

Estate Division of Adam Bumgardner. Recorded 15 Nov., 1779. Devisees: widow who had married John Baker; an orphan. Made by Benjamin Roberts, Jr., William Walker, Robert Alcock.

Inventory and Appraisal of Estate of Moses Green, dec'd. Recorded 20 Dec., 1779. Made by William Field, George Slaughter, Philip Gatewood.

Will of Frederick Kabler of St. Mark's Parish, Culpeper Co.
Dated 6 March, 1779. Proven 17 Jan., 1780.
Legatees: Son Nicholas Kabler. Grandsons: William Kabler, Frederick Watts, Frederick Kabler, son of Christopher. Granddau. Barbery Kabler, dau. of Nicholas Kabler. Sons: Christopher Kabler, Nicholas Kabler.
Executors: Son Nicholas Kabler and grandson William Kabler.
Wit.: Frederick Zimmerman, John Brown, Christopher Zimmerman.

Sales of Estate of William Mallory, dec'd. Recorded 21 Feb., 1780. Reported by David Baker.

Inquisition re escheats of Estate of John Glassell who returned to Great Britain in 1775 sometime after the 19th of April. List of Jurors included.

Inquisition re escheat of land of George William Fairfax who was out of the United States on 19 April, 1775. He was a British citizen. Recorded 21 Feb., 1780.

Inquisition re escheat of land of John Serjant who is a British subject. 30 Oct., 1779.

Inquisition re escheat of land of Susanna Anne Goodwin. She was determined to be a British subject. 19 Nov., 1779.

Inquisition re escheat of land of James Compton. He was determined to be a British subject. 19 Nov., 1779.

Inquisition re escheat of land of Andrew Cochrane and Co. Determined they were British subjects. 27 Oct., 1779.

Inquisition re escheat of land of William Cunningham. Determined he was a British subject. 17 March, 1780.

Will of Edward Ballenger of St. Mark's Parish, Culpeper Co.
Dated 9 Dec., 1779. Proven 20 March, 1780.
Legatees: Son Edward Ballenger, Son-in-law Stokely Towles, Dau. Margary Towles, Grandson Gabriel Wilhoit, Dau. Agathy Kilbee, Dau. Susanna Ballenger. My seven children: Frances, John, Edward, Mary, Margary and Agathy. (Note: He named only six.)
Executors: Son Edward Ballenger, John Bailley.
Wit.: Robert Coleman, Jr., Ann (X) Bailley, Hutt(?) Randolph.

Inventory and Appraisal of Estate of Frederick Kabler, dec'd. Recorded 20 March, 1780. Made by ___ (not named).

Will of John Campbell of Bromfield Parish, Culpeper Co.
Dated 6 Feb., 1780. Proven 20 March, 1780.
Legatees: Wife Margaret Campbell, Dau. Margaret Campbell (a minor).
Executor: Martin Nalle.
Wit.: John Slaughter, Richard Gaines, Peter Deal.
Court, 17 April, 1780, appointed George Wetherall, admr.

Inventory and Appraisal of Estate of Capt. Christopher Dicken, dec'd. Recorded 20 March, 1780. Made by William Chapman, Ambrose Bohannon, John Hume.

Account of Sales of Estate of Christopher Dicken, dec'd. Recorded 17 April, 1780. Made by William Chapman, George Hume, John Hume.
Purchasers: Thomas Harrison, John Hughs, John Yowell, Charles Carter, George Rowe, William Herndon, James Shurley, Benj. Lillard, Stephen Haynes, Samuel Fargeson, Capt. John Lillard, John Clark, Will Baxter, Joseph Henuley, Will Chapman, Ambrose Bohannon, John Garr, Henry Cremore, Capt. Rice, Fisher Rice, Elias Campbell, Adam Yager, Ben Haynes, Ruben Thomas, Anthony Hughs, Will Kelly, Mark Finks, Reginal Burdine, Robert McAlester, Will Henson, Morton Christopher, Isaac Smith, John Ascher(?), Andrew Glassell, Charles Creal, Nicholas Wilhoit, John Garret, Michael Garr, Adam Fisher, Robert Render, John Crow, Henry Chrisler, James Yowell, John Burdine, Mary Dicken, Richard Dicken, John Dicken, Benj. Dicken, Henry Lewis, John Bell, Will Grayson, John Yager, Thomas Graves, Stephen Fisher, John Thomas, Capt. John Banbever, John Yowell, John Preesons, Charles Henson, Jesse Thomas, Timothy Amiss, Joel Early, Elias Fisher, Will Baxter, Ambrose Bohannon, Frances Harvey, John Hume, Jasper Haynes, Tobias Wilhoit, James Hurt, Tobias Wilhoit, Henry Toles, Samuel Yowell, George Row, Elisha Berry, John Garret, Bernard Fisher, Aere(?) Berry, John Archer, Andrew Glassell, Michael Yager, Richard Dicken, Ben Dicken, Will Dicken, Will

Hurt, Francis Harvey, Nicholas Wilhoit, Michael Huffman, John Clore, Adam ____, Thomas Banks, Ruben Medley, Elias Campbell, Simeon Bluford, Joseph Delany, John Sampson, Jeremiah Kirtley, Lewis Garr, Henry Blankenbeeker, Michael Clore, Michael Yager, Henry Chrisler, Will Kirtley, Thomas Chapman, Samuel Yowell, Charles Henson, George May, Dennis Crow, Will Kelley, John Burdine, Joseph Render, Joshua Render, Mary Dicken, Jesse Thomas, David Yowell, Ruben Crigler, Jonathan Garret, Peter Cook, Jno. Lewis, Frederick Tanner, Isaac Smith, Charles Hendson, Henry Lewis, James Shearly, James Jones.

Inventory and Appraisal of Estate of Edward Ballenger, dec'd. Recorded 17 April, 1780. Made by Robert Coleman, Jr., George Haywood, William Allan.

Will of William Rice of Culpeper Co.
Dated 9 Feb., 1780. Proven 17 April, 1780.
Legatees: Wife Sarah Rice. Sons: Richard Rice, Benajah Rice, John Rice and Richard Rice. Daus.: Hannah Rice, Ann Graves, Sarah Graves wife of Edward Graves.
Executors: Sons Benajah Rice, John Rice, Richard Rice, son-in-law John Graves.
Wit.: John Gibbs, Richard Seebree, William Zackary, John Lindslay, Samuel Delp.

Dower Division of Estate of Rev. Thompson. Recorded 17 April, 1780. Made by Robert Green, James Duncanson, Henry Taliaferro, Reuben Long, William Bradley.

Will of Bryant Thornhill of St. Mark's Parish, Culpeper Co.
Dated 28 Dec., 1779. Proven 17 April, 1780.
Legatees: Wife Thomson Thornhill. Sons: Joseph Thornhill, John Thornhill, Ruben Thornhill (unmarried), William Thornhill. Dau. Elizabeth Boley.
Executors: Wife Thomson Thornhill, sons Joseph Thornhill and John Thornhill.
Wit.: William Allan, Jeremiah (X) Asher, William Claterbuck.

Inventory and Appraisal of Estate of John Campbell, dec'd. Recorded 15 May, 1780. Made by William Flowrence, William Hughes, Michell Slone.

Account of Estate Sales of John Berry. Recorded 19 June, 1780.
Purchasers: Anthony Berry, Elijah Berry, Aron Berry, Acrey Berry, Ambrose Barber, Elisha Berry, John Berry, Will Baxter, David Yowell, John Cave, Nicholas Leatherer, Malachia Berry, Wyatt Coleman, Samuel White, Robert Henseley, Samuel Yowell, Adam Yager, James Yowell, John Hughs, Ben Dicken, Benjamin Stennett, John Graves, Daniel Campbell, William Hughs, William Whitten, Paul Leatherer, Michael Zimmerman, John Wealkey, William Gaines, Samuel Leather, Elizabeth Henseley, Moses Garriot, William Jenkins, Robert Render, John Broyle, James White, John Crow, John McKenzie, Thomas Cubbage, Samuel Delp, Jonathan Garriot, Charles Henson, Michael Clore, John Turnham, Anne Whitten, James Crow, John Yowell, Will Herndon, Arjalon

Price, Will Campbell, James Ramsbottom, Jacob Crim, John Broyle, Joseph James, Jr., Joshua Shumate, Robert Nixon, Ruben Thomas, Rev. Thomas Harrison, Christopher Zimmerman, George Restall.

Inventory and Appraisal of Estate of Bryant Thornhill, dec'd. Recorded 19 June, 1780. Made by William Bradley, Ruben Zimmerman, John Boulley(?).

Inventory and Appraisal of Estate of Abraham Gibson, dec'd. Recorded 21 Aug., 1780. Made by John Bradford, James Humphrey, John Lawlor(?).

Inventory and Appraisal of Estate of John Cooper, dec'd. Recorded 21 Aug., 1780. Made by James Duncan, James Graves, William Duncan, Jr.

Inventory and Appraisal of Estate of John Scott Wood, dec'd. Recorded 21 Aug., 1780. Made by Alexander Waugh, Charles Brooking, William Watts.

Inventory and Appraisal of Estate of William Crawford, dec'd. Recorded 21 Aug., 1780. Made by Thomas Spelman, John Read, Vincent Tapp.

Will of Joseph Blackwell.
Dated 28 Jan., 1780. Proven 21 Aug., 1780.
Legatees: Wife Catey Blackwell. Children: William Blackwell, Benjamin Blackwell, Lucy Blackwell, Elizabeth Blackwell.

Will of William Allen.
Dated 23 March, 1780. Proven 18 Sept., 1780.
Legatees: Wife Mary Allen land he received from his father. "all my children" - not named.
Executors: Wife Mary Allen, Daniel Bradford.
Wit.: John Bradford, Enoch Bradford, Wm. Green.

Inventory and Appraisal of Estate of Gabriel Jones, dec'd. Recorded 18 Sept., 1780. Made by William Ball, Hezekiah Brown, William Hawkins.

Inventory and Appraisal of Estate of William Bell. Recorded 16 Oct., 1780. Made by Jacob Medley, Edward Tinsley, Ephraim Rucker.

Will of John Brown of Bromfield Parish, Culpeper Co.
Dated 7 Jan., 1774. Proven 20 May, 1780.
Legatees: Wife Elisabeth Brown. Sons: William Brown, Daniel Brown, Thomas Brown, Coleman Brown, Richard Brown, John Brown. Daus.: Ann Brown, Mary Brown, Elizabeth Dickerson.
Executors: Wife Elizabeth Brown, son Thomas Brown, son Daniel Brown.
Wit.: John Dillard, Sophia (X) Dillard.

Executor's Account of Estate of John Smith, dec'd. Recorded 28 ____, 1780. Made by Edward Watkins.

Will of Martin Nalle of Culpeper Co.
Dated 14 March, 1780. Proven 20 Nov., 1780.

Legatees: Brothers Richard Nalle, John Nalle, Francis Nalle, James Nalle.
Wit.: Thomas Brown, James Sims, Thomas Garriott.

Executor's Account of Estate of John Berry, dec'd. Recorded 21 Nov., 1780. Made by Malechiah Berry.

Division of Estate of Capt. Gabriel Jones, dec'd. Recorded 19 Feb., 1781. Inventory made by James Green and John Gray. Devisees: William Broadus who had married the widow of the decedent. Remainder divided among the four children, each child received the equivalent of 125£ 8s 6d. Division made by Robert Pollard, Robert Slaughter, Jr., William Ball.

Executor's Account of Estate of John Scott Wood, dec'd. Recorded 19 Feb., 1781. Made by Joseph Wood, Robert Alcock.

Will of Margaret Kirtley of Culpeper Co.
Dated 26 Feb., 1777. Proven 20 March, 1781.
Legatees: Grandau. Ann Collins, grandau. Marget Collins.
Executors: James Collins and son, Thomas Kirtley.
Wit.: Daniel Ray, Gideon (X) Crawford, Oliver Crawford.

Account of Sales of Estate of ___ Ping. Recorded 16 April, 1781. Purchasers: Jane Restall, Joseph Strother, Robert Slaughter, Amon B. Rice, James Graves, John Graves, Armistead White, William Pinegar, James Lillard, Daniel Brown, Hezekiah Boone, Benjamin Lillard, Thomas Shelton.

Will of Elliott Bohannon of Culpeper Co.
Dated __ April, 1781. Proven 21 May, 1781.
Legatees: Wife Ann Bohannon. Sons: Ambrose Bohannon, John Bohannon, Elliott Bohannon. Daus.: Mildred Gaines, Mary Herndon, Anne Kirtley. "my eight children." (Others were not named).
Executors: Sons Ambrose Bohannon, John Bohannon and Elliott Bohannon.
Wit.: James Archer, William Kirtley, Julius Gibbs.

Will of James Graves of Bromfield Parish, Culpeper Co.
Dated 27 April, 1781. Proven 21 May, 1781.
Legatees: Wife Sarah Graves. Daus.: Mary Parks, Jail Jones. Sons: John Graves. James Parks his surveyor's instruments. James Graves Jones.
Executors: Son John Graves and two sons-in-law Richard Parks and William Jones.
Wit.: Ben Gaines, John Deel.

Will of Jonathan Pratt of Culpeper Co.
Dated 24 Oct., 1777. Proven 21 May, 1781.
Legatees: Son Thomas Pratt. My wife's daughter, Katharine Redman.
Executor: Son Thomas Pratt.
Wit.: John Flint, Richard Flint.

Will of Hannah Triplett of Culpeper Co.
Dated 3 Sept., 1780. Proven 21 May, 1781.

Legatees: Son Thomas Triplett, a servant left her by her deceased husband.
Wit.: Thomas Slaughter, William Roberts, Larkin Field.

Inventory and Appraisal of William Allen, dec'd. Recorded 21 May, 1781. Made by William Roberts, John Corbin, Benjamin Elkins.

Oath of Allegiance - 1777 - a copy. Not signed.

Inventory and Appraisal of Estate of James Graves, dec'd. Recorded 18 June, 1781. Made by Ben Gaines, Robt. Slaughter, Cadwallader Slaughter.

Will of John Deer of Culpeper Co.
Dated 28 March, 1781. Proven 18 June, 1781.
Legatees: Wife Catharine Deer. Sons: Moses Deer, John Deer. Daus.: Mary Deer, Elisabeth Deer, Catharine Rider, Susanna Brown, Dorothy Fletcher(?), Eve Bohon.
Executors: Ambrose Bohannon and son, John Deer.
Wit.: George Lornven, Reuben Fleshman, Moses Fleshman.

Will of Christopher Zimmerman.
Dated 6 March, 1780. Proven 18 June, 1781.
Legatees: Pollard Brown, or if he dies without heirs, then to Robert Brown.
Executors: Thomas Brown and Robert Brown.
Wit.: Nicholas Kabler, John Brown, William Kabler.

Inventory and Appraisal of Estate of Elliott Bohannon, dec'd. Recorded 16 July, 1781. Made by Reuben Beale, John Gibbs.

Will of Christopher Blankinbeeker of Bromfield Parish, Culpeper Co.
Dated 26 April, 1781. Proven 16 July, 1781.
Legatees: Wife Christeenah Blankinbeeker. Sons: Ephraim Blankinbeeker, Lewis Blankinbeeker, Jonas Blankinbeeker.
Executors: friend Jacob Blankinbeeker, John Wayland, Jr.
Wit.: Henry Blankinbeeker, Michael (X) Utz, John (X) Blankinbeeker.

Will of Samuel Hening.
Dated (none). Proven 16 July, 1781.
Legatees: Bro. James Hening. Sisters: Nancy Hening, Nelly Hening, Salley Hening.
Executors: Bros. David Henning, James Henning.
Wit.: Samuel Clayton, James Gaines, David Hening.

Appraisal of Estate of Mrs. Margaret Kirtley, dec'd. Recorded 20 Aug., 1781. Made by Ephraim Rucker, William Harvey, Joel Larley.

Inventory and Appraisal of Estate of John Deer. Recorded 20 Aug., 1781. Made by Richard Major, Benajah Rice, Lewis Booten.

Will of William Sparks of Bromfield Parish, Culpeper Co.
Dated 6 July, 1781. Proven 20 Aug., 1781.
Legatees: Wife Elizabeth Sparks. Sons: Jasper Sparks (a minor), John Sparks, William Sparks, Joseph Sparks, Humphrey Sparks. Daus.: Mary Sparks, Elizabeth Sparks, Sary Sparks.
Executors: Wife and bros.-in-law Jasper Haynes and Joseph Haynes.
Wit.: Ann Clark, Milley (X) Sparks, John Willys(?).

Will of Thomas Bryand of Culpeper Co.
Dated 14 June, 1781. Proven 20 Aug., 1781.
Legatees: Wife Sarrah Briand. Sons: Benjamin Briand, Wilfre Briand, Bruenton Briand, Hackney Hunt.
Wit.: Joseph James, Daniel James, Mary James.

Will of James Collings of St. Mark's Parish, Culpeper Co.
Dated 6 April, 1781. Proven 21 Aug., 1781.
Legatees: Wife Mary Collings. Sons: Francis Collings (a minor), James Collings, Tandy Collings, Thomas Collings, John Collings. Daus.: Mary Collings, Milley Broadus, Margaret Collings.
Executors: Col. James Barbour, wife Mary Collings, son Francis Collings.
Wit.: Richard Broadus, William Crawford, Gideon (X) Crawford.

Will of Francis Fletcher.
Dated 25 March, 1781. Proven 20 Aug., 1781.
Legatees: Wife Nanny Fletcher, dau. of Thomas Colens. Children: Jenny, Jerry, White, Anne White, Billey and Sukey.
Executors: Thomas Allen, Daniel Field.
Wit.: John Rosson, Henry Elly, Francis Hume.

Will of Richard Ship of Culpeper Co.
Dated 9 Feb., 1781. Proven 20 Aug., 1781.
Legatees: Wife Isabel Ship. Sons: Ambrose Ship, Richard Ship, Josiah Ship, John Ship, Thomas Ship. Daus.: Lucy(?) Ship, Nancey Ship.
Executors: Job Popham, Joshua Shumate, George Witherall.
Wit.: William Pinnegar, Elizabeth (X) Pinnegar, Lucey (X) Thornhill.

Will of Nicholas Yager of Brumfield Parish, Culpeper Co.
Dated 12 Sept., 1779. Proven 20 Aug., 1781.
Legatees: Wife Susanna Yager. Sons: Solomon Yager, Nicholas Yager, Frederick Yager, Cornelius Yager, Absolom Yager, Benjamin Yager, Elijah Yager, Jessee Yager. Daus.: Peggy Yager, twins Rosanna Yager and Susanna Yager.
Executors: Nicholas Wilhoite, John Yager, John Gaar, wife Susanna Yager.
Wit.: Godfrey Yager, Nicholas (N) Yager, Cornelius Yager.

Will of Jane Prichard of Culpeper Co.
Dated 14 July, 1781. Proven 20 Aug., 1781.
Legatees: Isabella Hill, wife of John Hill; Lydia Hill, dau. of Isabella Hill; Mary Hill, dau. of Isabella Hill; Jenny Hill, dau. of Isa-

bella Hill; Elizabeth Page, Sarah Cook, Ann Trecley(?), Elisabeth Cambwell, William Mason, Mary Baron. (No relationship stated for any of the legatees.--DFW)
    Executors: none.
    Wit.: William Davis, John Hill, Elizabeth Maddox.

    Will of Mark Bryant of Culpeper Co.
    Dated 26 July, 1781. Proven 20 Aug., 1781.
    Legatees: Mary Monroe, Nella Monroe, Mary Cliffton, William Tool, Joseph Allen.
    Executors: William Tool, Joseph Allen.
    Wit.: William Tool, Charles Cliffton, Joseph Roberts.

    Will of Joel Watts of Culpeper Co.
    Dated 17 July, 1781. Proven 20 Aug., 1781.
    Legatees: Wife Isabel Watts. Son: Frederick Watts. Daus.: Lettice(?) Brown, Joanna Stewart. Grandchildren: Barbara Watts Thomas, ____ Thomas, John Thomas, Larkin Thomas, dau. and sons of my dau. Barbara Thomas.
    Executors: Son Frederick Watts, William Kabler.
    Wit.: John Brown, Reuben Doggett, William Kabler.

    Inventory and Appraisal of Estate of John Tibboo, dec'd. Recorded 20 Aug., 1781. Made by Ambrose Barbour, James Yowell, Jacob Blackinbeeker.

    Inventory and Appraisal of Estate of Jonathan Pratt, dec'd. Recorded 20 Aug., 1781. Made by Thomas Graves, John Flynt, Richard Flynt, Thomas Graves, Jr.

    Inventory and Appraisal of Estate of John Brown, dec'd. Recorded 20 Aug., 1781. Made by James Graves, Francis Nalle, William Hill.

    Inventory and Appraisal of Estate of Joel Watts, dec'd. Recorded 15 Oct., 1781. Made by John Wharton, William Kabler, Richard Chilton.

    Will of George Witherall.
    Dated 13 June, 1781. Proven 15 Oct., 1781.
    Legatees: Son John Witherall. Daus.: ____ Towls, Anne Witherall, Mary Witherall.
    Executors: Robert Shotwell, Job Ephraim, Henry Towles, Henry Hill.
    Wit.: Eve (X) Yager, Elizabeth (X) Yager, John Hume.

    Inventory and Appraisal of Estate of John Garriott, dec'd. Recorded 17 Nov., 1781. Made by John Gray, John Wallis, Leonard Barnes.

    Will of William Duncan of Brumfield Parish, Culpeper Co.
    Dated 24 Feb., 1781. Proven 15 Oct., 1781.
    Legatees: Sons: Charles Duncan, James Duncan, Rawley Duncan, William Duncan, John Duncan, dec'd., Joseph Duncan. Dau.: Anne Roberts, dec'd.
    Executors: Son Joseph Duncan, son James Duncan, John Bradford.
    Wit.: William Hughs, William Browning, Shadrach Browning.

Will of Adam Wayland of Brumfield Parish, Culpeper Co.
Dated 16 May, 1775. Proven 15 Oct., 1781.
Legatees: Wife Elizabeth Wayland. "among my children."
Executors: Son John Wayland, Godfrey Yeager.
Wit.: ____ Blankinbeeker, Henry (H. B.) Barlow, Barnett (B. F.) Fisher.

Will of Thomas Quinn of Culpeper Co.
Dated 10 Jan., 1781. Proven 19 Nov., 1781.
Legatees: Wife Jenny Quinn. Children: Frankey Quinn, Thomas Quinn and one on the way.
Executors: James Quinn, William Watts, William Rogers.
Wit.: Richard Quinn, William Glass, Elizabeth Quinn.

Inventory and Appraisal of Estate of William Cox, dec'd. Recorded 19 Nov., 1781. Made by Ben Pulliam, William Jones, Thomas Pulliam.

Inventory and Appraisal of Estate of William Sparks', dec'd. Recorded 19 Nov., 1781. Made by Ambrose Powell, James Clark, Absolom Bobo.

Inventory and Appraisal of Estate of Adam Wayland, dec'd. Recorded 19 Nov., 1781. Made by Henry Hill, Andrew Carpenter, Fisher Rice.

Inventory and Appraisal of Estate of Christopher Blankenbeeker, dec'd. Recorded 19 Nov., 1781. Made by Thomas Porter, Fisher Rice, Andrew Carpenter.

Will of Elijah Berry.
Dated 11 Sept., 1781. Proven 19 Nov., 1781.
Legatees: Wife Anne Berry. Leonard Berry, son of Malechiah Berry - two years schooling. Elijah Berry, son of Aaron Berry - two years schooling. At wife's death to four children of my bro. Acrey Berry - viz. Sary Berry, Jemimah Berry, Mary Berry, John Berry.
Executors: Wife Anne Berry, bro. Acrey Berry.
Wit.: William Grayson, Abrey Berry, James Grayson.

Will of James Hurt of Bromfield Parish, Culpeper Co.
Dated 10 Sept., 1781. Proven 19 Nov., 1781.
Legatee: Wife Jemima Hurt.
Executors: Wife's father, Richard Gaines, bro. William Hurt.
(Note: James Hurt was going into the militia and had no children.)
Wit.: John (X) Yowell, Elias Campbell, John Campbell.

Will of John Bacar Turner of Culpeper Co.
Dated 12 March, 1778. Proven 19 Nov., 1781.
(Note: After Culpeper Co. appears the word "Chililman" which has not been interpreted.--DFW)
Legatees: Wife Rebacah Turner. At her death, equally to Mary Bradford and Elisabeth Williams.
Executors: William Johnston and John Deal.
Wit.: Peter Deal, John Deal, Elisabeth (X) Deal.

Inventory and Appraisal of Estate of William Duncan, dec'd. Recorded 19 Nov., 1781. Made by John Lawlor, William Browning, John Corbin.

Inventory and Appraisal of Estate of Joseph Blackwell, dec'd. Recorded 19 Nov., 1781. Made by Hank Read, Thomas Spilman (?Coleman), Oliver Clark.

Inventory and Appraisal of Estate of Richard Doggett, dec'd. Recorded 19 Nov., 1781. Made by James Hackley, Capt. James Tutt and William Dulany.

Will of Alexander McQueen.
Dated 29 June 1774. Proven 19 Nov., 1781.
Legatees: Wife Henreter Cooper (alias McQueen). Refers to "my former wife" and children by both wives. Son John McQueen.
Executors: Wife Henreter Cooper (alias McQueen), a son by her, Charles McQueen.
Wit.: William Williams, Lucey Williams, James Williams.

Will of Ezekiel Hanes of Culpeper Co.
Dated 21 July, 1781. Proven 17 Dec., 1781.
Legatees: Wife. Sons: Jacob Hanes, Carlile Hanes, Isaac Hanes. Dau.: Sarah Painter. Grson.: Abraham Hanes, a minor.
Executors: Thomas McClanahan, John Strother.
Wit.: John Strother, Charles Browning, Samuel (X) Ashford.

Inventory and Appraisal of Estate of Thomas Bryant, dec'd. Recorded 17 Dec., 1781. Made by James Gaines, Thomas Pope, James Long.

Inventory and Appraisal of Estate of Job Popham, dec'd. Recorded 21 Jan., 1782. Made by Ben Gaines, William Murtle, Thomas Brown.

Inventory and Appraisal of Estate of Charles Carter, dec'd. Recorded 21 Jan., 1782. Made by John Long, William Pierce, James Branham.

Will of Jasper Haynes of Culpeper Co.
Dated 19 June, 1779. Proven 21 Jan., 1782.
Legatees: Wife. Sons: Joseph Haynes, Jasper Haynes, Stephen Haynes, Benjamin Haynes, James Haynes, William Haynes. Daus.: Elizabeth Moses, Mary Haynes, Anne Haynes.
Executors: Son Joseph Haynes, son Jasper Haynes.
Wit.: Alexander Waugh, Humphrey Sparks, William Phillips.

Will of William Roebuck of Brumfield Parish, Culpeper Co.
Dated 30 Oct., 1780. Proven 21 Jan., 1782.
Legatees: Wife Mary Roebuck. Son Rawleigh Roebuck. Daus.: Elisabeth Roebuck, Millie Roebuck, Lucey Roebuck. His father was Robert Roebuck.
Executors: John Walker, David Tinsley, bro. Robert Roebuck, wife Mary Roebuck.
Wit.: Joshua Lindsay, Lussy(?) Vernon, Sarah Vernon, Richard Vernon.

Inventory and Appraisal of Estate of William Cannon, dec'd. Recorded 18 Feb., 1782. Made by John Barbee, Patterson Fletcher, John Freeman.

Inventory and Appraisal of Estate of Simon Stone, dec'd. Recorded 18 Feb., 1782. Made by Hank Read, John Read, William Bowmer.

Inventory and Appraisal of Estate of William Roebuck, dec'd. Recorded 18 Feb., 1782. Made by Benjamin Zahary, Ambrose Medley, Zacharias Gibbs.

Will of Charles Morgan of St. Mark's Parish, Culpeper Co.
Dated 3 Feb., 1782. Proven 18 Feb., 1782.
Legatees: Daus.: Ann Wright, Milley Cornelius. Grandson Charles Morgan Thornhill (a minor). Mentions his son-in-law, Bryant Thornhill. Grandsons: Morgan Wright, Charles Cornelius. Elizabeth Jones, a legatee, apparently no relation. Mentions son-in-law Absolom Cornelius.
Executors: Harry Taliaferro, Thomas Wright, Absolom Cornelius.
Wit.: Reuben Thornhill, Absolom Bradley, Zachary Shackleford.

Will of Benjamin Roberts of Culpeper Co.
Dated 8 Aug., 1781. Proven 17 Dec., 1782.
Legatees: Wife Sarah Roberts. Sons: Joseph Roberts, Benjamin Roberts, John Roberts, George Roberts. Daus.: Elizabeth Roberts, Jemima Roberts, Sarah Roberts, Mary Roberts. Infant on the way.
Executors: Bro. Joseph Roberts, Daniel Field.
Wit.: James Sims, Joseph Roberts.

Will of Joseph Thornhill.
Dated 11 Oct., 1781. Proven 18 Feb., 1782.
Legatees: Wife Elizabeth Thornhill. My young children.
Executors: "my son Thomas if please God he returns from the Southward Army," bro. Reuben Thornhill, William Allen.
Wit.: Reuben Zimmerman, John Foshee, John Fletcher.

Inventory and Appraisal of Estate of Alexander McQueen, dec'd. Recorded 18 Feb., 1782. Made by John Yancey, Jr., Benjamin Tutt, James Whitehead.

Will of John Blakey of Culpeper Co.
Dated 30 Dec., 1781. Proven 18 March, 1782.
Legatees: Wife Jane Blakey. Sons: John Blakey, Churchill Blakey. Daus.: Frances Bush, heirs of dau. Martha Morriss, dec'd., Sarah Edins, Elizabeth Daviss.
Executors: Son John Blakey, Joel Earley.
Wit.: Jonathan Cowherd, Thomas Kirtley, Elisabeth Cowherd.

Will of Benjamin Roberts of St. Mark's Parish, Culpeper Co.
Dated 14 Feb., 1782. Proven 18 March, 1782.
Legatees: Son Benjamin Roberts, Joseph Roberts. Grandsons: Philla Gathous Roberts, Boanerges Roberts. Grandsons: Joseph Roberts, son of Benjamin Roberts; Benjamin Field, son of Daniel Field; Benjamin Dulany; and at dau. Mary's decease, divided amongst her four youngest children. (Note: in paragraph on Benjamin Dulany.) Dau. Jemima Kirtley and her

children. Daus.: Hannah Field, Anne Field, Mary Dulany. William Field, son of Hannah Field, not to receive anything but rest of Hannah's children do.

Executors: Son-in-law Daniel Field, son Joseph Roberts.
Wit.: Thomas Slaughter, Reuben Field, John Roberts.

Account of Sale of Estate of William Wright, dec'd. Recorded 18 March, 1782. Made by Henry Field, Jr.

Inventory and Appraisal of Estate of Joseph Thornhill, dec'd. Recorded 18 March, 1782. Made by John Brown, William Kabler, Nicholas Kabler.

Inventory and Appraisal of Estate of Ezekiel Haynes, dec'd. Recorded 18 March, 1782. Made by George Calvert, Sr., Alpheus Bell, John Calvert.

Inventory and Appraisal of Estate of Elijah Berry, dec'd. Recorded 18 March, 1782.

Inventory and Appraisal of Estate of Charles Morgan, dec'd. Recorded 18 March, 1782. Made by John Johnston, John Triplett, Reuben Zimmerman.

Inventory and Appraisal of Estate of Nicholas Yager, dec'd. Recorded 18 March, 1782. Made by Thomas Porter, John Major, Fisher Rice for part in Virginia. Made by William Dicken, Stephen Fisher, Nicholas Wilhoit for part in Kentucky.

Inventory and Appraisal of Estate of Richard Ship, dec'd. Recorded 18 March, 1782. Made by Robert Strother, Robert Jones, Joshua Shumate.

Inventory and Appraisal of Estate of William Gully, dec'd. Recorded 28 March, 1782. Made by Ambrose Barbour, Joseph James, Jr., Aaron Berry, John Triplett.

Inventory and Appraisal of Estate of Francis Fletcher, dec'd. Recorded 18 March, 1782. Made by Henry Elly, Bassil Hooe, Francis Hume. Also Account Sale filed same day.

Account Sale of Estate of Ezekiel Haynes, dec'd. Recorded 18 March, 1782. Made by John Strother.
Purchasers: John Ashford, Alpheus Beall, John C. Cocke, Elisha Cheek, John Chapman, John Calvert, Layton Cooper, Robert Covington, John Cadwallader, Col. William Champe, James Duncan, Mark Fulton, Reuben Finnell, Isaac Haynes, Anthony Hughs, William Hughs, LeeRoy Hitt(or Hill), Henry Hickman, Jacob Haines, George Johnston, Isaac Jackson, Martin Johnston, John Lawlor, George Mozingo, Bryant McGrath, William McQueen, Henry Manifee, Robert Nixon, Jeremiah Prest, Benjamin Reader, Jr., James Pinion, Daniel Peyton, Isaac Painter, John Riley, John Strother, Simon Vaught, William Watte, Thomas Yates, George Roberts.

Will of John Payton of Bromfield Parish, Culpeper Co.
Dated 14 Oct., 1781. Proven 18 March, 1782.

Legatees: Wife Ureth Payton. Sons: Thomas Payton, Charles Payton, Jeremiah Payton. Daus.: Nancey Payton, Marey Payton, Elizabeth Scogin. Granddau. Jemima Payton.
Executors: Son Thomas Payton, Thomas McClanahan.
Wit.: John Bradford, W. L. Jacobi, Katharine (X) Jacobi.

Will of Thomas Oxford of Culpaper Co.
Dated 14 Nov., 1781. Proven 15 April, 1782.
Legatees: Wife Elizabeth Oxford, dau. Molley Jennings, grdau. Elizabeth Jennings (a minor), grdau. Hannah Jennings, grson. Thomas Oxford Jennings.
Executors: Wife Elizabeth Oxford, Augustin Jennings.
Wit.: Daniel Farmer, William Field, John (F) Farmer.

Will of Ignatius Tureman of Culpeper Co.
Dated 28 March, 1781. Proven 15 April, 1782.
Legatees: Elener Tureman. Children: Susanah Tureman, Lucy Tureman (minors).
Executors: Wife, Jacob Medley, Ambrose Medley.
Wit.: Samuel Brooking, Ephraim Klug, Robert Brooking, Lydia (X) Klug.

Inventory of Estate of William Dillard, dec'd. Recorded 2 April, 1782. Made by John Barbee, John Lightfoot, John Jeffries.

Division of Estate of William Rice, dec'd. Dated 18 Oct., 1780. All Legatees present and of age have themselves agreeably divided the estate. Recorded 20 May, 1782. Reported by Reuben Beale, Joseph Easley, Edward Tinsley.

Inventory and Appraisal of Estate of Thomas Oxford, dec'd. Recorded 20 May, 1782. Made by John Roberts, Thomas Brown, Sr., Michael Marr.

Inventory and Appraisal of Estate of John Blakey, dec'd. Recorded 20 May, 1782. Made by John Blakey, Jr., Joel Earley.

Inventory and Appraisal of Estate of James Hurt, dec'd. Recorded 20 May, 1782. Made by George Row, Richard Dicken, Henry Lewis.

Inventory and Appraisal of Estate of George Witherall, dec'd. Recorded 20 May, 1782. Made by Fisher Rice, John Hume, George Hume.

Guardianship Account of Christopher Dicken with his brother Richard Dicken. Recorded 19 March, 1782(?). Made by Thomas Porter, George Hume, John Hume.

Estate Division, Abraham Gibson, dec'd. The widow's dower, Abfia Gibson, Ann Gibson - 3 equal parts. Recorded 20 May, 1782. Made by James Thomas, Daniel Grinnan, Greensby Waggoner.

Inventory and Appraisal of Estate of Jasper Haynes, dec'd. Recorded 17 June, 1782. Made by Humphrey Sparks, Lewis Conner, Ambrose Medley.

Will of William Courts of Culpeper Co.
Dated 31 March, 1780. Proven 19 Nov., 1781.
Legatees: Wife Mary Courts. Sons: Charles Courts, John Courts, William Courts, Walter Hanson(?) Courts.
Executors: Wife Mary Courts, Benjamin Gaines.
Wit.: Arjalon Price, John Strother, Jr., John Gatewood.

Will of William Gaines (going into the Army).
Dated none. Proven 17 June, 1783.
Legatees: Mother to live on his land until her death, then divided among all his sisters.
Executors: Thomas Watts, James Quinn.
Wit.: Thomas Watts, George Tomlinson, Richard Richardson, Sarah Gaines.

Will of David Davis of Culpeper Co.
Dated 17 Jan., 1782. Proven 17 June, 1782.
Legatees: Sons: Thomas Davis, Jessee Davis. Children to William Davis alias William Leonard and Fanny Davis alias Fanny Leonard, Liddy Davis, Richard Davis, Thomas Davis, Betty Davis, Jessee Davis (all minors).
Executors: William Sherrell, John Wigginton.
Wit.: David (D) Canaggee, Elender (X) Canaggee, John Wigginton.

Inventory and Appraisal of Estate of James Collins, dec'd. Recorded 15 July, 1782. Made by Ephraim Rucker, Joseph Earley, Elijah Kirtley.

Inventory and Appraisal of Estate of David Davis, dec'd. Recorded 26 June, 1782. Made by James Jett, John Barbee, David Carnagee.

Will of John Nalle of Bromfield Parish, Culpeper Co.
Dated 16 Sept., 1780. Proven 19 Aug., 1782.
Legatees: Wife Mary Nalle. Sons: Richard Nalle, John Nalle, William Nalle, Francis Nalle, James Nalle. Grandson John Nalle, son of my son John Nalle. Grandson John Nalle, son of my son William Nalle. Granddau. Mary Nalle, dau. of my son William Nalle and Susanna, his wife. Dau. Agatha Hitt ½ service of a negro woman, other half to "my grandson James Sims from the time of my daughter's marriage to Russell Hitt and after my daughter's decease.....to my grandson James Sims. Daus.: Mary Sims, Ann Burk, Elizabeth Sims, Gressel Parker, Amie Morriss. Grandson Martin Morriss, son of William Morriss and Amie Morriss. Son Martin Nalle if he appear "my will bearing date 1777 to take place."
Executors: Wife Mary Nalle, son John Nalle, son Francis Nalle.
Wit.: John Brown, Thomas Brown.

Guardian's Account for Lucy Ward. Recorded 20 Aug., 1782.

Inventory and Appraisal of Estate of George Calvert, dec'd. Recorded 20 Aug., 1782. Made by Thomas Jerdan, James Browning, James Browning, Jr.

Will of John Carpenter of Culpeper Co.
Dated 29 June, 1782. Proven 16 Sept., 1782.

Legatees: Wife Ann Barbara Carpenter. Children: John Carpenter, Andrew Carpenter, William Carpenter, Michael Carpenter.
Executors: Son John Carpenter, son Andrew Carpenter, son William Carpenter.

Will of Lawrence Catlett of St. Mark's Parish, Culpeper Co.
Dated 30 June, 1782. Proven 16 Sept., 1782.
Legatees: Wife Mary Catlett. Sons: Kemp Catlett, Thomas Catlett, George Catlett. Daus.: Mary Catlett, Sarah Catlett, Alice Catlett, Nancey Catlett. (Note: A Court suit is pending between Lawrence Catlett and Lawrence Taliaferro.)
Executors: Wife Mary Catlett, son Kemp Catlett, son Thomas Catlett, James Pendleton.
Wit.: Elizabeth Taliaferro, William Ball, John Hackley, Cadwallader Slaughter.

Inventory and Appraisal of Estate of John Payton, dec'd. Recorded 16 Sept., 1782. Made by John Bradford, James Browning, James Browning, Jr.

Will of John Lear of St. Mark's Parish.
Dated 12 Sept., 1780. Proven 16 Sept., 1782.
Legatees: Wife Susanna Lear. Children: John Lear, William Lear, Elizabeth Lear, Mary Lear. Grandson: William Lear, son of James Lear.
Executrix: Wife
Wit.: Amos Crane, Sabediah (X) Israel, Elizabeth (X) Weeks, John Spillaman.

Inventory and Appraisal of Estate of Thomas Quinn, dec'd. Recorded 16 Sept., 1782. Made by James Quinn, Extr.

Will of Frederick Fishback of Culpeper Co.
Dated 20 Sept., 1782. Proven 21 Oct., 1782.
Legatees: Wife Eve Fishback. Sons: Martin Fishback, John Fishback, Jacob Fishback, Frederick Fishback. Grandchildren: Children of my dau. Ann Elizabeth Smith, dec'd. Daus.: Elizabeth Spilman, Catharine Atwood, Sarah Button. Mary Fishback (relationship not stated).
Executors: Son John Fishback, son Jacob Fishback.
Wit.: Joseph Coons, Jr., Joseph (X) Coons, John Wigginton.

Will of Samuel Wood.
Dated 29 Jan., 1781. Proven 21 Oct., 1782.
Legatees: Wife. Son Samuel Wood. "estate to be equally divided amongst all my children."
Executors: Wife Alias Wood, Robert Latham, Sr.
Wit.: David (X) Davis, Robert Latham, Jr., David (X) Carnaggie.

Inventory and Appraisal of Estate of Ignatius Tureman, dec'd. Recorded 21 Oct., 1782. Made by Joseph Rogers, Joshua Willis, William Rogers.

Will of Jonas Menefee of Bromfield Parish, Culpeper Co.
Dated 23 Feb., 1779. Proven 18 Nov., 1782.

Legatees: Wife Elizabeth Menefee. He owned land in Hampshire Co. At wife's decease divided equally among all children then living.
Executors: Wife Elizabeth Menefee, son Henry Menefee.
Wit.: Edmund Duling, Henry Baker, Nancy Baker, Joseah Bryan.

Will of Thomas Payton of Culpeper Co.
Dated 4 Sept., 1782. Proven 18 Nov., 1782.
Legatees: Mother, wife Mary Payton, my children (all minors).
Executors: John Strother, John Browning.
Wit.: William (X) Ress, Ann (X) Ress, William Butler.

Inventory and Appraisal of Estate of William Courts, dec'd. Recorded 18 Nov., 1782. Made by Anthony Hughes, Joseph Strother, Francis Covington.

Inventory of Estate of Mark Bryant. Recorded 18 Nov., 1782.

Inventory and Appraisal of Estate of Thomas Chapman, dec'd. Recorded 18 Nov., 1782. Made by Henry Lewis, Joshua Render, Christopher Crigler.

Inventory and Appraisal of Estate of Fredrick Fishback, dec'd. Recorded 18 Nov., 1782. Made by Vincent Tapp, James Arnold, John Read, Joseph Coons.

Will of Thomas Griffin of Bromfield Parish, Culpeper Co.
Dated 9 Feb., 1781. Proven 21 Oct., 1782.
Legatees: Wife Elizabeth Griffin. Sons: Anthony Griffin, Zachariah Griffin. Daus.: Elizabeth Long, Mary Peters. "Elizabeth Kenney a young woman that I and my wife have raised."
Executors: Son Anthony Griffin, son Zachariah Griffin.
Wit.: Thomas Brown, James Sims.

Will of Barnard Rogers of Culpeper Co.
Dated 30 Oct., 1780. Proven 20 Jan., 1783.
Legatees: Bro. William Rogers, bro. Joseph Rogers, bro. John Rogers, sis. Ann Crittendon, sis. Sarah Ronsow, sis. Lency(?) Rawsow, sis. Elizabeth Garnett, Jeremiah Rogers and John Rogers, son of my bro. Joseph Rogers.
Executors: Bro. Joseph Rogers, Ambrose Medley, James Quinn.
Wit.: James Sebree, Joseph Rogers.

Inventory and Appraisal of Estate of Samuel Wood, dec'd. Recorded 20 Jan., 1783. Made by Robert Latham, John Lightfoot, David Carnagee.

Account of Sales of Estate of Benjamin Roberts, Gent., dec'd. Recorded 20 Jan., 1783. Made by Daniel Field, Extr.

Will of Alexander McDannold of St. Mark's Parish, Culpeper Co.
Dated 29 Jan., 1783. Proven 17 Feb., 1783.
Legatees: Sons: John McDaniel, Reubin McDannold, George McDannold. Daus.: Mary Turner, Sarah Drisdle, Nelley McDannold, Peggy Shropshire. Grandson Roddy Turner, son of Jeremiah Turner.
Executors: Capt. John Magers (clerk gives Major), Thomas Pourter.

Wit.: Jemimey (X) Crain, Vincent Allen, Richard (X) Turner.

Inventory and Appraisal of Estate of Thomas Payton. Recorded 17 Feb., 1783. Made by James Browning, William McClanahan, John Bradford.

Will of Joseph Towles of Bromfield Parish, Culpeper Co.
Dated 27 Jan., 1770. Proven 20 Aug., 1770.
    Legatees: Sons: Henry Towles, William Towles, Joseph Towles, Robert Towles (all minors). Other children: Mary Towles, Jane Towles, Ann Towles, Frances Towles, Sarah Towles.
    Executors: Oliver Towles, Reubin Terrell.
    Wit.: Ware Long.

ADDITIONS

Will Book B, p. 16 - Will of Francis Gaines - the following was omitted:
                Dated 26 Sept., 1775. Proven 15 July, 1776

Will Book B, p. 22 - Division of Estate of Courtney Norman - the following
                was omitted: 20 Oct., 1777.

47

CULPEPER COUNTY, VIRGINIA

Will Book C (1783-1791)

Will of John Matthews of St. Mark's Parish, Culpeper Co.
Dated 15 Feb., 1776. Proven 17 March, 1783.
Legatees: Wife Ann Matthews. Sons: Benjamin Matthews, John Matthews, Aquila Matthews, William Matthews, Elisha Matthews, Daniel Matthews, James Matthews (a minor). Daus.: Franky Matthews (a minor), Mary Matthews (a minor).
Executors: Cuthbert Bullitt, son John Matthews, wife Ann Matthews.
Wit.: John Wigginton, Patterson Fletcher, Thomas Clark Fletcher, William Sherril.

Inventory and Appraisal of Estate of John Lear, dec'd. Recorded 17 March, 1783. Made by Patterson Fletcher, John Freeman, David Cornaggie.

Will of John Faver, Sr., of St. Mark's Parish, Culpeper Co.
Dated 19 July, 1779. Proven 18 March, 1783.
Legatees: Wife Isabell Faver. Children of my son, William Faver, dec'd. Son John Faver who is married to Ann Covington, dau. of Thomas and Jael Covington. Mentions that dau. Henrietta Faver had married Lewis Yancey, Jun. Grdau. Isabel Faver, dau. of son William, dec'd. If she dies before marriage then to her sis. Alice Faver. Mentions Rosanna Faver as youngest child of his son William Faver, dec'd. Children of William Faver, dec'd., are Alice Faver, Henrietta Faver, Isabell Faver, Frances Faver and Rosanna Faver.
Executors: Birkett Davenport, John Williams.
Wit.: John Strother, Thomas Latham, Robert Coleman.

Inventory and Appraisal of Estate of Benjamin Roberts, Junr., dec'd. Recorded 21 April, 1783. Made by Joseph Stewart, James Sims, Henry Towles.

Inventory and Appraisal of Estate of William Houston, dec'd. Made 14 March, 1783 by William Pierce, James Gaines, John Long, Jr.
Separate Inventory for things in Culpeper Co. and those in Spotsylvania Co. Spotsylvania Co. made by John Herndon, John Chew, Henry Head, John Wiglesworth. 19 March, 1783.

Will of Joseph James of Culpeper Co.
Dated 31 Dec., 1778. Proven 21 April, 1783.
Legatees: "My present wife" Mary James. Sons: Joseph James, George James, Daniel James. Son Henry James had died.
Executors: Wife Mary James, Joseph Stuard, son Joseph James, Jr.
Wit.: Ambrose Coleman, Timothy Holdway, Ann (X) Holdway.

Inventory and Appraisal of Estate of Barnett Rogers, dec'd. Recorded 21 April, 1783. Made by John Cave, William Watts, Francis Gibbs.

Account of Sales and Administration of Estate of Francis Corbin, dec'd.

Recorded 19 May, 1783. Examination of Account made by William McClanahan, William Roberts, John Minor.

Inventory and Appraisal of Estate of Joseph James, dec'd. Recorded 19 May, 1783. Made by Ambrose Coleman, Thomas Wright, James Long.

Inventory and Appraisal of Estate of Alexander McDanold, dec'd. Recorded 19 May, 1783. Made by John Long, James Willis, David Hening.

Inventory and Appraisal of Estate of John Nalle, dec'd. Recorded 19 May, 1783. Made by John Tutt, John Brown, Richard Parks.

Inventory and Appraisal of Estate of Martin Nalle, dec'd. Recorded 19 May, 1783. Mde by John Tutt, John Brown, Daniel Brown.

Inventory and Appraisal of Estate of Thomas Griffin, dec'd. Recorded 19 May, 1783. Made by John Nalle, Francis Nalle.

Will of Lewis Wilhoit.
Dated 20 March, 1783. Proven 19 May, 1783.
Legatees: Bros.: Tobias Wilhoit, Jessee Wilhoit, William Wilhoit, Joel Wilhoit. Mentions that William Wilhoit and Caty Cook have his mare between them.

Inventory and Appraisal of Estate of Jonathan Fennell, dec'd. Recorded 19 May, 1783. Made by James Clark, John Wever, William Clark.

Inventory and Appraisal of Estate of Isaac Davis, dec'd. Recorded 19 May, 1783. Made by Ben Lowin, John Threlkheld, Reuben Doggett.

Will of Edward Leavell of Culpeper Co.
Dated 2 June, 1781. Proven 19 May, 1783.
Legatee: Mother Sarah Leavell.
Produced in Court by Edward Leavell, Lee Roy Canaday. Handwriting proven by Charles Garner, William Watson, George Cordell. Court ordered that Robert Leavell, uncle and heir-at-law be summoned to next court.

Inventory and Appraisal of Estate of William Gaines, dec'd. Recorded 16 June, 1783. Made by William Watts, William Rogers, Joseph Rogers.

Inventory and Appraisal of Estate of John Carter, dec'd. Recorded 21 July, 1783. Made by James Whitehead, Alexander McQueen, Henry Duvall.

Will of John Hord of Culpeper Co.
Dated 11 July, 1783. Proven 21 July, 1783.
Legatees: Son Ambrose Hord. Dau, Frances Watts. Mentions bro. Ambrose Hord had left him some slaves.
Executors: Barnett Watts, William Watts.
Wit.: Thomas Watts, Jr., John Watts, Julius Watts.

Inventory and Appraisal of Estate of Edward Leavell. Recorded 21

July, 1783. Made by James Finney, Hadley Head, Edward Herndon.

Report states "which said slaves and personal estate descended to the said Edward Leavell from his father Joseph Leavell, dec'd., and is subject to the dower of Sarah Canaday mother of the said Edward Leavell, dec'd., and formerly the wife of the said Joseph."

Will of John Oneal of St. Mark's Parish, Culpeper Co.
Dated 11 May, 1783. Proven 18 Aug., 1783.
Legatee: Wife Sarah Oneal.
Wit.: William Gray, William Ball, George Kinnard.

Guardian's Account, John Wayland guardian of Lewis Wayland, son of Adam Wayland, dec'd. Recorded 15 Sept., 1783.

Will of Harmon Fishback.
Dated 25 Feb., 1776. Proven 18 Aug., 1783.
Legatees: Son Harmon Fishback money rec'd. for land sold in Fauquier Co. Grandson Jacob Fishback (a minor). Daus.: Mary Wilhoit, Cathoran Roberson, Alse Huphman.
Executors: Son Harmon Fishback, John Huphman.
Wit.: John Wilhoit, Richard Flynt, Moses Wilhoit.

Will of William Covington of Culpeper Co.
Dated 11 Feb., 1783. Proven 18 Aug., 1784 (Believe should be 1783. DFW).
Legatees: Son Robert Covington. Dau. Ellener Hensley. Mentions Francis Covington's meadow and bro. Richard Covington. My three youngest daus.: Grizzel Coper, Elizabeth Covington, Lucy Covington.
Executors: Son Robert Covington, Robert Hensley, William Covington.
Wit.: Francis Covington, Ezekiel Wright, John Wright, Agness (X) Hensley.

Inventory and Appraisal of Estate of John Faver, dec'd. Recorded 19 Aug., 1783. Made by P. Slaughter, James Slaughter, Jr., James Whighthead.

Inventory and Appraisal of Estate of Lawrence Catlett, dec'd. Recorded 20 Aug., 1783. Made by Gabriel Long, Robert Coleman, Jr., Robert Key.

Inventory and Appraisal of Estate of William Thompson, dec'd. Recorded 20 Aug., 1783. Made by Harry Taliaferro, Reuben Zimmerman, William Allen.

Will of Richard Wright of St. Mark's Parish, Culpeper Co.
Dated 19 Aug., 1783. Proven 15 Sept., 1783.
Legatees: Wife Sarah Wright. Sons: William Wright and Richard Wright, John Wright.
Executors: Wife Sarah Wright, Thomas Wright, Robert Pollard.
Wit.: Frederick Zimmerman, Harry Taliaferro, Susanna King.

Will of Henry Huffman of St. Mark's Parish, Culpeper Co.
Dated 25 April, 1767. Proven 15 Sept., 1783.
Legatees: Wife Margaret Huffman. Sons: Thomas Huffman, John Huffman, Henry Huffman, Joseph Huffman, Herman Huffman, James Huffman. "Son-in-law John Young who married my daughter Elizabeth." Dau. Catharine Huffman. Daus.: Mary, Elizabeth, Alice, Elsibeth, Susanna, Eve.
Executors: Son John Huffman, son-in-law John Young.
Wit.: James Pendleton, James (X) Blackwell, Charles Spilman.
(Note: Almost in German script and not really legible as to spelling. DFW)
6 Sept., 1783. Tilman Huffman, eldest son and heir of Henry Huffman, dec'd., relinquished his claim.
Wit.: James Arnold, Henry Hufman.

Will of William George.
Dated 4 April, 1781. Proven 15 Sept., 1783.
Legatees: Wife, eldest dau. Mary Ann Hopper, dau. Elizabeth Corder, Susannah Butten (relationship was not stated). Remainder at wife's death divided between two daughters named above.
Wit.: James Arnold, Vincent Tapp, William Tapp.
Postscript - Left his orphan boy James Bryan to Mary Ann Hopper.

Will of Joseph Early of Culpeper Co.
Dated 12 Feb., 1780. Proven 20 Oct., 1783.
Legatees: Wife Jane Earley. Sons: Paschal Early (land testator had received by will from his father), William Early (a minor), Whitefield Early, Joseph Early. Daus.: Julianer Early, Mary Early. To my six children, when Whitefield Early shall come of age all my lands in the County of Kentucky equally divided.
Executors: Capt. Johnny Scott, Elijah Craig and Adam Banks.
Wit.: Thomas Spolden, Daniel (X) McClayland, one not legible, Margeret (X) Moyer.

Will of Henry Miller of Culpeper Co.
Dated 20 Sept., 1780. Proven 20 Oct., 1783.
Legatees: Wife Margit Miller. Two youngest children: John Miller and Henry Miller. "equally divided among all my children."
Executors: Charles Brooking, Thomas Canaday, William Watts.
Wit.: William Brooking, Robert Brooking, John Brooking.

Will of William Clift.
Dated 15 May, 1783. Proven 20 Oct., 1783.
Legatees: Wife Jemima Clift during her life-time and then return to Leijah Roberts. Bro. William Abbett, bro. Joseph Abbett.
Executors: John Field, William Abbett, Larkin Field.
Wit.: Joseph Sanford, Joseph Roberts, Harwood (X) Abbett.

Inventory and Appraisal of Estate of Richard Wright, dec'd. Recorded 20 Oct., 1783. Made by Frederick Zimmerman, Harry Taliaferro, George Gray.

Inventory and Appraisal of Estate of Henry Huffman. Recorded 20 Oct., 1783. Made by John ____ (?Jett, Hitt), Jacob Coones, Henry Coones.

Guardian's Account. Richard Young Wigginton in account with John Wigginton, guardian. Recorded 17 Nov., 1783.

Will of James Marshall.
Dated 5 Sept., 1775. Proven 17 Nov., 1783.
"As I am soon to be Exposed to the dangers of the Sea & human Life, subject to Many Casualties......"
Legatees: To my brother for use of mother. At death of mother, ½ to brother and ½ divided equally among his sisters. Dr. Marsden not to have any direction of his property.
Wit.: Colen Campbell, Thomas Aubenthnot.

Division of Estate of William Williams, dec'd., "according to the will of the decedant." Devisees: equally to James Williams, Lucy Green, Susanna Williams, Mary Williams, William Clayton Williams, Philip Williams. Recorded 17 Nov., 1783. Made by Robert Coleman, Edward Watkins, Gabriel Long.

Inventory and Appraisal of Estate of Joseph Early, dec'd. Recorded 17 Nov., 1783. Made by Ephraim Rucker, John Gibbs, Henry Gaines.

Allotment of Dower to widow of Peter Presley Thornton, dec'd. Included lots in possession under tenure of John Ashford, Samuel Jones, William Moore, Philip Eastham, John Johnston, in all 824 acres. Recorded 17 Nov., 1783. Made by Thomas Jordan, Henry Ward, James Hickman.

Inventory and Appraisal of Estate of Isaac Settle, dec'd. Recorded 17 Nov., 1783. Made by Thomas McClanahan, Francis Jacobie, John Calvert.

Inventory and Appraisal of Estate of William George, dec'd. Recorded 17 Nov., 1783. Made by John Fishback, Vincent Tapp, John Read, James Arnold.

Account of Sales of Estate of George Calvert, recorded 18 Nov., 1783. Purchasers: Archibald Bigbie, Mary Calvert, Owen Minor, John Calvert, Robert Hensley, Isaac Haines, John Carter, Jacob Haines, Carlile Haines, Capt. John Strother, John Pinnall, Hezekiah Boon, Simeon Daniel, George Calvert, Jr., Benjamin Sandes, William Wall, William Moore, John Griffith, Marshall Jones, Solomon Strother, William Crain, William Pinnall, Isaac Settle, Reuben Finnell, James Pinnall, William Covinton, Henry Ward, William Grigsbie, Thomas Johnston, Owing Camble, John Kidwalleder.

Will of John Edwards of Culpeper Co.
Dated 31 Oct., 1775. Proven 15 Dec., 1783.
Legatees: Wife Barbary Edwards (included some land in Augusta Co.); Friend Joseph Ball of Northumberland Co.; Friend Capt. Benjamin Harrison; nephew George Edwards, niece Mary Edwards, son and dau. of Robert Edwards and Elizabeth, his wife.
Executors: William Ball and Ambrous Barbour.
Wit.: William Ball, Joseph Ball, Jr., Benjamin Crump, Frances Ball.

Inventory and Appraisal of Estate of Lewis Wilhoit, dec'd. Recorded 15 Dec., 1783. Made by Thomas Sparks, John Crigler, Matthias (X) House.

Inventory and Appraisal of Estate of James Blackwell, dec'd. Recorded 15 Dec., 1783. Made by John Spilman, Vinson Tapp, Sr., Joseph Coones, Jr.

Inventory and Appraisal of Estate of Jonas Manifee, dec'd. Recorded 16 Feb., 1784. Made by Anthony Hughes, William Covington, Charles Browning.

Inventory and Appraisal of Estate of Mrs. Margaret Marshall, dec'd. Recorded 15 March, 1784. Made by Francis Apperson, James Duval, Micajah Stevens.

Inventory and Appraisal of Estate of John Nooe, dec'd. Recorded 19 April, 1784. Made by Thomas Allen, John Proctor, Joshua Jennings.

Will of James Brown of St. Mark's Parish, Culpeper Co.
Dated 7 April, 1784. Proven 19 April, 1784.
Legatees: Wife Elizabeth Brown. Sons: Hezekiah Brown, James Brown, Henry Brown and George Brown. Daus.: Elizabeth Brown, Sarah Brown, Ann Brown. Grchildren: James Brown Rice and Elizabeth Rice.
Wit.: Robert Pollard, Thomas (X) Mitchell, Susannah (X) Mitchell.

Settlement of Estate of Jasper Haynes, dec'd. Recorded 19 April, 1784. A child's part to each of the following: Joseph Haynes, Jasper Haynes, Stephen Haynes, Elizabeth Sparks, Moses Haynes, Benjamin Haynes, James Haynes, Mary Haynes, Ann Clark, William Haynes. Division made by Henry Hitt, Henry Field, Jr., John Gillison.

Will of Christian Ryner of Bromfield Parish, Culpeper Co.
Dated 3 Sept., 1777. Proven 15 Dec., 1783, finally proven 17 May, 1784.
Legatees: Wife Elizabeth Rynor (given as Riner when recorded.). Sons: John Riner, Daniel Riner, Christian Riner. After wife's death, rest divided equally among three daughters: Mary Riner, Elizabeth Riner, Sarah Riner.
Executors: Wife Elizabeth Riner, John Fleshman, Jacob Medley, son John Riner.
Wit.: Charles Brooking, Abberhart Riner, Tapley Wilson.
Codicil: 25 Aug., 1783. Son Christian Riner not to have any part of land unless older brothers and his mother thinks proper.
Wit.: Robert Fleshman (German script), Aberhard Riner.

Inventory and Appraisal of Estate of Edward Sims, dec'd. Recorded 19 April, 1784. Made by Bushrod Dogett, James Pattie, William Dulaney, James Broaddus.

Will of Susannah Chiles of Culpeper Co.
Dated 8 March, 1784. Proven 17 May, 1784.
Legatees: "all the estate I had by my first husband John Graves to

be equally divided between by four sons which I had by the said John Graves: Thomas Graves, John Graves, Isaac Graves, Edward Graves." "estate of my last husband Henry Chiles" is to be equally divided between my two daughters, Elizabeth Car and Ann Davis.
    Executor: Walter Car of part which came from Henry Chiles.
    Wit.: James Powell, Henry Delph, Conret (X) Delph, Sr.

Will of Henry Souther of Bromfield Parish, Culpeper Co.
Dated 2 Sept., 1783. Proven 17 May, 1784.
    Legatees: Sons: Stephen Souther, Michael Souther, Jacob Souther. Daus. Barbary Hufman, Catharine Cannada.
    Executor: Son Michael Souther.
    Wit.: Henry Wayland, Henry (X) Cristler, Joseph Cristler.

Inventory and Appraisal of Estate of John White, dec'd. Recorded 17 May, 1784. Made by John Minor, Benjamin Elkins, John Corbin.

Inventory and Appraisal of Estate of Andrew Norwood, dec'd. (Items in the hands of Richard Reynolds.) Recorded 17 May, 1784. Made by John Wharton, Ben Lowen, Daniel Brown.

Inventory and Appraisal of Estate of Edwin Smith, dec'd. Recorded 17 May, 1784. Made by Thomas Kirtley, George Anderson, William Simpson (or Sampson).

Division of slaves of Gabriel Jones, dec'd. Only sets off number to William Broadus intermarried with the widow. Recorded 17 May, 1784. Made by Robert Pollard, Robert Slaughter, Sr., William Ball.

Will of Robert Jones of Culpeper Co.
Dated 3 Jan., 1784. Proven 17 May, 1784.
    Legatees: Wife Mary Jones, son Thomas Jones, dau. Lucy Thornhill. Part to wife during her lifetime and then divided "among all my children."
    Executors: Robert Strother, John Thornhill.
    Wit.: John Dillard, Robert Strother, John Thornhill, Thomas Jones.

Settlement of Estate of William Crawford, dec'd. Mentions amount delivered to Rosanna Crawford, legatee, and Mary Crawford, legatee. Balance carried on. Recorded 17 May, 1784. Made by Cornelius Mershon, extr.

Inventory and Appraisal of Estate of Henry Souther, dec'd. Recorded 21 June, 1784. Made by Henry Crisler, Michael Gaar, George Crisler.

Inventory and Appraisal of Estate of James Brown, dec'd. Recorded 16 Aug., 1784. Made by Robert Pollard, William Broadus, Richard Waugh.

Inventory and Appraisal of Estate of William Covington, dec'd. Recorded 16 Aug., 1784. Made by Francis Covington, Anthony Hughes, William Covington.

Will of William Champe of Culpeper Co.
Dated 10 April, 1784. Proven 16 June, 1784.
Legatees: Wife Mary Champe; nephew Henry Willis, land in King George Co.; dau. of Col. William Fleming, land in King George Co.; friend William Chadwell, land in King George Co., where he now lives; Mary Gaitskill, land she lives on during her natural life.
Executors: Wife Mary Champe, bro.-in-law William Flemin and Francis Thornton.
Wit.: John Thornton, Henry Gaitskill, Rowland Gaines.

Inventory and Appraisal of Estate of John Edwards, dec'd. Recorded 16 Aug., 1784. Made by William Hughes, Aaron Berry, William Green.

Will of John Reynolds, Sr., of Culpeper Co.
Dated 12 June, 1784. Proven 16 Aug., 1784.
Legatees: Wife Jennet Reynolds. Sons: William Reynolds, John Reynolds, Edward Reynolds. Dau. Mildred Wilhite. "all my children."
Executors: Col. Henry Hill, Capt. Henry Field.
Wit.: P. Marye, Ben (X) Hawkins, Zachariah Wall.

Will of Nathan Turner of St. Mark's Parish, Culpeper Co.
Dated 13 April, 1783. Proven 16 Aug., 1784.
Legatees: Wife Judith Turner. Five of youngest children: Jeremiah Turner, Richard Turner, Nathan Turner, Elizabeth Jones and Hezekiah Bush.
Wit.: John (X) McDannald, Jeremiah (X) Turner, Vincent Allen.

Inventory and Appraisal of Estate of Carlisle Haynes, dec'd. Recorded 17 Aug., 1784. Made by George Calvert, Robert Hensley, Robert Covington.

Inventory and Appraisal of Estate of Judith Cooper, dec'd. Recorded 17 Aug., 1784. Made by Charles Browning, Frances Covington, William Covington.

Will of William Butts of Culpeper Co.
Dated 27 Feb., 1780. Proven 20 Nov., 1780 (partially). Proven 17 Aug., 1784 (fully).
Legatees: Wife Alender Butt. My children: Elizabeth Butt, Samuel Butt, Rose Butt, John Butt, William Butt, Alender Butt, Thomas Butt. Some land was in Culpeper Co. and some in Shenandoah Co.
Executors: Wife Alender Butt, John Menefee.
Wit.: Thomas Jordan, John Calvert, George Jordan.

Inventory and Appraisal of Estate of Samuel Hening, dec'd. Recorded 18 Oct., 1784. Made by John Long, John Rogers, Nicholas Long.

Will of Lewis Yancey of Culpeper Co.
Dated 6 Oct., 1784. Proven 18 Oct., 1784.
Legatees: Wife Henrietta Yancey. Sons: George Yancey, Birkett Garland Yancey. Daus.: Winifred Yancey, wife of Thomas Yancey; Isabella Tutt, wife of Lewis Tutt; Henrietta Tutt, wife of Hansford Tutt; Lucy Yancey, Eleanor Yancey, Nancy Yancey (minors).

Executors: Wife Henrietta Yancey, bro. Richard Yancey, son-in-law Lewis Tutt.
Wit.: James Pendleton, Bushrod Doggett, Gabriel Tutt.

Will of James Rucker of Bromfield Parish, Culpeper Co.
Dated 31 May, 1784. Proven 15 Nov., 1784.
Legatees: Wife Milley Rucker, bro. Wisdom Rucker, father Thomas Rucker.
Executors: Father Thomas Rucker, John Tinsley.
Wit.: Joseph Rucker, William Rucker, William Pearcy.

Will of Israel Robinson of St. Mark's Parish, Culpeper Co.
Dated 4 Nov., 1784. Proven 15 Nov., 1784.
Legatees: Wife Sarah Robinson, bro. Joseph Robinson, father Israel Robinson.
Wit.: Adam Newall, Mary Reveley, Benj. (X) Payton.

Estate Settlement of Thomas Monteith, dec'd. Recorded 15 Nov., 1784. Made by William McClanahan, James Browning, Stephen Morriss, Thompson Ashford.
Legatees: Son ___ Monteith, John Grigsby who married a daughter, Jonathan Fennell who married another daughter.

Inventory and Appraisal of Estate of Robert Jones, dec'd. Recorded 15 Nov., 1784. Made by Benjamin Gaines, Benjamin Pulliam, Richard Gaines.

Division of Estate of Robert Jones, dec'd. Recorded 15 Oct., 1784. Made by Ben Gaines, John Slaughter, Benjamin Pulliam. Legacies to Thomas Jones and Lucy Thornhill.

Will of Edmund Terrill.
Dated 1 June, 1784. Proven 15 Nov., 1784.
Legatees: My children Elizabeth Terrill, Mary Terrill, John Terrill, Edmund Terrill, Sarah Terrill, Jean Terrill, Robert Terrill, James Terrill, Nancy Terrill, Fanny Terrill, Lucy Terrill.
Executors: John Terrill, Robert Garnett, William Willis.
Wit.: John Terrill, William Willis, John Waugh, John Willis, Ann Terrill.

Inventory and Appraisal of Estate of William Butt, dec'd. Recorded 15 Nov., 1784. Made by Thomas Jordon, Robert Johnston, John Johnston.

Inventory and Appraisal of Estate of Henry Miller, dec'd. Recorded 15 Nov., 1784. Made by Joseph Roggers, John Yager, John Fitzpatrick.

Inventory and Appraisal of Estate of Lewis Yancey, dec'd. Recorded 17 Jan., 1785. Made by James Tutt, Benjamin Tutt, John Dillard Jones.

Inventory and Appraisal of Estate of Christian Ryner. Recorded 21 Feb., 1785. Made by Ambrose Medley, Benjamin Powell, Richard Flint.

Report of Capt. William Green as guardian of Estate of Francis Wyatt Green. Recorded 17 Jan., 1785.

Will of John Thomas of Bromfield Parish, Culpeper Co.
Dated 29 April, 1782. Proven 21 Feb., 1785.
Legatees: Sons: John Thomas, Benjamin Thomas. Sons-in-law: William Powell, Robert McKey, Jeremiah Kirk. Dau.-in-law Elizabeth Thomas, widow of my son Massey Thomas; great granddau. Lucy Thomas, dau. of my grandson, John Thomas, son of Massey Thomas; grandson-in-law who married my granddau., Susanna now residing in Maryland; grandson John Thomas, son of Massey Thomas; grandson Jessey Thomas, son of John Thomas; grandson Reuben Thomas. Residue of Estate to be sold and cash divided equally among my following children: Benjamin Thomas, John Thomas, representatives of Massey Thomas, William Thomas, Robert McKey who married my dau. Margaret, William Powell who married my dau. Sarah, Jeremiah Kirk who married my dau. Ann.
Executors: Son John Thomas, grandson John Thomas son of Massey, William Wallace.
Wit.: Henry Lewis, William Lewis.

Will of Christopher Hoomes of Culpeper Co.
Dated 20 May, 1780. Proven 21 Feb., 1785.
Legatees: "my reputed son and whom I have raised from his infancy William Sherril, son of Margaret Sherril alias Margery Perkins - land where I now live and one-seventh part of slaves, cattle and hogs." "my reputed son Thomas Freeman, son of Elizabeth Freeman who now lives with me - land and one-seventh part of personal property." "my reputed son George Freeman, son of Elizabeth aforesaid." "my reputed daughter Ann Spilman, wife of Nathaniel Spilman - one-seventh etc." "my reputed daughter Sarah Anderson, wife of Isaac Anderson - one-fourteenth...." "my reputed daughter Elizabeth Garner, wife of Jonas Garner - one-fourteenth....." "my reputed daughter Mary Freeman, dau. of Elizabeth Freeman who now lives with me - one-seventh." "my reputed daughter Frances Freeman, dau. of Elizabeth Freeman, aforesaid - one-seventh...." Elizabeth Freeman to live on land given to Thomas and George Freeman until George comes of age or marries.
Executors: Henry Pendleton, James Pendleton, John Wigginton, William Sherrill.
Wit.: John Wigginton, William Davis, David (X) Carnaggie, James (X) Carnaggie.

Inventory and Appraisal of Estate of John Finnell, dec'd. Recorded 21 March, 1785. Made by William Hill, Russell Hill, Charles Taylor.

Inventory and Appraisal of Estate of Lewis Tapp, dec'd. Recorded 21 March, 1785. Made by Jacob Coones, John Fishback, Joseph Coones, Jr.

Will of Joseph Steward of St. George's Parish, Spotsylvania Co.
Dated 21 Feb., 1778. Proven 21 March, 1785.
Legatees: Wife. Sons: William Steward, part was land in Stafford Co., adjoining land where he lived; Joseph Steward, already received part; John Steward.
Executor: John Steward.
Wit.: Samuel Todd, John Sills.

Inventory and Appraisal of Estate of Jane Simpson, dec'd. Recorded 22 March, 1785. Made by Thomas Cortly, Elijah Kirtley, Thomas Sampson.

Inventory and Appraisal of Estate of James Rucker, dec'd. Recorded 22 March, 1785. Made by Merry Walker, John Rowzee, George Alexander.

Executor's Account of Estate of Dr. Thomas Howison. Recorded 22 March, 1785. Made by John Slaughter, extr. An objection was raised by John Thompson who intermarried with the heiress of said Howison.

Will of Bowles Armistead.
Dated none. Proven 21 June, 1785.
Legatees: Wife Mary Anne Armistead, pregnant. Sons: William Armistead (a minor), Peter Fontaine Armistead (a minor). Daus.: Elizabeth Armistead, Mary Bowles Armistead (minors). Owned land in Halifax Co. in right of his wife.
Executors: Bro. John Armistead, bro.-in-law William Fontaine, wife Mary Ann Armistead, Capt. John Spotswood.
Wit.: William Fontaine, Mary Thornton, Lawrence Brooke, George Hume, Jr.

Will of John Zachary, Jr., of Bromfield Parish, Culpeper Co.
Dated 25 March, 1785. Proven 16 May, 1785.
Legatees: Two brothers and five sisters equally. Benjamin Zachary, William Zachary, Elizabeth Bledsoe, Esther Burbridge, Hannah Burbridge, Sarah Eastham, Milley Wright.
Executors: Bros. Benjamin Zachary, William Zachary.
Wit.: Daniel Farmer, Richard Shackleford, Evan Brown.

Will of Joseph Norman of Culpeper Co.
Dated 20 Nov., 1783. Proven 16 Feb., 1784.
Legatees: Wife Sarah Norman. Sons: Thomas Norman, John Norman (a minor), William Norman, James Norman. Grandson Isaac Norman. Sarah Norman, wife of my son Isaac Norman. Daus.: Mary Dillard, Winifred Bywater, Peggy Calvert, Sally Norman, Fanny Norman, Mimey(?) Norman, Kisiah Norman.
Executors: Wife Sarah Norman, Thomas Norman.
Wit.: John Triplett, Thomas Norman Fanny(?) (X) Norman.

Inventory and Appraisal of Estate of John Reynolds, dec'd. Recorded 17 May, 1785. Made by John Henshaw, Henry Towles, Zachariah Wall.

Will of James Pattie of Culpeper Co.
Dated 25 Feb., 1783. Proven 16 May, 1785.
Legatees: Wife Sarah Pattie, son John Pattie, dau. Sally Saunders.
Executors: Sarah Pattie, William Pendleton.

Will of John Clore of Culpeper Co.
Dated 2 Dec., 1779. Proven 20 June, 1785.
Legatees: Wife Katherine Clore. Sons: George Clore, Michael Clore, John Clore. Daus.: Milley Clore, Anne Clore, Frances Clore. "my nine children."

Executors: Son Michael Clore, son John Clore, son-in-law John Stonsiver.
Wit.: John Hume, Airey Berry, Philip (X) Chelf, Henry Lewis, one in German script, Christopher Crigler.

Inventory and Appraisal of Estate of Edmund Terrill, dec'd. Recorded 20 June, 1785. Made by Robert Garnett, Thomas Garnett, Alexander Dawney(?).

Inventory and Appraisal of Estate of Christopher Hoomes, dec'd. Recorded 20 June, 1785. Made by John Dillard, Patterson Fletcher, Robert Latham.

Inventory and Appraisal of Estate of Joseph Norman, dec'd. Recorded 20 June, 1785. Made by Harry Taliaferro, William Vaughan, George Gray.

Inventory and Appraisal of Estate of John Carder, dec'd. Recorded 18 July, 1785. Made by Francis Irwin, Harry Taliaferro, William Ball.

Inventory and Appraisal of Estate of John Thomas, dec'd. Recorded 18 July, 1785. Made by George Hume, Henry Lewis, Michael Yager.

Will of Thomas Sims, Sr., of Bromfield Parish, Culpeper Co. Dated 21 April, 1784. Proven 18 July, 1785.
Legatees: Sons: Eldest Thomas Sims, Jr., children of dec'd. son William Sims, son James Sims, Elizabeth Sims, wife of James Sims, son Elijah Sims and sons of his (Elijah's) first wife, son Zachariah Sims, son Richard Sims. Daus.: Amay Bobo, Ann Graves. Grdaus.: Lucy Jones, Anna Jones, daus. of my dau. Sarah Jones, dec'd.
Executors: Son Thomas Sims, son James Sims.
Wit.: James Sims, Edward Sims, William Mason.

Inventory and Appraisal of Estate of James Pattie, dec'd. Recorded 18 July, 1785. Made by Bushrod Doggett, William Delaney, James Tutt.

Inventory and Appraisal of Estate of John Broyle, dec'd. Recorded 18 July, 1785. Made by Zachariah Walle, George Parsons, Henry Towles.

Inventory and Appraisal of Estate of William Tapp, dec'd. Recorded 18 July, 1785. Made by John Read, Hank Read, Jacob Coones.

Inventory and Appraisal of Estate of John Button, dec'd. Recorded 15 Aug., 1785. Made by John Read, John Pullen, Joseph Utterbach, Randolph Stallard.

Inventory and Appraisal of Estate of Esther Rucker, dec'd. Recorded 15 Aug., 1785. Made by William Alexander, Edward Herndon, Joseph Henderson.

Guardian's Account for Robert Piper, orphan of David Piper. Reported by John Piper. Recorded 15 Aug., 1785.

James Williams, guardian of William C. Williams, Account Report. Recorded Aug., 1785.

James Williams, guardian of Philip Williams, Account Report. Recorded Aug., 1785.

William Lewis' receipt to John Brown, guardian, 3441b in bonds and paper currency and slaves in full of all my wife's, Mary Lewis, estate. Recorded 15 Aug., 1785.

Account Report from Adam Utz, guardian to Hanah Wayland, orphan of Adam Wayland, dec'd. Recorded Aug., 1785.

Report of Ambrose Barbour, George Hume and John Hume of Account of Mrs. Mary Sampson as guardian of orphans of John Sampson, dec'd. Recorded 19 Sept., 1785.

Bazil Nooe, guardian of orphans of George Bourn, dec'd. Account Report. Recorded 19 Sept., 1785. Some orphans named were Betsy Bourn, Sarah Bourn, Leucy(?) Bourn. He has entry for "my wife's share of the personal estate."

Inventory and Appraisal of Estate of William Mitchell, dec'd. Recorded 19 Sept., 1785. Made by James Hickman, Benjar Douglass, John Norman.

Will of Henry Green of Fauquier Co.
Dated 6 Sept., 1782. Proven 19 Sept., 1785.
Legatees: Mother, Mrs. Ann Green of Fauquier Co., bro. Willis Green, bro. William Green, sis. Elenor Duff Green.
Executor: Willis Green.
Wit.: John Lee, A. Madison, Mary Madison.

Will of John Maddox.
Dated 21 May, 1782. Proven 19 Oct., 1785.
Legatees: Wife Mary Maddox, "all my children." "To my children my lawful right of my uncle John Maddox's estate."
Executrix: Wife Mary Maddox.
Wit.: William Davis, James Withers, James Hord, Jr.

Account Report of Russell Vawter(?), guardian of Fanny Towles. Recorded 17 Oct., 1785.

Nun-cupative will of Henry Green, dec'd., late of the County of Fayette, made at house of Major James Green.
Legatees: Mother Ann Green during her life-time, then divided between his bro. William Green and sis. Eleanor Duff Green. Said he had a written will filed in Orange Co.
Wit.: James Green, Benjamin Field, Joel Gustine, John Green, 30 July, 1785 - Certified same day. Recorded 17 Oct., 1785.

Will of Henry George of Culpeper Co. "going into regular service."
Dated 19 Jan., 1776. Proven 17 Oct., 1785.
Legatees: "Equally between my six sisters."

Wit.: Richard George Gaines, James Gaines.

"Henry George who enlisted in the Army in 1776 and was made prisoner 1779 and has not been heard of since in a presumption of his death."

Inventory and Appraisal of Estate of John Clore, dec'd. Recorded 21 Nov., 1785. Made by Henry Lewis, George Hume, John Hume.

Will of Paul Leatherer of Culpeper Co.
Dated 5 Nov., 1780. Proven 21 Nov., 1785.
Legatees: Wife Margaret Leatherer. Sons: Michael Leatherer, Nicholas Leatherer, Samuel Leatherer, John Leatherer, Paul Leatherer, Joshua Leatherer. Daus.: Margaret Leatherer, Susanna Leatherer, Mary Yowell.
Executors: Wife Margaret Leatherer, son John Leatherer, son Joshua Leatherer.
Wit.: John Hume, James (X) Crain.

Will of Robert Shotwell of Culpeper Co.
Dated 5 Oct., 1785. Proven 21 Nov., 1785.
Legatees: Wife Hannah Shotwell, "all my children," eldest son Reuben Shotwell, eldest dau. Anne Shotwell.
Wit.: O. Minor (Owen).

Inventory and Appraisal of Estate of Thomas Sims, dec'd. Recorded 22 Nov., 1785. Made by Joseph Steward, William Newton, Stephen Baughan.

Inventory and Appraisal of Estate of Thomas Bywaters, dec'd. Recorded 22 Nov., 1785. Made by Hank Read, John Read, Joseph Duncan.

Will of George Woolfenbargo of St. Mark's Parish, Culpeper Co.
Dated 29 Sept., 1785. Proven 23 Nov., 1785.
Legatees: Wife Elizabeth Woolfenbargo. My six children: Eliza Woolfenbargo, Catharine Woolfenbargo, Sally Woolfenbargo, George Woolfenbargo, Hannah Woolfenbargo, John Woolfenbargo.
Executors: Wife Elizabeth Woolfenbargo, uncle Philip Woolfenbargo, bro. Frederick Woolfenbargo, bro.-in-law John Thomas.
Wit.: William Willis, Alexander Dawney.

Will of Edward Wood.
Dated 2 Sept., 1782. Proven 19 Dec., 1785.
Legatees: Sis. Ginney, clothes to William Martain, bro. Peter Wood. Mentions Peggy Martain when sis. "Genney" dies.
Wit.: William Acre, James Hagan, John Coppage.

Will of Jacob Hanback of Culpeper Co.
Dated 1 Nov., 1785. Proven 19 Dec., 1785.
Legatees: Sons: John Hanback, Jacob Hanback. Daus.: Susanna Hanback, Elizabeth Coones wife of Jacob Coones, Mary Coones wife of Henry Coones, children of my dau. Catharine, dec'd.
Executors: Wife Mary Hanback, Jacob Coones.
Wit.: Amos Crane, James Stevenson, John Wigginton.

Administrator's Account of Estate of Leond Ziglar, dec'd. Recorded 19 Dec., 1785.

Will of Thomas Washbourne of Culpeper Co.
Dated 22 Jan., 1772. Proven 19 Dec., 1785.
Legatees: Wife Lucy Washbourn, dau. ___(?Seena) wife of Robert Bywaters, dau. Haney wife of Ely Washbourn.
Executors: Wife Lucy Washbourn, son-in-law Robert Bywaters, son-in-law Ely Washbourn.
Wit.: James Pendleton, Catharine Pendleton.

Inventory and Appraisal of Estate of Jacob Hanback, dec'd. Recorded Jan., 1786. Made by John Fishback, Joseph Wayman, Joseph Coon__(Coonze).

Inventory and Appraisal of Estate of Robert Shotwell, dec'd. Recorded 6 Jan., 1786. Made by Henry Lewis, Sr., Louis Render, O. Minor.

Inventory and Appraisal of Estate of Adam Barlow, dec'd. Recorded Jan., 1786. Made by Charles Taylor, Adam Snyder, Moses Broyles.

Executor's Account of Estate of William Courts, dec'd., for years 1781 through 1785. Recorded 20 Feb., 1786. Made by Ben Gaines.

Inventory and Appraisal of Estate of John Maddox, dec'd. Recorded 17 April, 1786.

Inventory and Appraisal of Estate of George Wolfenbargo, dec'd. Recorded 17 April, 1786. Made by William Willis, Alexander Downey, John Alfred Head.

Will of John Burdyne of Bromfield Parish, Culpeper Co.
Dated 28 March, 1786. Proven April, 1786.
Legatees: Wife Betty Burdyne land in Cantuckey bought of John Dicken, known as Cartwright Tract and all of estate. At her death divided equally among eight children: Benjamin Burdyne, Susanner Burdyne, Catherine Burdyne, Sarah Burdyne, Betty Burdyne, Amos Burdyne, Nancy Burdyne, Agnes Burdyne (all minors). 30₺ in trust to William Chapman for support of his mother, Catherine Burdyne.
Executors: Wife Betty Burdyne, John Dicken, Joseph Dicken.
Wit.: William Chapman, John Sampson, James Hume, John Wright, Ephraim Dicken, John Hughs.

Inventory and Appraisal of Estate of James Gaines, dec'd. Recorded 17 April, 1786. Made by Alexander Waugh, Thomas Garnett, Absalom Cornelious.

Will of William Fooshee (indexed Foushee).
Dated 26 Jan., 1786. Proven 17 April, 1786.
Legatees: Wife Susannah Fooshee his estate and part willed to him by his father at his mother's death. At death or marriage of wife, one half to Philip Fooshee and Frances Fooshee, two eldest children of bro.

Charles Fooshee. Other half to wife or her heirs.
    Executors: Bro. Thornton Fooshee, friend Daniel Grinnan.
    Wit.: William Sneed, George Fooshee, J. Price.

    Inventory and Appraisal of Estate of John Burdyne, dec'd. Recorded 19 June, 1786. Made by John Sampson, Andrew Glassell, William Dicken.

    Inventory and Appraisal of Estate of Bowles Armistead. Recorded 19 June, 1786. Made by Gabriel Long, Basel Nooe, William Richards.

    Inventory and Appraisal of Estate of William Clift, dec'd. Recorded 19 June, 1786. Made by Joseph Sanford, Roger Abbett, Leonard Barns.

    Inventory and Appraisal of Estate of William Fooshe, dec'd. Recorded 19 June, 1786. Made by Zachariah Petty, James Branham, John Lightfoot.

    Inventory and Appraisal of Estate of James Jarrell, dec'd. Recorded 19 June, 1786. Made by Thomas Graves, Joseph Eddins, Reuben Clark.

    Will of Elijah Finnell of Culpeper Co.
    Dated 7 Feb., 1786. Proven 19 June, 1786.
    Legatee: Wife Frances Finnell.
    Executor: Frances Finnell.
    Wit.: Ephraim Dicken, Zachariah Wall, John Finnell.

    Will of Barbary Edwards of Culpeper Co.
    Dated 5 April, 1786. Proven 19 June, 1786.
    Legatees: Dau. Nancy Rice, "among my children now living and my three Grand Daughters," grandson James B. Zigler land at Cantuck.
    Executor: Amon B. Rice
    Wit.: Ben Weeks, James Maxwell, Sarah Rice.

    Will of Doratha Gaines.
    Dated 24 April, 1786. Proven 19 June, 1786.
    Legatees: Daus.: Doratha Gaines, Susannah Carter, Anne Martin, Elizabeth Yates. Son James Gaines. These were all of her living children.
    Executors: Nephew Richard Gaines, friend George Cordell.
    Wit.: Ambrose Coleman, John Underwood, Joseph Gaines.

    Administrator's Account of Estate of John Garrott, dec'd. Recorded 19 June, 1786. Made by F. Zimmerman.

    Inventory and Appraisal of Estate of Alex Rider, dec'd. Recorded 19 June, 1786. Made by Thomas Lillard, James Lillard, Benjamin Lillard.

    Inventory and Appraisal of Estate of Barbary Edwards, dec'd. Recorded 19 June, 1786. Made by John Butler, William Jones, Benjamin Stinnett.

    Will of Thomas Mitchell of St. Mark's Parish, Culpeper Co.
    Dated 24 Nov., 1785. Proven 17 July, 1786. (In book as 1787 between

all entries of 1786.).
Legatees: Wife Susannah Mitchell, "amongst all my children."
Executors: Wife Susannah Mitchell, son Willis Mitchell.
Wit.: Thomas Farish, Robert Long, Hezekiah Brown, Gabriel Chism.
Court appointed James Branham co-executor during the minority of Willis Mitchell.

Inventory and Appraisal of Estate of Doratha Gaines, dec'd. Recorded 17 July, 1786. Made by John Camp, John M. Bell, John Long, Sr.

Executor's Account of Estate of John Scott Wood, dec'd. Recorded 17 July, 1786.

Inventory and Appraisal of Estate of Thomas Mitchell, dec'd. Recorded 18 Sept., 1786. Made by Benjamin Long, John Waters, William Hawkins.

Inventory and Appraisal of Estate of Thomas Washburn, dec'd. Recorded 16 Oct., 1786. Made by William Dulaney, William Smith, Joseph Duncan.

Will of Susanna Williams of St. Mark's Parish, Culpeper Co.
Dated 24 Feb., 1786. Proven 26 March, 1786.
Legatees: "To pay my father's debts." Remainder equally between my brothers and sisters.
Executors: Bro. John Williams, James Williams.
Wit.: George Yates, John Williams, Mary Williams.

Inventory and Appraisal of slaves of Susanna Williams, dec'd. Recorded 16 Oct., 1786. Made by R. Slaughter, John Mason, James Slaughter, Jr.

Will of John Gordon of Culpeper Co.
Dated 31 Dec., 1782. Proven 16 Oct., 1786.
Legatees: Wife Elizabeth Gordon all estate "except a pied heifer of four grasses old." Daus.: Sarah Compton, Mary Gordon. Son William Gordon.
Executor: William Gordon.
Wit.: John Nince, Isaac Willson, Alexander Willson.

Inventory and Appraisal of Estate of Robert Spilman, dec'd. Recorded 16 Oct., 1786. Made by Hanks Read, John Lightfoot, Patterson Fletcher.

Account of Sales of Estate of Robert Spilman. Recorded 16 Oct., 1786. Made by Thomas Spilman, Admr. Purchasers: Widow Winifred Spilman, George Clerk, Griffin Read, Lewis Corbin, James Spilman, Benjamin Spilman, Ann Wall, John Freeman, Francis Morgan, Jessee Smith, Abner Newman, Thomas Spilman.

Will of James Cotton of Culpeper Co.
Dated 7 March, 1785. Proven 16 Oct., 1786.
Legatees: Wife Elizabeth Cotton. My children: Edward Cotton, James Cotton, Jonathan Cotton, Polly Cotton and one expected.

Executors: Wife Elizabeth Cotton, James Thomas.
Wit.: Zachariah Delany, Thomas (TG) Ginn, Thomas (X) Blackwell.

Inventory and Appraisal of Estate of Elijah Finnell, dec'd. Recorded 25 Aug., 1786. Made by Zachariah Wall, Henry Field, Jr., Henry Towles.

Inventory and Appraisal of Estate of Paul Leatherer, dec'd. Recorded 16 Oct., 1786. Made by George Hume, John Sampson, Henry Lewis.

Inventory and Appraisal of Estate of Joseph McCurdy, dec'd. Recorded 16 Oct., 1786. Made by Henry Elley, Thomas Dillen, Francis Hume.

Executor's Account of Estate of Francis Gaines. Recorded 16 Oct., 1786. Made by James Gaines, Extr.

Will of Ann White of Culpeper Co.
Dated 14 Dec., 1785. Proven 16 Oct., 1786.
Legatees: Sons: John White, William White, Jonathan White, Daniel White. Daus.: Rachel White, Susannah White, Agatha Jones.
Executors: Son John White, David Henning.
Wit.: Vincent Allen, John (X) Hill, Samuel Trascey, John Barnett.

Will of Richard Nalle of Bromfield Parish, Culpeper Co.
Dated 7 Dec., 1785. Proven 18 Dec., 1786.
Legatees: Wife Judah Nall, John Beverly Carter. "my part of my father's estate that is coming to me" to wife. Dau. Susannah Burk "land at Cantuckey in Jefferson County on Sott River."
Executors: Wife Judah Nall, bro. Francis Nall.
Wit.: Charles Avery, John (X) Snyder, John Parks.

Will of Thomas Brown of St. Mark's Parish, Culpeper Co.
Dated 29 Oct., 1786. Proven 15 Jan., 1787.
Legatees: Wife Sarah Brown. Sons: John Brown, Evan Brown, Thomas Brown, James Brown, Gideon Brown. Dau. Salley Kenaday. Grson. Thomas Brown, son of John Brown.
Executors: Wife Sarah Brown, son John Brown, son Thomas Brown.
Wit.: James Wheatley, Daniel Farmar, Richard (X) Hudson.

Inventory and Appraisal of Estate of Ann White, dec'd. Recorded 15 Jan., 1787. Made by William Steward, Daniell Grinnan.

Will of Jeremiah Early of Culpeper Co.
Dated 16 Jan., 1786. Proven 19 Feb., 1787.
Legatees: Sons: "to the lawfull heir of my son Jeremiah Early, dec'd." Joshua Early - one-ninth, Jacob Early, Joel Early. Daus.: Sarah Kirtley, Ann Rogers, Hannah Scott. Grandson Paschel Early. Dau.-in-law Jane Early, loan of land. Grandsons: Whitfield Early and Joseph Early, sons of my son Joseph, dec'd., land lent to their mother, Jane Early. Grandson William Early, son of Joseph, dec'd.
Executor: Son Joel Early. If he cannot, then grandsons Elijah Kirtley and Jeremiah Kirtley.
Wit.: John Spoldin, Joel Harvey, Abigale (X) Harriss.

Will of Thomas Sparks of Culpeper Co.
Dated 10 Dec., 1784. Proven 19 Feb., 1787.
Legatees: Wife Mary Sparks. Humphrey Sparks, John Sparks, James Kilby, Russell Vawter, Henry Sparks, Jacob Aylor, "after my wife's decease or second marriage the land and plantation I now live on." "At wife's decease or second marriage equally divided among all my children namely John, Ann, Humphrey, Lucy, Henry, Thomas, Mary and Frankey."
Executor: Henry Hill
Codicil, dated 30 Dec., 1785.
Executors: Wife Mary Sparks, Adam Snider.
Wit.: Thomas Ward, Patty (X) Ward, George Head.

Inventory and Appraisal of Estate of Thomas Brown, dec'd. Recorded 19 Feb., 1787. Made by (not recorded).

Will of Mary Maddox of Culpeper Co.
Dated 5 June, 1786. Proven 16 April, 1787.
Legatees: Sons: Samuel Maddox, Notley Maddox, Thomas Maddox, Matthew Maddox. Daus.: Mary Harrell, Sally Conn, Maggrater Wilson. At death of dau. Maggrater Wilson, to her son James Wilson and if he die, to Sally Wilson.
Executor: Son Matthew Maddox.
Wit.: Thomas Magruder, Thomas (X) Hurley, James Withers.

Will of William Booten of Bromfield Parish, Culpeper Co.
Dated 13 Nov., 1779. Proven 17 April, 1787.
Legatees: Wife Judah Booten. Sons: William Booten (a minor), Lewis Booten. Son-in-law James Bohannon. Children of son, Ambrose Booten, dec'd.
Executors: Wife Judah Booten, Russell Hill, Ephraim Rucker, Henry Hill.
Wit.: Jacob Ward, Augustin Rucker, John (X) Deer, Richard Vernon.

Estate Account of Richard Tutt. Recorded 17 April, 1787. Made by Edward Watkins, an executor. Report covered period 1770 through 1779.

Inventory and Appraisal of Estate of Jeremiah Early, dec'd. Recorded 17 April, 1787. Made by Ephraim Rucker, Adam Banks, William Harvey.

Administrator's Account of Estate of George Doggett, dec'd. Recorded 17 April, 1787. Made by James Bramham, admr.

Will of James Gaines of Culpeper Co.
Dated 24 May, 1781. Proven 20 March, 1786.
Legatees: Wife Mary Gaines. Dau. Isabella Gaines (youngest). All my children: Harry Gaines, James Gaines, Richard Emund Gaines, Joseph Gaines, Francis Thomas Gaines, Mary Herndon, Sarah Broades, and the children of my daughter Catherine Broades and the daughter of my son William Gaines.
Executors: Son Henry Gaines, son James Gaines, son Richard Gaines, Edward Watkins.
Wit.: Thomas Garnett, James Garnett, John Garnett.

Will of John Corbin, Sr., of Culpeper Co.
Dated 10 Jan., 1786. Proven 20 March, 1786.
Legatees: Wife Frances Corbin. Thirteen children: William Corbin, John Corbin, Catherine Corbin, Magdely Corbin, Betsey Corbin, Charles Corbin, George Corbin, Joseph Corbin, Francis Corbin, Nancey Corbin, Sarah Corbin, Harry Corbin, Lucy Corbin.
Wit.: William Corbin, Sr., John Brown, George Fant, John Minor.

Appraisal for dower of widow of Brumfield Long, dec'd. Recorded 18 Dec., 1786. Made by Richard Waugh, John Wharton, Robert Slaughter, Jr.

Inventory and Appraisal of Estate of John Zachary, dec'd. Recorded 21 March, 1786. Made by Am. Bohannan, Edward Tindsley, John Gibbs.
Further inventory made by Am. Bohannon, John Gibbs, Michael Gaar.

Will of Philip Clayton of St. Mark's Parish, Culpeper Co.
Dated _____, 1779. Proven 21 March, 1786.
Legatees: Wife Ann Clayton. Son Samuel Clayton. Daus.: Lucy Williams, Susannah Slaughter.
Executors: Son Samuel Clayton, son-in-law James Slaughter.
Wit.: Samuel Clayton, Robert Slaughter, John Rawlings.

Account of dower of Ann Tapp, widow of Lewis Tapp, dec'd. Agreed to by other heir: Philip Amiss on behalf of his wife the said Ann Tapp (now Amiss), Vincent Tapp, guardian to Lewis Tapp, son and heir-at-law of the dec'd. Dated 5 May, 1787. Signed by Wm. McClanahan, John Wigginton, James Jett. Recorded 18 June, 1787.

Inventory and Appraisal of Estate of Thomas Sparks, dec'd. Recorded 18 June, 1787. Made by Zachariah Wall, George Passons, John Henshaw.

Inventory and Appraisal of Estate of Richard Nalle, dec'd. Recorded 18 June, 1787. Made by Peter Casper, Humphrey Sparks, John Tutt.

Inventory and Appraisal of Estate of William Booten, dec'd. Recorded 16 July, 1787. Made by Am. Bohannon, Edward Tindsley, Henry Gaines.

Inventory and Appraisal of Estate of John Clore, dec'd. Recorded 16 July, 1787. Made by John Hume, William Chapman, Henry Lewis.

Will of Edward Watkins of St. Mark's Parish, Culpeper Co.
Dated 6 Jan., 1787. Proven 17 Sept., 1787.
Legatees: Wife Sarah Watkins; "50₤ for schooling poor children and orphans in St. Mark's Parish...."; Niece Sarah Watkins Cowne. If she die without heirs, to be divided between her two sisters. Niece Elizabeth Tutt, Nephew James Broadus, Godson John. At wife's death, "two-thirds of proceeds of sale be divided between living children of my sister Elizabeth Campbell and of my brother Nathaniel Pendleton."
Executors: Wife Sarah Watkins, William Pendleton, Thomas Wright.
Wit.: N. Brown, Robt. Cowne, Jno. Stevens, Daniel Colvin, William C. Brown, John Sanders, Edward Stevens, Henry Pendleton.

Will of John Buford of Culpeper Co.
Dated 13 Sept., 1785. Proven 17 Sept., 1787.
Legatees: Sons: Abraham Buford land..."I had of Henry Lewis"; Simeon Buford, James Buford. Grandson, John Buford, son of Simeon. Grandson, William Buford, son of Simeon.
Executors: Sons: Abraham Buford, Simeon Buford.
Wit.: Jacob Ward, William Zachary, John Rhodifer, James Bledsoe.

Inventory and Appraisal of Estate of John Fleshman. Recorded 17 Sept. 1787. Made by Jacob Blankenbaker, Samuel Blankenbaker, Jacob Rouze.

Administrator's Account of Estate of William Dulany, dec'd. Recorded 1 Sept., 1787. William Hensley, admr.

Will of Robert Floyd of Bromfield Parish, Culpeper Co.
Dated 1 Dec., 1786. Proven 15 Oct., 1787.
Legatees: Wife, son Henry Floyd. At wife's death, "amongst all my children."
Executors: Wife and wife's bro. Henry Hoffman.
Wit.: Henry Field, Jr., Adam Huffman, Ambrose Huffman.

Will of William Payton of Culpeper Co.
Dated 6 Oct., 1786. Proven 17 April, 1787.
Legatees: Wife Sarah Payton. Sons: Valentine Payton, William Parfield Payton (minors).
Executors: Wife Sarah Payton, Joseph Roberts.
Wit.: William Burton, John (X) Barbey, Joseph Roberts.

Will of Henry Field, Jr., of Culpeper Co.
Dated 7 Nov., 1785. Proven 15 Oct., 1787.
Legatees: Wife Mary Field. Son Daniel Field, included land in Kentucky, being one half of Ambrose Coffer's Tract of 1100 acres. Son Henry William S. Field included land in Lincoln County. Sons: George Field, Joseph Field, Thomas Field, John Field. Daus.: Dianah Field, Suze Field, Nancy Field, Elizabeth Field, Mary Field, Sarah Field, Nancy Delany, Molley Field. Executors to sell 1,000 acres out of his tract of 3,400 acres in Kentucky in Huston's Fork. Minor children were John, Thomas, Joseph, George and Sarah Field.
Executors: Son Daniel Field, son Henry William S. Field.
No witnesses.

Account of Sales of Estate of Jeremiah Early, dec'd. Recorded 17 Dec., 1787. Reported by Joel Early, Extr. Purchasers: George Eve, Frank Harvy, Edmond Burton, William Bates, Jr., Joseph James, Christopher Crigler, Lewis Snell, Mordecai Barbour, Robert Roebuck, Charles Walker, Valentine Johnston, Thomas Kirtley, Anthony Foster, William Dalton, Henry Lewis, George Copher, Micajah Neale, Thomas Sampson, Adam Snyder, James Walker, Henry Field, Jr., Merry Walke, Samuel Dedman, Daniel Hollenback, John Spalden, John Hume, Edmond Gaines, Edward Graves, Joseph Edins, Solomon Gorrel, Abigale Harriss, Jonathan Cowherd, Isaac Smith, Edmond Shackleford, Isaac Davis, Ambrose Dowell, John Graves, Augustin Anderson, William Sims,

Elijah Kirtley, William Stowers, Adam Banks, Armistead Minor, James Early, Ellick Bohannon, Joseph Strother, James Head, Thomas Maxwell, Jeremiah Jarrel, Jacob Powers, Isaac Davis, Jr., Dawning Smith, Reuben Clark, William Chapman, Susannah Handley(?), Ben. Quin, Prettyman Merry, Paul Leatherer, Frances Vawter, Matthias Mank, William Broadus, George Hume, Jr., John Clore, William Huse, Molten(?) Christopher, Benajah Rice, John Sampson, John Rouzee, James Scott, Joel Early, William Kirtley, Joshua Early.

Administrator's Account of George Harden. Recorded 17 Dec., 1787. Made by George Thomas, John Peper, Brian Magrath.

Will of William Clark of Culpeper Co.
Dated 29 Oct., 1787. Proven 17 Dec., 1787.
Legatees: Wife. Sons: Joseph Clark, George Clark, Reuben Clark, Robert Clark, Ambrose Clark, Larkin Clark. Daus.: Sarah Clark, Lucy Beck, Ann Griffen.
Executors: Son Reuben Clark, son Joseph Clark.
Wit.: Lewis Conner, Robert Terrell, Thomas Hughes, James Jones.

Executor's Account of Estate of John Edwards, dec'd. Recorded 17 Dec., 1787. Made by Ambrose Barbour, extr.

Account of William Walker, guardian of Henderson orphans. Recorded 18 June, 1787.

Inventory and Appraisal of Estate of Edward Watkins, dec'd. Recorded 21 Jan., 1788. Made by Reuben (X) Long, Stephen Threlkheld, Thomas Latham.

Inventory and Appraisal of Estate of William Clark, dec'd. Recorded 21 Jan., 1787. Made by Charles Hume, Thomas Hughes, Ambrose Powell.

Account of Settlement of Estate of Francis Browning, dec'd. Recorded 21 Jan., 1788. Made by Charles Browning and Frances Browning, admrs.

Will of Sarah Barbour of Culpeper Co.
Dated 19 May, 1781. Proven 18 Feb., 1788.
Legatees: Sons: James Barbour, Thomas Barbour, Phillip Barbour, Ambrose Barbour. Grandson Mordecai Barbour. If he die without heir, then divided between his two sisters, Mary Barbour and Frances Barbour. Granddau. Sarah Barbour. If she die without heir, then to her sister, Mary Barbour. Dau. Mary Thompson. If her children die without heirs, then to be divided among son James Barbour's children: Mordecai Barbour, Thomas Barbour, Frances Barbour. Dau. Betty Johnston. Granddau. Lucy Johnston. Granddau. Lucy Todd. Grandson James Barbour. Grandson Philip Barbour, son of Ambrose Barbour.
Executors: Son James Barbour, son Thomas Barbour, son Ambrose Barbour.
Wit.: Curtis Ballard, Richard Quinn, Thomas Scott.

Will of John Christian Lips.
Whereas I feel meself in an declining state of Health I tink proper

for the Sake of Mortalite to despose in Regard of my Properte and leave my will behind and I declare by these presents that this is my finall will and Testament.

I To my sons Georg and Henry I lieve all my rights, Titles, Inheritances what may fall to my Share and come to in Germanie in the Mark and Eteetmat of Brandenburg in the Town of Frenenbriegen and adiacent Naiburhood likewise all Legacies and what might be made over to me during my absence. My Vader was John Georg Lips and my Mother Elonora Sophia Daughter of Deceased Fredick Capport. My curator was Master Schallge in Frenenbriegen. Having Numbers of Relations I tink proper to state these Things here for their Instruction after my Death and to make use of this.

II I declare that Mary Daughter dec'd. Charles Ewald in Philadelphia is my Lawfull wife and lieve and make over therefore my present tittle State to her: That is to say the Plantation whereon I now live House Effects Horses and Cattle likewise on Lot ground on the Robinson River; and I declare by these presents & that no Body else shall have Right Possession of the said Plantation House Effects Horses and Cattle and Lot but my wife Mary.

III The Money wich will arise from the Sale of on Gray Stallion left in the Hands of Daniel Fisher Planter in Chehassewan(?) South Carolina ____
____ past; the said Money shall be employed to pay the Account ofe Messrs. Lillies and James Foshee, Merchants of Fredericksburg against me and my wife shall be obliged to pay the Ballances out of the Debts in the Naebarhood as Specified in an Led, and signed my Nam. Finally I recommend my Being to the Peace of the independant and Almighty Being through the Mercie of my Savior Jesus Christ. Don at Culpeper November 25th in the year of Our Lord on Thousand seven hundred Eighty Seven.

Test.: Michael Gaar, William Eastham, Henry Miller.

This will was proven 21 April, 1788.

Estate Division of Adam Wayland, dec'd. Heirs: Widow, John Wayland, Godfrey Yager, Joshua Wayland, Anney Wayland, Lewis Wayland, Morton Christopher, Adam Wayland, Hannah Wayland.

The Court recorded that the widow was the 2nd wife of the dec'd and the children Adam and Hannah were hers. Instead of the dower right of one-third she is entitled by law to a child's part. She was guardian to her children.

Division made by James Barbour, H. Hill, Thos. (?) Porter. Recorded 21 April, 1788.

Will of Lewis Davis Yancey of Culpeper Co.
Dated 17 April, 1778. Proven 22 April, 1788.

Legatees: Wife Winifred Yancey. One shilling to the following children who had received their portion of slaves and personal estate: Charles Yancey, Lewis Yancey, Richard Yancey, John Yancey, Philemon Yancey, Ann Nalle, Winifred Nalle. Sons: James Yancey (apparently in parts unknown). If he does not return and apply for his part of slaves, they were to go to son Robert Yancey. Divided among "all my children," if Robert "should die in the Service of his Country."

Executors: Sons Lewis Yancey, Richard Yancey, Robert Yancey.

Wit.: James Pendleton, Henry Pendleton, Elizabeth Yancey.

Codicil, dated 2 May, 1782, proven 16 June, 1788, altered bequests

to Robert Yancey and James Yancey but showed they survived the War.
    Wit.: Birkett Davenport, Hered Freeman, Frances (x) Miller.

Will of John Peter Fox of Culpeper Co.
Dated 24 Dec., 1787. Proven 16 June, 1788.
Legatees: Wife Mary Ann Fox, granddau. Mary Gray (a minor), dau. Ann Gray. Estate to be divided into 12 parts; 10 children and grandson John Taylor to have 11 parts, other twelfth to the first grandchildren, children of Molly Bails. Ten children: Mary Rains, Matthias Fox, Joseph Fox, John Fox, Peggy Clunt, Eve Benger, Margaret Wiswell, Elizabeth Courts, Ann Gray, Anthony Fox. John Taylor to live with his wife, maintain her and have the rest of the profits.
    Wit.: Joshua Ginnens, Benjamin Partlow, Mary (X) Gray.

Will of Lawrence Bradley of Bromfield Parish of Culpeper Co.
Dated 1 June, 1784. Proven 16 June, 1788.
Legatees: Wife Elizabeth Bradley, son Augustin Bradley.
Executrix: Wife Elizabeth Bradley.
    Wit.: James James, Archabud Rider, William Brown, William Ambrose Brown.

Will of George Yates of Culpeper Co.
Dated 13 March, 1788. Proven 16 June, 1788.
Legatees: Wife Mary Yates, son Lawrence Catlett Yates (minor). His grandfather, George Yates, dec'd., made him a Deed of Gift in Caroline Co. If that land can be recovered by his bro. William Yates and cousin John Yates, it is to be equally divided to son Lawrence Catlett Yates, my brothers and sister, and the children of Uncle George Yates, dec'd.
    Executors: Bro.-in-law Kemp Catlett, friend David Jameson.
    Wit.: Sally Catlett, Gabriel Jones, R. Y. Wigginton.

Executor's Account of Estate of William Johnston, dec'd. Items cover period 1765 through 1783. Recorded 16 June, 1788. Made by William Roberts, extr.
    Payments 1765 (partial list). Made by executor of William Johnston, dec'd. Richard Brooks for sawing, Mr. Lawlor for brandy for harvest, Will. Acree for keeping the mill, Rice Duncan for mowing and making shoes, James Baker for keeping school, Will. Duncan for provisions, Dr. Herman, Mr. Irion for wine.
    Payments 1766. Thomas Dowdy for keeping the mill, Francis Birk 1 quire paper, Thomas Bywaters for inspecting tobacco, Robert Scott, Wm. Lyon, Ben. Morgan, Levina Spicer, servant, to boarding the schoolmaster, James Duncanson, John Kennedy, Dr. Knave, Francis Browning for corn, James Humphreys, Rawley Duncan, William Ludspike, Nicholas Browning for sawing, John Moore, Robert Scott.
    Payments 1767. Abraham Cooper for rebuilding the mill, Hawkins Castle for sawing, Francis Walle, Abraham Cooper for iron work for the mill, Isaac Wall for making 6 pairs of shoes, Philip Clayton for Judgment and costs, Will. Allason, Richard Nalle, Alexander Wright for tobacco, Gabriel Jones, Jr., for land, Dixon Brown for bacon, John Roberts for corn, Peter Russell for corn, William Daniel for pailing the grave and finishing the

house, Daniel Jacoby, Jno. Chapman, Abraham Cooper for Smith's work, James Nash, James Graves.

Payments 1768. Cornelius Mitchell for brandy, Capt. Ben Roberts for bacon, John Cooper brandy for the sale, Amrey Day for smith's works, Woodrow & Nelson.

Payments 1769. William Russell, Jno. White, Joseph Jones, Alex. Bush, Jno. Corbin, to rum and sugar for the burial of John Corbin, Tilman Wisecarver for weaving 38 yds. cloth.

Payments 1771. Henry Stringfellow for Smith's work, George Carder for making 5 pairs of shoes, James Graves laying of the Widow's dower, Edwin Hickman, James Robinson, Michael Sloan for making 14 pairs of shoes, Alex Bush, Will. Gambill, William Walker, Thomas Bywaters, Isaac Smith, William Kiretey, John Fields.

1766 Received from James Graves, Daniel Richardson, Capt. James Slaughter, Edward Bush, Francis Browning, Aron Jones, Francis Meale, William Duncan, John Norman, Richard Yancey, James Shakleford, Will. Edwards, Richard Parks, Capt. Will. Ball, John Sanders, Col. Thomas Slaughter, John Bush, Birkett Davenport, Henry Pendleton, John Cooper, John Slaughter, James Pendleton, John Corbin, Mathew Hawkins, Mary Settle, William Dulaney, James Crow, Tilman Wisecarver, French Strother, Samuel Fargeson, Charles Mozingo, Samuel Moore, Francis Slaughter, Herman Wisecarver, Thomas Washburn, Will. Edwards, John Roberts.

Inventory and Appraisal of Estate of John Christian Lips, dec'd. Recorded 16 June, 1788. Made by Elliott Bohannon, Michael Garr, Henry Miller, John Wilhoite.

Executor's Account of Estate of Samuel Hening, dec'd. Recorded 16 June, 1788. Made by David Hening, Extr., son of the deceased.

Division of Estate of Francis Gaines, dec'd. (Division of slaves only.) Legatees (in equal amounts): Dolly Gaines, James Gaines, John Yates, Sally Brasfield, George Bourne estate, Thomas Carter. (All were his children or sons-in-law.) Recorded 21 July, 1788. Made by Robert Coleman, Jr., David Hening, Philip Slaughter.

Division of Estate of John Smith, dec'd. Recorded 21 July, 1788. Made by Thomas Wright, extr. William Barber surveyed the land of John Smith, dec'd., for his son William Smith. A plat is shown of the 100 acres in Culpeper Co.

Will of Thomas Magruder of Culpeper Co.
Dated 21 July, 1787. Proven 21 July, 1788.
Legatees: Wife Prissiller Magruder. At her death or remarriage to be divided among all his children.
Executors: Thomas Jurden, Presiller Magruder.
Wit.: Robert Johnston, Notley Maddox.

Will of John Gray of Culpeper Co.
Dated 31 May, 1785. Proven 15 Sept., 1788.
Legatees: Wife. Sons: William Gray, Gabriel Gray, John Gray (a

minor). Daus.: Mary Gray, Peggy Gray, Dorothy Gray. Mother (not named).
Executors: Wife, son William Gray, son Gabriel Gray.
Wit.: William Ball, John Hackley.

Will of George Field.
Dated 21 Sept., 1787. Proven 15 Sept., 1788.
Legatee: Mother Sarah Field.
Executor: Capt. William Grant.
Wit.: Joseph Roberts, James Vowles.
Executor refused to act and Sarah Field was appointed administrator.

Inventory and Appraisal of Estate of Henry Field, Jr., dec'd. Recorded 15 Sept., 1788. Made by Henry Towles, James Sims, William Newton. They met first at the late dwelling of the deceased, 30 Oct., 1787. They met there again, 11 June, 1788, to appraise the slaves and personal property "which came from Kentucky." The latter list mentioned four slaves, 2 horses, a bull, a pair of money scales, pair of pistols, a pair of saddle bags, a pair of scales and weights and a Map of Kentucky Western valued at 12 shillings.

Inventory and Appraisal of Estate of Henry Field, dec'd. Recorded 15 Sept., 1788. Made by H. Marshall, John Craig, John Marshall. This property was in Fayette County, Va. (later Kentucky). Among such items as slaves, cattle, hogs, corn was included "Salmon's Geographical Grammer."

Will of Martin Nalle of Culpeper Co.
Dated 9 March, 1783. Proven 15 Sept., 1788.
Legatees: Wife Isabell Nalle. Sons: William Nalle, Martin Nalle. Daus.: Ann Nalle, Rachel Nalle, Clary Nalle, Winny Nalle, Milly Nalle. Granddau. Catey Parks, one-eighth of estate. If granddau. should die without heirs her part return to Mary Holloday's other children.
Executors: Wife Isabelle Nalle, son William Nalle, son Martin Nalle, son-in-law Humphrey Sparks.
Codicil: "To John Sanders part willed to his late wife, Winifred, for the use of his children by my daughter Winny." Dated 9 March, 1783.
Wit.: (same to will and codicil) Richard Parks, William Purvis, John Tutt.
(Note: It is possible that others or all of his daughters were married as he mentioned them only by their Christian name and this compiler inserted the name "Nalle" for facility in indexing. DFW).

Inventory and Appraisal of Estate of Martin Nalle, dec'd. Recorded 20 Oct., 1788. Made by John Tutt, Robert Cowne, John Nalle.

Will of Ann Strother of Culpeper Co.
Dated 24 Sept., 1787. Proven 20 Oct., 1788.
Legatees: Sons: Jeremiah Strother (a minor), George Strother, John Strother. Daus.: Caty Strother, Mary Strother.
Executors: Father John Strother, bro. John Strother, Jr.
Wit.: William Hughes, Thomas Hughes, Charles Browning.

Will of Ambrose Powell of Culpeper Co.
Dated 26 Jan., 1782. Proven 20 Oct., 1788.
Legatees: Wife Mary Powell. Sons: Robert Powell, William Powell. Daus.: Ann Hill, Fanny Sutton, dec'd. "My warrant for two thousand acres of land as an officer in the last war, I give to my two sons Robert and William and my son-in-law Henry Hill...." Grandchildren: John Sutton and Mary Bledsoe Sutton.
Executors: Wife Mary Powell, son Robert Powell, son William Powell, son-in-law Henry Hill.
Wit.: Henry Field, Jr., Lewis Conner, Humphrey Sparks.

Account of Estate of William Courts, dec'd. Recorded 20 Oct., 1788. Made by Mary Courts, extrx.

Will of John Kirk.
Dated 14 Sept., 1787. Proven 15 Dec., 1788.
Legatees: Wife Margret Kirk, dau. Judah Kirk. At wife's decease "if William Brooks' father nor Thomas Kirk's father never comes in they share all share equally with all my children...."
Wit.: Leeroy Canady, Edward Herndon, Abram Ehart.

Will of James Rush of Bromfield Parish, Culpeper Co.
Dated 7 June, 1788. Proven 15 Dec., 1788.
Legatee: Niece Anne McCallester, "land whereon William Rush now lives...."
Wit.: John Smith, Elizabeth Smith, Margot Crim.
Ann McCallester was appointed administrator.

Inventory and Appraisal of Estate of John Lacey, dec'd. Recorded 19 Jan., 1789. Made by John Finnell, Joshua Barler, Moses Broyles.

Inventory and Appraisal and Division of Estate of Lawrence Catlett, dec'd. Recorded 19 Jan., 1789. Reported by Gabriel Long, William Lightfoot, Reuben Zimmerman. Legatees: Kemp Catlett, Thomas Catlett, Sally Catlett, orphans of the deceased.

Inventory and Appraisal of Estate of John Quinn, dec'd. Recorded 21 April, 1789. Made by John Taliaferro, John Stockdell, Zachariah Gibbs.

Will of William Plummer Thurston of Culpeper Co.
Dated 12 March, 1789. Proven 21 April, 1789.
Legatee: Wife Lucy Mary Thurston. Had already given to daughters Mary and Ann.
Executors: Lawrence Taliaferro, John Taliaferro, Nicholas Taliaferro.
Wit.: Andrew Shepherd, Charles Taylor, George Porter, Margaret Wood.

Inventory and Appraisal of Estate of Thomas McGruder, dec'd. Recorded 21 April, 1789. Made by Walter Compton, Barton Thorn, Peregrine Thorn.

Inventory and Appraisal of Estate of John Kirk, dec'd. Recorded 15 June, 1789. Made by Leeroy Canaday, Hadly Head, Abram Ahart.

Will of James Hurt of Culpeper Co.
Dated 28 March, 1785. Proven 15 June, 1789.
Legatees: Wife Sarah Hurt. Son William Hurt land at his mother's death. Daus.: Frances Grayson, Anna Berry, Mary Berry. Children of deceased dau. Sarah Yowell.
Executors: Wife Sarah Hurt, son William Hurt, son-in-law Acre Berry.
Wit.: James (X) Crow, Reuben Thomas, John Hume.

Inventory and Appraisal of Estate of James Rush, dec'd. Recorded 15 June, 1789. Made by A. Berry, E. Berry, J. Smith.

Will of Michael Ehart.
Dated 7 May, 1788. Proven 15 June, 1789.
Legatees: Wife Katharine Ehart. Sons: Abraham Ehart, Adam Michal Ehart, Jacob John Ehart. Daus.: Christeene Brooce, Katharine Rucker, Susanna Herndon.
Executors: "my three sons, Abraham, Adam and John Ehart."
Wit.: Belfield Cave, Wisdom Rucker, Edward Herndon.

Inventory and Appraisal of Estate of Mary Browning, dec'd. Recorded 15 June, 1789. Made by John Minor, Benjamin Elkin, Jr., Stephen Morrison.

Inventory and Appraisal of Estate of Capt. Ambrose Powell, dec'd. Recorded 15 June, 1789. Made by Goodrich Lightfoot, Charles Hume, Lewis Conner, Ambrose Medley.

Division of Estate of Ambrose Powell, dec'd. Recorded 15 June, 1789. Made by same as those above. Legatees: John and Mary Bledsoe Sutton, Mrs. Mary Powell, Robert Powell, William Powell, Mrs. Anne Hill.

Inventory and Appraisal of Estate of Philemon Yancey, dec'd. Recorded 15 June, 1789. Made by James Duval, Henry Duval, James Slaughter, Jr.

Administrator's Account of Estate of Philemon Yancey, dec'd., by John Strode, admr. Recorded 15 June, 1789.

Jointure of Sarah Williams, widow of Paul Williams, dec'd. Made 9 May, 1789. Recorded 20 July, 1790. Court allotted her one half of land, slaves, military certificates, etc., in accordance with a pre-nuptial agreement recorded in Fauquier Co. Division signed by James Jett, Henry Ward, Thomas Edwards.

Will of Robert Green.
Dated 30 June, 1789. Proven 20 July, 1789.
Legatees: Wife Frances Green "all the estate I got by her to her and her heirs forever." Dau. Susanna Elizabeth Green (infant).
Executors: William Edmunds, James Williams.
Wit.: George Latham, James Hoomes Sherrel, Robert Latham, Jr.

Will of James Clark of Culpeper Co.
Dated 2 June, 1789. Proven 21 Sept., 1789.

Legatees: Wife Mary Clark. Sons: Ambrose Clark, Thomas Clark, Reuben Clark, Joseph Clark, John Clark, James Clark. Bro. Joseph Clark "for use of my dau. Elizabeth." Daus.: Lucy Clark, Nancy Clark, Molly Clark, Sucky Clark, Joannah Clark, Fanny Clark, Rhoda Clark.
Executors: Wife Mary Clark, bro. William Clark, bro. Joseph Clark.
Wit.: William Porter, Joseph Clark, Henry Sparks.
Some of his land was in Orange Co.

Will of Robert Stuart of Culpeper Co.
Dated 14 May, 1770. Proven 21 Sept., 1789.
Legatees: Wife Mary Stewart. Son: Robert Stuart. Daus.: Lucy Pulliam, Nancy Strother.
Executors: Wife Mary Stewart, George Witherall, Benjamin Pulliam.
Wit.: John Dillard, William Jones, Joseph (X) Cammel.

Will of James Tutt of Culpeper Co.
Dated 20 Jan., 1786. Proven 21 Sept., 1789.
Legatees: Wife Ann Tutt. Sons: Benjamin Tutt, Richard Tutt, Lewis Tutt, Gabriel Tutt, Hansford Tutt. Daus.: Mille Lynch, Elizabeth Sanders, Mary Tutt, Ann Williams, wife of Paul Williams. Granddau.: Mille Tutt.
Executors: Wife Ann Tutt, son Lewis Tutt, son Gabriel Tutt.
Wit.: John Routt, John Barnes, George Doggett.

Inventory and Appraisal of Estate of Ann Strother, dec'd. Recorded 21 Sept., 1789. Made by James Green, Jr., Gabriel Green, Anthony Hughes.

Inventory and Appraisal of Estate of Lewis D. Yancey, dec'd. Recorded 21 Sept., 1789. Made by James DuVal, Francis Slaughter, James Slaughter, Jr.

Inventory and Appraisal of Estate of Michael Ehart, dec'd. Recorded 21 Sept., 1789. Made by Leeroy Canaday, Hadley Head, John Rowzee.

Division of Estate of William Foushee, dec'd. Relict's portion to Mrs. Susanna Ficklin, late wife of the deceased. Recorded 21 Sept., 1789. Made by Nicholas Taliaferro, James Thomas, Daniel Grinnan.

Inventory and Appraisal of Estate of Nicholas Crigler, dec'd. Recorded 19 Oct., 1789. Made by Mark Finks, Reuben Crigler, Zachy Broyle.

Inventory and Appraisal of Estate of Capt. James Clark, dec'd. Recorded 19 Oct., 1789. Made by Benjamin Porter, George Proctor, Peirce Sanford. Personal in Orange Co., same but in Culpeper Co. Made by John Terrill, Alexander Waugh, William Twyman.

Inventory and Appraisal of Estate of Charles Duncan, dec'd. Recorded 19 Oct., 1780. Made by Anthony Hughes, Francis Covington, William Covington.

Inventory and Appraisal of Estate of Francis Willis, dec'd. Recorded 19 Oct., 1789. Made by Armistead White, Francis Covington, John Hisle.

Inventory and Appraisal of Estate of Robert Green, dec'd. Recorded 21 Dec., 1789. Made by Cornelius Mershon, John Dillard, Andrew Mershon.

Inventory and Appraisal of Estate of James Tutt, dec'd. Recorded 19 Oct., 1789. Made by James Tutt, Henry Stringfellow, Richard Yancey.

Inventory and Appraisal of Estate of James Hurt, dec'd. Recorded 21 Dec., 1789. Made by H. Lewis, A. Berry, Christopher Crigler.

Will of Andrew Bourn of Culpeper Co.
Dated 22 Aug., 1788. Proven 18 Jan., 1790.
Legatees: Wife Jane Bourn. "Children of my dau. Elizabeth Hawkins, deceased." Daus.: Ann Hawkins, Sarah Price, Jane Hawkins, Frances Newman, Judith Zimmerman, Polly Bourn. Sons: Andrew Bourn, William Bourn.
Executors: William Morton, William Pannill.
Wit.: John Bourn, Benjamin (X) Thornton, Reuben Newman, William Bourn.

Will of John Calvert of Culpeper Co.
Dated 24 April, 1789. Proven 18 Jan., 1790.
Legatees: Wife Helen Calvert. Son Cealius Calvert. Daus.: Sarah Calvert and Anna Calvert "Land formerly belonging to my father whereon his widow now lives...."; Elizabeth Calvert, Hannah Calvert, Delilah Calvert and Gettah Calvert.
Executors: Son Cealius Calvert, bro. George Calvert, James Browning.
Wit.: Wm. McClanahan, Thomas Deatherage, William (X) Sizeson.

Will of Frances Latham of Culpeper Co.
Dated 28 Oct., 1789. Proven 18 Jan., 1790.
Legatees: Daus.: Susanna Freeman, wife of Thomas Freeman; Frances Sharpe, wife of Lynfield Sharpe. Sons: Robert Latham, George Latham, Philip Latham.
Executors: Son George Latham, son Philip Latham.
Wit.: James Pendleton, George Freeman, Robert (X) Wilkerson.

Division of Estate of Gabriel Jones, dec'd. (Slaves only divided at this time). Legatees: Gabriel Jones received one-third. No other legatee was named. Recorded 15 Feb., 1790. Made by John Strode, William Ball, Robert Coleman, Jr.

Will of Benjamin Head of Orange Co.
Dated 20 Dec., 1784. Proven 15 Feb., 1790.
Legatees: Wife Grace Head. Sons: Benjamin Head (youngest), Francis Head (eldest). Dau.: Molly Perry.
Executors: Wife Grace Head, son Benjamin Head.
Wit.: Edmund Row, Zachariah (X) Jones, Elizabeth (X) Jones.

Inventory and Appraisal of Estate of George Field, dec'd. Recorded 15 Feb., 1790. Made by John Field, Charles Clifton, Reuben Field.

Nun-cupative will of John Faver.
Dated 23 July, 1789. Proven 15 Feb., 1790.

Legatees: Wife Elizabeth Faver, during her life and then to her child (not baptized but to be called) Isabella Faver.
Written by Nathaniel Pendleton, proven by Alexander McQueen, William Bowen.
Court appointed Elizabeth Faver, widow of the deceased as administrator.

Account of Henry Gaines, guardian of Henry George. Recorded 19 April, 1790.

Inventory and Appraisal of Estate of Zachariah Compton, dec'd. Recorded 19 April, 1790. Made by James Withers, Daniel Love, Barton Thorn, Mary Compton.

Division of Estate of John Scott Wood, dec'd. Recorded 19 April, 1790. Made by William Twyman, John Terrill, Francis Madison. "Deed from James Barbour and Sarah, his wife, to John Scott Wood, dec'd., ... being one-third part of the land the said John Scott Wood died seized and possessed of, and also one-third part of his negroes...." Legatees: one-third each to William Evans, Judith Woods, James Wood. A final settlement to be made later, also a guardian's account report.

Survey of Dower of Sarah Norman, widow of Joseph Norman. Recorded 19 April, 1790. Made by Gabriel Long, Reuben Zimmerman, Absalom Bradley.

Inventory and Appraisal of Estate of Frances Latham, dec'd. Recorded 15 Feb., 1790. Made by William Sherrill, George Freeman, John Freeman.

Inventory and Appraisal of Estate of John Gray, dec'd. Recorded 21 June, 1790. Made by William Ball, John Hackley, William Hawkins. Memorandum from executors, William Gray and Gabriel Gray, that 29 head of cattle had been sold to Col. Burgess Ball to satisfy a debt to William Taylor, owed by the deceased's estate.

Will of Michael Utz of Culpeper Co.
Dated 13 Oct., 1785. Proven 21 June, 1790.
Legatees: Wife Susanna Utz. Sons: George Utz, Michael Utz, Adam Utz, Daniel Utz. Dau. Elizabeth Swindel. Six children of dau. Margaret Broyle, dec'd.: Susanna Broyle, Rosanna Broyle, Michael Broyle, Elizabeth Broyle, Margaret Broyle, Nancy Broyle.
Executors: Son George Utz, son Adam Utz, son Michael Utz, son Daniel Utz.
Wit.: John Hume, Reuben Crigler, Lewis (X) Blankenbaker.

Will of Patrick Cockrane of Culpeper Co.
Dated 3 Aug., 1789. Proven 21 June, 1790.
Legatees: Son John Cockrane. Daus.: Elizabeth Cockrane, Mary Cockrane. (All children were minors).
Executors: James Robb, Andrew Shepherd, William Morton.
Wit.: Alexander Waugh, William Clark, Hugh Walker.
Executors refused to act. Eleanor Garnett, late Eleanor Cockrane,

claimed her dower at law. Admr. granted to Robert Garnett and Eleanor Garnett.

Inventory and Appraisal of Estate of Daniel Wilhoit, dec'd. Recorded 21 June, 1790. Made by Reuben Crigler, Henry Wayman, Mark Finks.

Will of George Clayton Slaughter of Culpeper Co.
Dated 5 May, 1790. Proven 21 June, 1790.
Legatees: Wife Betsy Slaughter. Bro. Thomas Smith Slaughter. Land in Kentucky given to him by William Knox to be given to bro. Philip Slaughter, bro. Thomas Smith Slaughter, three youngest sisters, Susanna Slaughter, Patsey Slaughter, Sally Slaughter.
Executor: Bro. Philip Slaughter.
Wit.: James Slaughter, Thomas Marston, Robert Slaughter.

Will of Richard Corley of Culpeper Co.
Dated 14 Dec., 1789. Proven 19 July, 1790.
Legatees: Wife Effie Corley. Sons: Menoah Corley, Curtis Corley, children of my son Aquilla Corley. Daus.: Drucylla Corley, Effie Jordon, Lucy Duncan. Granddaus.: Lucy Jordon, Lucy Robertson. Grandson John Corley.
Executors: Son Menoah Corley, son-in-law William Duncan, son Curtis Corley.
Wit.: Henry Mauzy, William Garrard, Patty Harris.
Memorandum: If Lucy Jordon dies before she receives her legacy the same to be paid to granddau. Jenny Jordan.

Inventory and Appraisal of Estate of John Triplett, dec'd. Recorded 19 July, 1790. Made by Lawrence Slaughter, Frederick Kline, Joseph Roberts.

Executor's Account of Estate of George Woolfenberger, dec'd. Recorded 19 July, 1790. Made by John Woolfenberger, Extr. New executor, Alexander Dawney received the balance.

Inventory and Appraisal of Estate of Michael Utz, dec'd. Recorded 20 Sept., 1790. Made by Henry Miller, Andras Carpenter, John Weber, Sr.

Inventory and Appraisal of Estate of William P. Thurston, dec'd. Recorded 20 Sept., 1790. Made by William Robertson, William Robertson, Jr., George Scott.

Will of Armistead Minor of Culpeper Co.
Dated 5 Feb., 1790. Proven 20 Sept., 1790.
Legatees: Wife Margaret Minor. Son Elliott Minor (had received a gift from his grandfather, Joseph Minor.); Joseph Minor. Dau. Mary Allen Minor. All children were underage.
Executors: Wife Margaret Minor, Edmund Gaines, Elijah Kirtley.
Wit.: Augus Rucker, Ambrose Booton, George Allen.

Inventory and Appraisal of Estate of Andrew Bourn, dec'd. Recorded 20 Sept., 1790. Made by Harbin Moore, Churchill Gordon, James Morton.

Inventory and Appraisal of Estate of Benjamin Head, dec'd. Recorded 20 Sept., 1790. Made by Ambrose Barbour, Benjamin Cave, Joshua Willis.

Inventory and Appraisal of Estate of Patrick Cockran, dec'd. Recorded 20 Sept., 1790. Made by Nathaniel Welch, William Clark, Oliver Terrill.

Executor's Account of Estate of Charles Morgan. Recorded 20 Sept., 1790. Made by Thomas Wright, extr. Only amounts paid to legatees according to designation in the listing were paid to Morgan Thornhill, Absolum Cornelius, Thomas Wright. Dates included 1783 through 1787.

Will of John Rodeheaver of Culpeper Co.
Dated 30 May, 1790. Proven 20 Sept., 1790.
Legatees: Wife Sarah Rodeheaver. Sons: John Rodeheaver, Joseph Rodeheaver, David Rodeheaver.
Executors: Wife Sarah Rodeheaver, Benjamin Zachary, James Yeager.
Wit.: Anna (X) Ward, Peter Mountague, Richard Vernon.

Inventory and Appraisal of Estate of John Turnham, dec'd. Recorded 20 Sept., 1790. Made by Francis Apperson, William Threlkeld, John Whitehead.

Will of George Dillard of St. Mark's Parish, Culpeper Co.
Dated 2 March, 1790. Proven 20 Sept., 1790.
Legatees: Sons: Major Dillard, John Dillard, Samuel Dillard, James Dillard. Daus.: Ann Freeman, wife of Robert Freeman, Jr.; Liza Duncan, wife of Charles Duncan; Sarah Colvin, wife of John Colvin.
Executors: Son John Dillard, son-in-law Charles Duncan, son-in-law Robert Freeman, Jr. (He called the last two executors "step-sons", a term used more frequently in early records.)
Wit.: William Chowning, Nancy Kay(X) Apperson, Francis Apperson.
Sons-in-law refused to act as executors.

Administrator's Account of Estate of John Latham, dec'd. Recorded 20 Sept., 1790. Made by Thomas Latham, admr.

Inventory and Appraisal of Estate of Jeremiah Corbin, dec'd. Recorded 20 Sept., 1790. Made by John Puller, Joseph Basye, William McClanahan, Jr.

Account of Sales of Estate of William Marquess, dec'd. Recorded 18 Oct., 1790. Made by ____ ____ (not recorded.)

Inventory and Appraisal of Estate of John Terrill, dec'd. Recorded 18 Oct., 1790. Made by Joseph Steward, Thomas Pratt, Thomas Graves, William Powell.

Will of Ann Powers of St. Mark's Parish, Culpeper Co.
Dated 26 April, 1787. Proven 18 Oct., 1790.
Legatee: Dau. Elizabeth Yancey, wife of Charles Yancey.
Executors: Son-in-law Charles Yancey, Francis Apperson, grandson

William Yancey.
    Wit.: Thomas Yancey, Betty (X) Apperson.
    Charles Yancey, executor. Others refused to act.

Will of Benjamin Watts of Culpeper Co.
Dated 10 July, 1790. Proven 18 Oct., 1790.
    Legatees: Wife Anne Watts. At death of wife, land to Jeremiah White of Orange Co., son of Henry White. Elizabeth Snell, dau. of Lewis Snell. At death of wife, remainder of personal estate equally among bro. John Watts, bro. Thomas Watts, bro. Jacob Watts, sis. Sarah Gaines, each of their youngest children.
    Executors: Wife Anne Watts, nephew Barnard Watts, nephew Thomas Watts, nephew James Watts.
    Wit.: George Eve, William Broaddus, Molley (X) Lamb.

Will of Richard Quinn of Culpeper Co.
Dated 17 Feb., 1789. Proven 18 Oct., 1790.
    Legatees: Wife Elizabeth Quinn. Mary Offer (relationship not stated). Son Richard Quinn. Grandson John Offer.
    Executors: Leeroy Canaday, Edward Herndon.
    Wit.: Henry White, James Kirk, Hadley Head.

Inventory and Appraisal of Estate of Joel Smith, dec'd. Recorded 18 Oct., 1790. Made by Henry Taliaferro, William Lightfoot, Reuben Zimmerman.

Inventory and Appraisal of Estate of George Dillard, dec'd. Recorded 20 Dec., 1790. Made by William Threlkeld, William Chowning, Francis Apperson.

Will of James Williams of Culpeper Co.
Dated (not dated). Proven 20 Dec., 1790.
    Legatees: James Hog, plantation and one-fourth of personal estate. Jemimah Collings, slave and one-fourth of personal estate. Sarah Williams, slave and one-fourth of personal estate. Mary Hog, sis. of above-named James Hog, slave and one-fourth of personal estate. All legatees were minors. Robert Hooton(?), Elizabeth Williams land equally divided between them.
    Executrix: Elizabeth Williams.
    Wit.: Gabriel Green, John Strother, John Pratt, Able Griffith.

Inventory and Appraisal of Estate of John Favour, dec'd. Recorded 20 Dec., 1790. Made by James Whitehead, Henry Duval, Lunsford Carter.

Will of Daniel White of St. Mark's Parish, Culpeper Co.
Dated 23 Nov., 1788. Proven 20 Dec., 1790.
    Legatees: Sons: Henry White, John White. Granddau. Polly White, dau. of son John. Dau. Tabitha Rogers. Six grandchildren: Reuben Harrison, John Harrison, Richard Harrison, James Harrison, Elizabeth Tindsley wife of William Tindsley, Frances Lee wife of Richard Lee - children of dau. Frances Harrison, dec'd. Granddau. Elizabeth Todd Rogers, dau. of

dau. Tabitha Rogers.
Executor: Son John White.
Wit.: Hall Randolph, James Randolph, Jediah Randolph.

Inventory and Appraisal of Estate of Robert Stewart, dec'd. Recorded 20 Dec., 1790. Made by William Gaines, Cad W. Slaughter, William Slaughter.

Inventory and Appraisal of Estate of Benjamin Watts, dec'd. Recorded 20 Dec., 1790. Made by James Walker, Jr., Ephraim Rucker, Jonathan Cowherd.

Estate Division of Patrick Cochran, dec'd. Recorded 17 Jan., 1791. Made by Goodrich Lightfoot, John Terrill, Francis Madison, William Madison. Legatees: Widow, her dower; John Cochran, Elizabeth Cochran, Mary Cochran.

Will of William Tapp of Culpeper Co.
Dated 27 June, 1780. Proven 17 Jan., 1796.
Legatees: Wife Christian Tapp. Sons: Vincent Tapp, William Tapp, Lewis Tapp. Grandson William Tapp, son of Vincent Tapp. Dau. Ann Cunninghame, wife of John Cunninghame. Dau. Alice Graham, wife of John Graham. Dau. Elizabeth Green. Dau. Sarah Jett, wife of John Jett. William Yates, son of Mary Yates, dec'd.
Executors: Son Vincent Tapp, James Jett.
Wit.: Thomas Hopper, Jacob Wall, Ann (X) Walle.
Disannulled in a codicil, the bequest to William Yates. 10 Sept., 1789.
Wit.: Moses Tapp, Sias Tapp.
James Jett refused to act as executor.

Will of Vincent Tapp of Culpeper Co.
Dated 22 Nov., 1790. Proven 17 Jan., 1791.
Legatees: Wife Molly Tapp. Sons: Elias Tapp, William Tapp, John Tapp, Vincent Tapp, Moses Tapp, James Tapp, Nimrod Tapp. Daus.: Suckey Tapp, Ann Tapp, Molly Tapp, Sally Tapp.
Executors: Son William Tapp, James Jett.
Wit.: John Jett, James Arnold, Harmon (X) Hufman.

Will of Timothy Holdway.
Dated 24 Sept., 1787. Proven 17 Jan., 1791.
Legatees: Wife. Daus.: Anne Holdway, Abigail Holdway, Elizabeth Holdway, Phebe Holdway.
Wit.: Daniel James, Benjamin Roberts, Mary Jameson.

Division of Estate of George Dillard, dec'd. Recorded 17 Jan., 1791. Made by James Pendleton, James Jett. Legatees: Samuel Dillard, Robert Freeman, James Dillard, Charles Duncan, John Colvin, John Dillard in equal shares.

Will of James Spilman of Culpeper Co.
Dated 7 May, 1784. Proven 20 Sept., 1790.

Legatees: Wife Alice Spilman. Sons: Nathaniel Spilman (eldest), Charles Spilman (next eldest), next son Thomas Spilman, next son William Spilman, son John Spilman. "Other five children now young": Henry Spilman, Phillip Spilman, Elizabeth Spilman, Susanah Spilman, Peggy Spilman.
Executors: Wife Alice Spilman, son Thomas Spilman.
Wit.: None.
Thomas Spilman refused to act as executor.

Inventory and Appraisal of Estate of James Williams, dec'd. Recorded 17 Jan., 1791. Made by Richard Gaines, William Gaines, Cadwallader Slaughter.

Division of Personal Estate of Ambrose Powell, dec'd. Recorded 17 Jan., 1791. Made by Goodrich Lightfoot, Charles Hume, Lewis Conner, Ambrose Medley. Legatees: Mrs. Mary Rowe, late widow of Ambrose Powell, dec'd.; Major Robert Powell; Capt. William Powell; Col. Henry Hill.

Division of land of John Faver, dec'd. Recorded 18 April, 1791. Made by Robert Coleman, R. Slaughter, John Williams. Legatees: Rosanna Faver, Isabella Faver, Frances Faver, John Faver, John Apperson. Signed by John Grinnan and Sam Clayton who surveyed and drew the plat which appears on p. 416.

Will of John Fray of Bromfield Parish, Culpeper Co.
Dated 10 Sept., 1790. Proven 18 April, 1791.
Legatees: Wife Rebekah Fray. Sons: Ephraim Fray, Aaron Fray. Daus.: Mary Fray, Elizabeth Fray, Anne Fray, Marget Fray.
Executors: Son Ephraim Fray, Daniel Weaver.
Wit.: John Wayland, Jr., Henry Back.

Agreement and Division of Estate of Michael Blankenbaker. Recorded 21 June, 1790. He had died intestate. Heirs agreed to have George Hume, Mark Finks, George Chrisler divide the estate. Legatees: Elizabeth Blankenbaker, widow of Michael Blankenbaker, dec'd.; John Wilhoit, John Clore, Ephraim Utz, Elias Chrisler, Lewis Wilhoit, Jemima Crigler, Mary Wilhoit - all of Culpeper Co.

Inventory and Appraisal of Estate of Nicholas Crigler, Jr., dec'd. Recorded 19 Oct., 1789. Made by Mark Finks, Reuben Crigler, Zachary Broyle.

Inventory and Appraisal of Estate of Henry Delph, dec'd. Recorded 18 Jan., 1791. Made by John Graves, Michael Glove, Herry Terrell.

Agreement of heirs of George Dillard, dec'd., for division to be made by James Pendleton and James Jett. Signed by John Dillard, Samuel Dillard, James Dillard, Charles Duncan, Robert Freeman, Jr., John Colvin. Recorded 17 Jan., 1791.

Inventory and Appraisal of Estate of Richard Cooley, dec'd. Recorded 19 April, 1791. Made by James Browning, Stephen Movesoon(?), Charles Haney.

Inventory and Appraisal of Estate of John Calvert, dec'd. Recorded 19 April, 1791. Made by James Browning, Charles Browning, William Brooke.

Will of William Shaw.
Dated 25 March, 1791. Proven 19 April, 1791.
Legatee: Friend Zachariah Petty including his "pension due for 1790."
Executors: Zachariah Petty, William Edzard.
Wit.: William Edzard, Susanna Lightfoot, John Pettey, Robert Brown.

Will of Benjamin Lowen of Culpeper Co.
Dated 29 Nov., 1789. Proven 20 June, 1791.
Legatees: Wife Mary Lowen. All my children - eldest dau. Betsy Lowen still a minor.
Executors: Joseph Porter, Sr., wife Mary Lowen.
Wit.: Churchill Gordon, John Wharton, Elizabeth (X) Sisson.

Will of Jacob Ward of Culpeper Co.
Dated 31 March, 1791. Proven 20 June, 1791.
Legatees: Wife Anne Ward. Sons: John Ward, William Ward, Jacob Ward, Mitchell Ward. Daus.: Frankey Vawter, Judah Ward, Anne Ward, Sarah Yager. Granddau. Anne Rodifer, dau. of Sarah Yager.
Executors: William Booton, Hadley Head.
Wit.: Mildred Head, Mary Head.

Will of John Wiley of Culpeper Co.
Dated 18 April, 1791. Proven 20 June, 1791.
Legatees: Sis. Martha Wiley; Thomas Wiley, Vincent Wiley, Isaac Wiley, three sons of bro. Vincent Wiley, dec'd. All legatees were minors.
Executors: John Garwood, Robert Hunt.
Wit.: Merrick Starr, Jessee Penrose, Joshua Hunt.

Inventory of Estate of James Spilman, dec'd. Recorded 20 June, 1791. Made by Patterson Fletcher, John Fletcher, William Smith.

Inventory and Appraisal of Estate of John Fray, dec'd. Recorded 20 June, 1791. Made by John Weaver, Matthew Weaver, Tilman Huffman.

Administrator's Account of Estate of James Garrell, dec'd. Recorded 20 June, 1791. Made by Jeremiah Garrell, admr.

Inventory and Appraisal of Estate of Christian Ish(?), dec'd. Recorded 20 June, 1791. Made by John Wharton, Richard Chilton, Daniel Brown.

Inventory and Appraisal of Estate of John Rodeaver, dec'd. Recorded 20 June, 1791. Made by Ambrose Medley, Am Bohannon, John Gibbs.

Inventory and Appraisal of Estate of Alexander Thom, dec'd. Recorded 20 June, 1791. Made by Francis Irwin, ____ Slaughter, Joseph Roberts.

Inventory and Appraisal of Estate of James Shirley, dec'd. Recorded 20 June, 1791. Made by John Clore, Jonathan Smith, George Hume.

Inventory and Appraisal of Estate of John Wiley, dec'd. Recorded 18 July, 1791. Made by Merrick Starr, Jesse Penrose, Caleb Autrain, Robert Hunt.

Division of Estate (slaves only) of Gabriel Jones, dec'd. Recorded 18 July, 1791. Made by John Strode, William Ball, John Wharton, Robert Coleman, Jr. Legatees: Richard Y. Wigginton who intermarried with Mary Jones, one of the parties; Robert Slaughter, Gent., guardian of Frances Jones.

Inventory and Appraisal of Estate of William Shaw, dec'd. Recorded 18 July, 1791. Made by John Marshall, James Branham, Robert Brown.

Will of Oliver Clark.
Dated 11 Sept., 1777. Proven 18 July, 1791.
Legatees: Wife Mary Clark. At her decease equally divided among his children.
Wit.: James Read, John Read, James (X) Shakelford.

Inventory and Appraisal of Estate of Joseph Minor, dec'd. Recorded 19 Sept., 1791. Made by Alexander Bradford, James Archer, Joel Cofer.

Inventory and Appraisal of Estate of Armistead Minor, dec'd. Recorded 19 Sept., 1791. Made by John Bradford, Augustin Rucker, Angus Rucker.

Inventory and Appraisal of Estate of Jacob Ward, dec'd. Recorded 19 Sept., 1791. Made by Ambrose Medley, Am. Bohannon, Henry Gaines.

Inventory and Appraisal of Estate of William Marquess. Recorded 19 Sept., 1791. Made by James Hord, Robert Branham, William Richards.

Division of Estate of Michael Utz, dec'd. Recorded 19 Sept., 1791. Made by Robert Roebuck, Mark Finks, Lewis Conner. Legatees: Michael Utz, Lawrence Gaar, George Utz, Michael Swindle, Daniel Utz, Adam Utz.

CULPEPER COUNTY, VIRGINIA

Will Book G (1813-1817)

This book is missing but an Index is available.

ALDERS
  Francis. Inventory
ABBOTT
  Ann. Will
ADAMS
  Henrietta. Will   p. 178
    Inventory   p. 217
    Executor's Account   p. 221
ALLEN
  James. Will   p. 256*
  Thomas. Will   p. 270
    Inventory   p. 260
AMISS
  Ann. Account Sales
    Inventory   p. 324
    Account Sales   p. 416
ANDERSON
  James. Administrator's
    Account
  Eliza. Administrator's
    Account
BARNES
  Leonard. Account Sales p. 47
    Executor's Account   p. 52
BARROW
  John. Account Sales   p. 26
    Inventory   p. 34
BASYE
  Ethelbert. Will   p. 236
  Joseph. Inventory   p. 252
    Appraisal   p. 255
    Executor's Account   p. 257
  Elijah. Inventory   p. 257
    Executor's Account   p. 265
BECKHAM
  Abner. Administrator's
    Account   p. 92
  Elijah. Inventory   p. 180**
    Account Sales   p. 316
    Administrator's
      Account   p. 368
BERRY
  Aaron. Inventory   p. 417
    Account Sales   p. 418

BLACKWELL
  Catharine. Inventory   p. 7
BOALS
  Kate R. et als Guardian
    Account   p. 431
  James R. et als Guardian
    Account   p. 431
BOWERS
  Thomas. Will   p. 284
BRADFORD
  John. Will   p. 134
BRANHAM
  James. Will   p. 105
BROADUS
  Thomas. Administrator's
    Account   p. 19
    Inventory   p. 340
BROWN
  Thomas. Will   p. 67
    Inventory   p. 102
BROWNING
  John. Will   p. 61
    Inventory   p. 68
  Shadrock. Will   p. 296
    Inventory   p. 336
BURNLEY
  John. Inventory   p. 36
BUTT
  Eleanor. Will   p. 360
    Inventory   p. 366
CALVERT
  Rall. Will   p. 100*
  R. S. Inventory   p. 341
CAMP
  William. Will   p. 146
    Inventory   p. 230
CANNADY
  James. Will   p. 145
    Account Sales   p. 439
CANNON
  John. Will   p. 269
CASTALAS
  Robert. Will   p. 246
CHEEK
  Elizabeth. Will   p. 95

*Original in Box 1 in vault.
**Will in Bk "A".

*Copied in Suit Spiller vs Calvert.

85

CHICK
  Francis. Inventory   p. 63
COLLINS
  William. Will   p. 119
COMPTON
  Henrietta. Will   p. 431
COOPER
  Francis. Will   p. 81
    Inventory   p. 310
CORBIN
  John. Will   p. 36
    Inventory   p. 71
  William. Inventory   p. 170
  John. Executor's Account p. 358
  William. Executor's
    Account   p. 452
COVINGTON
  Margaret. Inventory   p. 239
CRUMM
  Lewis. Will   p. 436
    Account Sales   p. 437
    Administrator's
      Account   p. 438
CRUSER
  Mary. Will   p. 192
    Inventory   p. 245
    Account Sales   p. 289
    Administrator's
      Account   p. 411
DELPH
  Samuel. Inventory   p. 176
    Account Sales   p. 178
DILLARD
  John. Executor's
    Account   p. 312
  Ann. Will   p. 234
    Inventory   p. 359
DOWDALL
  Mary. Inventory   p. 386
    Account Sales   p. 388
DOWNEY
  Alexander. Account
    Sales   p. 149
DUKE
  William. Will   p. 315
  John. Inventory   p. 397
DULANEY
  John. Inventory   p. 307
DUNAWAY
  Isaac. Will   p. 344
    Account Sales   p. 455

DUNCAN
  James. Inventory   p. 182
    Account Sales   p. 185
EDGE
  Lott. Inventory   p. 165
EDWARDS
  Peggy. Inventory   p. 284
EGGBORN
  Jacob. Administratrix'
    Account   p. 4
  Ann. Will   p. 198
    Inventory   p. 270
FARMER
  Daniel. Will   p. 271
FINKS
  John. Will   p. 371
    Inventory   p. 382
FICKLIN
  Fielding. Inventory   p. 139
    Guardian's Account p. 392
  Sarah. Guardian's Account p. 392
  Eliza A. Guardian's
    Account   p. 394
  Fielding. Executor's
    Account   p. 443
FISHBACK
  Martin. Guardian's Account p. 8*
    Guardian's Account p. 10
  Elliott. Inventory   p. 279
  Mary. Administrator's
    Account   p. 353
FLETCHER
  John. Inventory   p. 225
    Will   p. 135
FOREACUS
  Herekiel. Inventory   p. 44
FOUSHEE
  John. Administrator's
    Account   p. 114
    Administrator's
      Account   p. 413
FREEMAN
  Thomas. Inventory   p. 5
    Administrator's Account p. 89
GAINES
  Richard. Executor's
    Account   p. 14
GREGG
  Roberts. Inventory   p. 467

*Previous one in Bk "F"

GREEN
    Aaron. Inventory   p. 279
    James. Executor's
        Account   p. 373
HAINES
    Isaac. Administrator's
        Account   p. 408
HANSBROUGH
    William. Will   p. 335
HAYNIE
    Anthony. Account Sales   p. 157
        Inventory   p. 160
        Guardian's Account   p. 298
        Administrator's
            Account   p. 354
        Administrator's
            Account   p. 356
HAWKINS
    Benjamin. Inventory   p. 420
        Account Sales   p. 421
HEATH
    Mildred. Will   p. 282
HICKERSON
    William. Inventory   p. 285
HILL
    William. Account Sales   p. 27
HOPPER
    Thomas. Inventory and
        Account Sales   p. 442
HUMPHREY
    John. Inventory   p. 224
HUME
    Armistead. Inventory   p. 432
JENKINS
    Richard. Inventory   p. 414
JEFFRIES
    John. Will   p. 103
    Joseph. Inventory and
        Account Sales   p. 375
JETT
    John. Executor's Account   p. 59
JOHNSON
    Allen. Inventory   p. 399
        Account Sales   p. 402
JOHNSTON
    Nathaniel. Inventory   p. 21
        Account Sales   p. 23
JONES
    James. Inventory   p. 133
    Mishall. Inventory   p. 226
        Will   p. 240

LATHAM
    Robert. Will   p. 109
        Inventory   p. 115
    Philip. Will   p. 172
        Inventory   p. 247
        Account Sales   p. 346
        Division of Slaves   p. 363
    Frances. Will   p. 472
LILLARD
    Thomas. Will   p. 181
        Inventory   p. 228
LEWIS
    Benjamin. Guardian's
        Account   p. 75
MARYE
    Peter. Division   p. 317
MARKHAM
    I. L. Division Inventory   p. 299
MASON
    Joel. Inventory   p. 112
    Elizabeth. Inventory   p. 121
MATTHEWS
    John. Executor's Account   p. 232
McKENNEY
    William. Account Sales   p. 85
McKELLUP
    Hughes. Executor's
        Account   p. 117
MILLER
    William. Inventory   p. 123
    John. Inventory   p. 127
        Account Sales   p. 128
        Administrator's
            Account   p. 323
MITCHELL
    Fisher. Administrator's
        Account   p. 17
MOORE
    Joseph. Division of
        Estate   p. 58
MURRY
    James. Will   p. 33
        Inventory   p. 39
NASH
    John. Inventory   p. 187
NALLE
    Frances. Account of
        Sales   p. 378
OZELL
    Jeremiah. Inventory   p. 462
ORMO
    Thomas. Inventory   p. 25

PARSONS
  Elizabeth. Will   p. 92
    Account Sales   p. 315
    Inventory   p. 190
PERRY
  Ann. Inventory   p. 43
PENDLETON
  Catherine. Will   p. 425
    Inventory   p. 451
PETTY
  Rawleigh. Will   p. 141*
POE
  Samuel. Inventory and
    Account   p. 454
POLLARD
  William. Inventory p. 244
POPHAM
  John. Inventory   p. 443
    Account Sales   p. 444
PORTER
  William. Will   p. 261
    Inventory   p. 337
  Samuel. Will   p. 412
PRATT
  Thomas. Will   p. 155
    Inventory   p. 168
RAKESTRAW
  I. Inventory   p. 290
    Account Sales   p. 292
    Administrator's
      Accounts   p. 294
READ
  Samuel. Division of
    Land   p. 110
RICHARDS
  Eliza. Will   p. 332
    Inventory   p. 365
SETTLE
  Merriman. Will   p. 122**
    Inventory   p. 154
  Frances. Will   p. 414
SINGLETON
  James. Will   p. 142
    Inventory   p. 366

*Found in Chancery Box 14. Suit of Settle's Administrator vs Petty.

**Certified copy on file in Chancery Records, Rappahannock Co.

SMITH
  Weeden. Administrator's
    Account   p. 42
    Will   p. 125
    Inventory   p. 137
    Inventory   p. 175
  L. P. Will   p. 359
    Inventory   p. 398
SPENNY
  James. Will   p. 350
STARKE
  William. Inventory p. 274
STOKESBERRY
  William. Inventory p. 288
SUDDOTH
  Benjamin. Account Sales p. 4
STRINGFELLOW
  Henry. Will   p. 130
    Inventory   p. 199
    Account Sales   p. 324
STROTHER
  John. Inventory   p. 434
TAYLOR
  John. Will   p. 276
    Inventory   p. 341
THRELKELD
  James. Will   p. 42
    Inventory   p. 322
TOWLES
  Mary. Inventory   p. 56
TRIPLETT
  E. Will   p. 104
TUCKES
  Moses. Will   p. 78
    Inventory   p. 86
TUCKER
  Moses. Account Sales p. 96
  Reuben. Will   p. 422
  John. Will   p. 450*
  Moses. Division of
    Estate   p. 457
    Executor's Account p. 458
  John. Will   p. 469
TURNER
  George. Will   p. 231
    Inventory   p. 266
TUTT
  John. Inventory   p. 20

*For copy see Chancery Box 19 O'Bannon vs Tucker.

TUTT (cont.)
  James. Will   p. 45
    Inventory   p. 58
    Administrator's
      Account   p. 64
    Inventory   p. 131
    Inventory   p. 132
VOSS
  Bob B. Executor's
    Account   p. 203
  Susan F. Guardian's
    Account   p. 209
  Benjamin F. Guardian's
    Account   p. 212
  Bob S. Guardian's
    Account   p. 217
  William E. Guardian's
    Account   p. 220
VAUGHAN
  William. Inventory   p. 54
    Administrator's
      Account   p. 390
WALE
  Lawson. Inventory   p. 66
WALL
  Isaac. Will   p. 143
    Inventory   p. 308
    Administrator's
      Account   p. 314
WHITE
  John A. Inventory   p. 228
  Presley J. Inventory   p. 242
    Administrator's
      Account   p. 277
WILEY
  Edward. Will   p. 409
    Inventory   p. 470*
WILLETT
  Richard. Will   p. 12
    Inventory   p. 79
WILHOITE
  Gabriel. Inventory   p. 237
  N. Trustee's Account   p. 333
  Edward. Inventory   p. 386
WOODWARD
  William. Inventory   p. 251
WOOD
  Joseph. Inventory   p. 148

WRIGHT
  Robert. Will   p. 91
    Inventory   p. 174
YANCEY
  William. Will   p. 238
  Eliza. Will   p. 241
  William. Inventory   p. 343
YATES
  Richard. Will   p. 189
    Inventory   p. 384
ZIMMERMAN
  Reuben. Administrator's
    Account   p. 81
  Mary. Administrator's
    Account   p. 113
    Inventory   p. 250

*Given as Willey.

CULPEPER COUNTY, VIRGINIA

OLD MISCELLANEOUS PAPERS

A packet of loose papers stored in a
cabinet in the County Clerk's office

PACKAGE No. 1

20 Sept., 1865. Bond of Thomas O. Flint, when elected Clerk of the Circuit Court of Culpeper County. Co-signers: John H. Rixey by Edward H. Lane, his attorney and James Barbour by the same. Amount $10,000.

9 Aug., 1865. $1300 note to Joseph Nalle from James M. Griffin. Nalle had filed suit to collect a $1300 debt.

29 April, 1851. Robert G. Ward, clerk of court, to Sheriff of Culpeper Co. to summon Winfield S. Coons to answer suit brought by Matthew Jett, Phoebe Doores, Dicey Tapp, Zepheniah Williams, Edmund Christian, assignee of Edgar Doores, William I. Doores, James Corbin and Jane his wife. A Suit re slaves, giving names and value of each.

1863. James Bickers requested permission to invest funds in his hands as administrator of Estate of Powhatan Massey, dec'd. It could not be distributed then because there were several claimants. Permission granted by Richard H. Field, Judge of the 10th Federal Circuit Court, 14 July, 1863.

3 June, 1851. Papers in Suit of Jameson's Administrator vs Thompson's Administrator give following statements: George W. Jameson, administrator of David Jameson, dec'd., recovered against Sarah Thompson, executrix, and John Thompson, executor, of Philip R. Thompson, dec'd., $2329.58 with 6% interest from 29 Sept., 1845, and court costs of $36.59.

17 Oct., 1855. George W. Jameson had died, so the Court took possession of unadministered assets of David Jameson, dec'd. Sarah Thompson, executrix, and John Thompson, executor of Philip R. Thompson, dec'd., had both died and administration had been granted to Francis Thompson, who was summoned re judgment granted in 1851 but not paid. Francis Thompson lived in Kanawha Co. 25 Oct., 1855, when he replied by appointing Thomas O. Flint of Culpeper attorney.

17 Nov., 1854. William Green acknowledges receipt of the $700 payment. No indication as to his relationship.

7 Nov., 1864. Order to summon John S. Pemberton, Lewis P. Nelson, Alfred L. Ashby, James Keys, Robert Triplett, William C. Jameson, James W. Inskeep, Robert Williams, John Williams, B. U. McCoy, A. J. Stofer, Walter Robertson, Kemp Beckham to give evidence before the Grand Jury.

5 Feb., 1846. Date of signature of John Thom to his will, a copy of which is in this package. Proven 4 June, 1855.

7 Nov., 1865. Brief paper in suit of William Colbert and Patsy, his wife, vs Sarah Watson and others.

10 Nov., 1856. Perry J. Eggborn, administrator of George Eggborn, re due bill of Mary Dulaney, dated 17 April, 1847, to George Eggborn. Mary Dulaney died before 10 Nov., 1856, and James G. or Y. Field was her administrator.

15 Nov., 1847. Promissory note of George Eggborn to Mary Dulaney for $150. Marked paid.

15 Nov., 1856. Affidavit from J. Y. Field re Capt. George Eggborn's debt to Mrs. Mary Dulaney.

Oct., 1855. Petition for appointment of George D. Gray as one of the Commissioners in Chancery in the place of John S. Shackleford, resigned. Contains 20 signatures.

10 Sept., 1856. Letter from James G. Field, administrator of Mary Dulaney to Perry I. Eggborn indicates that she was the widow of French C. Dulaney.

20 March, 1837. Summons to John Gordon for a re-hearing of a decree of 19 Dec., 1834 in his case against Margaret R. Gordon, Sarah Gordon and Joseph F. Gordon, orphan children of Francis Gordon who are still infants under the age of twenty-one years. Case brought by Sarah Gordon, orphan, by Washington Bailey, her next friend.

5 Nov., 1842. A few papers in case of Edward Williams vs Alfred S. Ashby for trespass, assault and battery and false imprisonment. Williams resided in Madison Co. and Ashby in Culpeper Co. Case settled in 1845.

2 Nov., 1860. Summons of Thomas Flint, executor of Elizabeth W. Petty, who had interest in estate of Marshall Petty, dec'd., which she had acquired by transfer from John S. Petty, one of the legatees of Marshall Petty. A bill in Chancery vs Thomas Flint, executor, exhibited by John D. Hudson, assignee of William H. Moore.

11 Nov., 1858. James A. English vs Samuel Russell. Court order to English to file answers to questions propounded by Russell.

17 Oct., 1864. Lewis P. Nelson took oath that Thomas Fitzhugh, a non-resident of the State owed him and James S. Grinnan, trading as Lewis and Grinnan, $422.87. A writ of attachment on estate of Thomas Fitzhugh issued the same day. Announcement of suit appeared in The Sentinel, Richmond, Virginia.

3 May, 1863. Statement of fees for appeal of Case of Edward B. Hill, executor of Thomas Hill, dec'd., vs Joseph M. Simms and Sallie M., his wife.

5 March, 1846. Summons. Walter O'Bannon to answer complaint of Andrew Jackson Wall.

June, 1849. Summons for John Shackleford to appear before the Superior Court re obstructing by fencing and ditching the road from Pottsville to Kelly's Mill upon evidence given by John P. Kelly, prosecutor.

15 Feb., 1853 - 11 March, 1855. Account pages presented by Plank Walk Way to prove indebtedness to them of L. P. Nelson.

27 Aug., 1864. Summons. Susan Wigginton, Sally Wigginton, Willie Yancey, John W. Mitchell, Mary J. Spencer, Sallie Yancey, Edward Yancey, Charles Yancey, Co___ Yancey, Edmonia Wigginton, Joseph D. Brown and Pamaly his wife, William Yancey and Elizabeth Miller to answer a bill in Chancery exhibited against them by Benjamin M. Yancey, executor of Susan T. Yancey, dec'd. It seems that Elizabeth Miller was a non-resident.

28 Feb., 1862. Summons. Abraham Lucas and William Stringfellow to answer Happy W. Lucas' plea of Debt for $500. Abraham Lucas not a resident on this date had given a note, 24 Jan., 1860, and William Stringfellow had signed it and entered Court and confessed the indebtedness.

14 Jan., 1862. Summons. Benjamin Higgason, of Orange Co., executor of Esther Higgason, dec'd., to answer a charge of trespass made by William Higgason and Catharine, his wife.

14 Jan., 1862. Summons. William R. Barber to answer Mark Bird.

7 Sept., 1864. Summons. Eastham Jordan to answer John Cole.

27 Sept., 1864. Summons. Benjamin Wigginton to answer, with others, James M. Yancey, executor of Susan M. Yancey, dec'd.

23 June, 1863. Summons. John H. Rixey, Robert T. Bowen, James M. Allan, George W. Jamison, Lewis P. Nelson, John S. Berry, Richard Abbott, William H. Ward to give evidence before the Grand Jury. John S. Berry was not found.

29 March, 1859. A request to "My Friend" from Sallie W. Gray of Madison for some money for provisions. W. Gray is ill.

11 Nov., 1865. H. Anne Robertson vs John C. Green, administrator of William Robertson and others. John C. Green has died and James W. Green is administrator of Wm. Robertson. Authorized public notice to creditors of Wm. Robertson and private notice to heirs.

A package of authorizations for amount allowed each person for Jury Duty for years 1850 through 1863. All signed by Thomas O. Flint, clerk. 140 separate authorizations. Names were not copied as 1850 and 1860 Census give names of residents with greater accuracy.

30 Sept., 1859. Joseph W. Roberts filed suit against John P. Kelly for trespassing through Roberts' attorney, Shackleford Gibron.

1 June, 1860. A neat, carefully marked plot of the Day tract owned by John P. Kelly. County Surveyor: James G. Broadus. The disputed area lay between Kelly's and the dower tract of Susanna Roberts which Kelly had acquired. 5 identical copies; each hand-drawn and hand-lettered.

13 July, 1860. A less professional copy on lighter weight paper. 6 copies. Copy of description of land sold 28 Aug., 1818, by Edward Day to P. Roberts.

8 March, 1856. Exemplification of "Papers", No. "81". To the Honorable the Judges of the Orphans' Court, in and for Allegheny County in the Commonwealth of Pennsylvania:
Petition of Godfrey, Martha Ann, Lewis Champ and Charles Edward, minor children under the age of fourteen years of Harriet Whiting by their mother and next friend. They petition for $100 each from executor of Philip Lightfoot, late of Culpeper Co. and that the Court appoint a guardian for them. The Court appointed A. M. Brown of Pittsburgh. James K. Brown and William M. Brown were co-signers of his guardianship bond.

17 Dec., 1855. Exemplification of "Papers" No. "82". Petition of Sarah, a minor child of Lucy Roberts to the Judges of the Orphans' Court in and for the County of Allegheny in the Commonwealth of Pennsylvania.
She is entitled to $100 from estate of Philip Lightfoot, dec'd, late of Culpeper Co. and requests a guardian be appointed for her. The Court appointed A. M. Brown of Pittsburgh who gave bond with James K. Brown and William M. Brown as co-signers.

18 Sept., 1855. Exemplification of "Papers" No. "59". Same paper--Allegheny Co., Pennsylvania for Samuel Pelham, John Pelham and Fanny Pelham, minors under fourteen years, children of Harriet Pelham for their part of estate of Philip Lightfoot, dec'd., late of Culpeper Co. The Court appointed A. M. Brown of Pittsburgh, who gave bond with James K. Brown and W. M. Brown as co-signers.

7 Nov., 1865. Court accepted affidavit of Lucy Ann Jameson that Fanny B. Jameson and Minnie Jameson had attained the age of twenty-one years and ordered that certificates of Stock of State of Virginia standing in their names be delivered to them.

18 Jan., 1859. Simpson Park of Platte County in Missouri stated to Judge R. H. Field, Judge of Circuit Court of Culpeper Co., that 10 May, 1856, he had qualified in Platte Co. as guardian of William H. Field, infant son of Albert Field, dec'd., and had given bond with William A. Fox as security. S. Park seeks for his ward about $800 in hand of his ward's guardian in Culpeper Co., James G. Field. Simpson Park's petition was accepted and recorded and payment to be sued for.

6 Nov., 1854. Summons. Fayette M. Latham to answer Thomas A. Foushee

and John W. Foushee late joint merchants in firm of Foushee and Co. a bill in Chancery filed by them against Rufus K. Vinson, Fayette M. Latham and others.

29 April, 1865. Summons. James Bickers to answer Richard Miles in trespassing.

26 April, 1862. Summons. David G. Wise to answer Edwin R. Gaines re trespassing.

5 July, 1853. Rutherford Co., Tennessee, in Town of Murfreesboro, John Clark, previously appointed by that Court as guardian of John H., William, Ferdinand, James and Elizabeth V. Hudson, infant children of Enoch M. Hudson. John Clark suggested to the Court that his wards were entitled to receive from the estate of Ezckiel Hudson, dec'd., late of Culpeper Co. and Clark gave an additional bond with John N. Clark and Samuel B. Robison, his sureties.

16 Sept., 1861. Summons. Benjamin Higgason, executor of Esther Higgason, dec'd., Joseph Embry and Travis Shipham to answer William M. Smith and Catharine his wife. Notation on back: B. Higgason is not a resident of this county.

14 Jan., 1862. Summons. Spotsylvania Co. Benjamin Higgason, executor of Esther Higgason, dec'd., to answer William M. Smith and Catharine, his wife.

14 Jan., 1862. Summons. Spotsylvania Co. Benjamin Higgason, executor of Esther Higgason, dec'd., to answer William Higgason re: trespassing.

5 Dec., 1850. At Court of Appeals, Richmond, Virginia. Henry Hill, executor of Samuel Wilhoite, dec'd., Susannah Wilhoite, Lawrence Pope, Sanford Pope, Henry Pope, Jane Pope, Emily Pope and Otway Garrett Pope, the last three being infants by the said Susannah Wilhoite, their next friend against Joseph Hume and George Clarke, assignees of Moses Wilhoite, Rodham ____ and Elizabeth his wife and John Wilhoite. The appellees were plaintiffs and the appellants were defendants in a Chancery suit in Culpeper, 18 Nov., 1836. It was struck from the docket because there had been no order nor proceeding regarding it for a period of seven years.

26 Aug., 1864. Summons. Fluvanna Co. Susan Wigginton, Sallie Wigginton and Willie Yancey to answer Benjamin M. Yancey, executor of Susan T. Yancey, dec'd. Sallie Wigginton not found.

14 July, 1855. Summons. William A. Bowen to answer George T. Fitzhugh.

Aug., 1858. J. S. alias Jacob S. Eggborn vs Wm. alias William Major and B. W. alias Bleecher W. Hansbrough for payment of an over-due note of $1200 dated 15 July, 1857.

28 Nov., 1859. Summons. Jacob S. Eggborn to testify in case where

he sues for benefit of Walter O'Bannon, plaintiff, and Bleecher.W. Hansbrough, defendant. Note is in the file signed by W. Major and B. W. Hansbrough, 1200 to J. S. Eggborn - dated 15 July, 1857.

19 July, 1858. Summons. Wm. alias William Major and B. W. alias Bleecher Hansbrough to answer J. S. alias Jacob S. Eggborn re unpaid note.

12 Nov., 1844. Richard H. Field, Judge of the Eleventh Federal Circuit and John Scott, Judge of the Sixth Federal Circuit signed an agreement to a temporary exchange of circuits from that date until "midnight on Saturday next."

29 Feb., 1864. State Supreme Court of Appeals. James F. Brown vs James R. Hume and James O. Harris, Sheriff re case 3 Feb., 1860, in Circuit Court of Culpeper Co. The Supreme Court reversed the decision of the County Court.

18 Jan., 1859. Re sale of property of Julius M. Hunt and disposal of the proceeds.

4 May, 1857. Fairfax Lodge of free and accepted Masons No. 43 ordered the worshipful Master to apply to the Judge of the next Circuit Court to have new trustees appointed for the property of the Lodge.
Exhibit: Deed dated 3 Dec., 1802. Edward Stevens and Grissell his wife of Culpeper Co. to Benjamin Shackelford, Philip Lightfoot, John Shackelford, John Jameson and Henry Clagett of Culpeper Co. for Lots 13 and 14 in the Town of Fairfax where the Lodge had already built a Masonic Hall, for five shillings. Wit.: William Ashby, Richard Norris, Thomas Jefferies. Signed by all seven parties.
In 1857 the original five trustees were all dead and Fayette Mauzy petitioned for the Lodge to the Judge of the Circuit to appoint new trustees and suggested Robert S. Lewis, George D. Gray, Jesse S. Burroughs, Lewis P. Nelson and Charles E. Lightfoot. They were appointed.

1 Jan., 1858. Mrs. Mary Pemberton in account with Leonard Wharton for goods charged in 1852 plus interest.

4 Dec., 1843. State Court of Appeals. Philip Harrison vs William Major and William Emison re case in Culpeper, 10 Nov., 1837. Court upheld the decree of the Circuit Court and ordered Harrison to pay costs of $27.86.

29 April, 1853. Clipping from the Culpeper Observer giving notice that the guardian appointed in Rutherford Co., Tennessee, for orphans of Enoch W. Hudson will apply in Circuit Court of Culpeper, 6 June, 1853, for money or property due the orphans, especially to Abner Hudson, executor of Ezekiel Hudson, dec'd. Signed by John Clark.

22 July, 1863. Lewis P. Nelson, guardian since Nov., 1854 of George E. Nelson and James I. Nelson, infant sons of Arthur B. Nelson, petitioned to invest the funds in bonds. Permission granted.

30 Jan., 1867. Brown vs Brown et al. Court appointed a Commissioner to rent out a lot in Stevensburg known as the Cole lot and land in Orange Co. Report given that the former was rented to Harris Freeman and the latter is woodland and not rentable.

1 June, 1868. Elizabeth Garnett of Culpeper Co. appointed C. T. Crittenden attorney to execute, sign and deliver a surety for Jeremiah C. Garnett to be guardian of his infant children, Etheline Garnett and Florence C. Garnett.

4 June, 1868. Affidavit of A. G. Garnett that he knows Elizabeth Garnett and that she is worth far more than the $5,000 guaranteed on the bond for her son, Jeremiah C. Garnett to become guardian of his children.

5 June, 1868. Guardianship bond signed by Jeremiah C. Garnett and Elizabeth Garnett, his security.

17 Dec., 1861. Summons. William H. Ward to answer Thomas Hill re a debt. Judgment granted Hill.

28 Jan., 1837. Appeal to Hon. John Scott, one of the Judges of the General Court of Virginia by Sarah Gordon, infant daughter of Francis Gordon, dec'd., by Washington Bailey her next friend re error in transcript of Case of Gordon vs Gordon in County Court of Culpeper. June 13, 1837. Decree was reversed because of errors.

Will of Charles Jones of Culpeper Co.
Dated 21 Jan., 1851 (or 1857?).
Legatees: John Rixey has received about $2,000 already in right of his wife, Matilda. Presley M. Rixey has received about $1,500 already in right of his wife, Mary F. Bequeaths $500. Jones Rixey, grandson and child of Presley M. and Mary F. Rixey. Son John T. (?Turner) Jones; son William R. Jones; son E. Jones; son Charles Samuel Jones, a minor; son Powhatan E. Jones, a minor; son Henry B. Jones, a minor; son Philip M. Jones, a minor. Wife Jane Jones. Dau. E. E. Jones, a minor.
Executors: Sons John T. Jones and Wm. R. Jones.
Wit.: J. Y. Field.

16 July, 1866. Bond of Charles T. Crittenden, J. R. Smoot and George D. Gray. $8,000. Charles T. Crittenden's bond as clerk of Circuit Court of Culpeper Co.

No date. A paper in the Case of Thomas et al vs Rixey et al. Petition of Robert A. Thomas, Reuben S. Thomas, James P. Thomas and George S. Thomas and Ann C. Thomas, Eliza F. Thomas and Sarah E. Thomas, infant children of Reuben Thomas, dec'd., late of Madison Co. by their guardian and next friend, Eliza Thomas, and the said Eliza Thomas, widow of the said Reuben Thomas for distribution of land in Culpeper Co. owned jointly by Reuben Thomas, dec'd., and Thomas H. Rixey. Reuben Thomas d. 1850 intestate. Reuben Thomas left two other children, Catharine M. Thomas and Esterline V. Thomas. The latter died before age 21. They ask that

Thomas H. Rixey and Catharine M. Thomas be made defendants. (Note by D. F. W.: relationship of Catharine M. Thomas is not stated.)

4 May, 1853. Shelby County, Illinois. Bushrod W. Henry applied for and received letters of guardianship for James O. Henry, Brice M. Henry, Peyton W. Henry, Elvira Henry and Beverly W. Henry, who had legal claim to portion of the estate of Ezekiel Hudson, dec'd., late of Virginia. William Headen was security on the guardianship bond, 22 March, 1853, when Bushrod W. Henry was appointed by the Court.

8 June, 1868. A small slip of paper. One side shows E. Williams due 1.26 from Madison Sheriff for serving 6 supoenas. Other side of paper in large illegible hand-writing: "James Bukus is out of all hope of this Jury ever deciding on this case and here confined without one mothful to eat or drink poor fellow."

29 Sept., 1860. Summons. A. J. Stofer to answer Lewis P. Nelson. Unpaid note. 2 June, 1860. Notification to Lewis P. Nelson, endorser of note of A. J. Stofer that the latter had defaulted. 1 Feb., 1860. The note signed by A. J. Stofer, endorsed by Lewis P. Nelson. Nelson vs Stofer. Declaration of intent to sue. Notice of protest in the file, assigned by Lewis P. Nelson to George Clark.

19 March, 1854. Note from Thomas J. Humphreys to Thomas O. Flint requesting enclosed Bill in Chancery be filed and supoenas issued at once in case of Thomas vs Rixey. States C. M. Thomas lives in Madison Co. and defendant Rixey lives in Caroline Co.

PACKAGE No. 2

1866. White vs Chismond. Alexandria, Virginia. Itemized account rendered by George E. White to R. E. Chrismond for purchases and credits from Jan. 12, 1866 through Oct. 5, 1866.

29 April, 1868. Summons. R. E. Chrismond to answer George E. White of a plea of trespass on the case. Reported R. E. Chrismond not now an inhabitant of Culpeper Co.

20 Aug., 1870. Bond of Fayette M. Latham with F. Mauzy, security. Latham had been appointed commissioner to sell the land in the case of Bickers vs Farish et al.

7 July, 1842. Moore's executor vs Petty's administrator. Bond by Elizabeth Petty, administratrix of Marshall Petty, dec'd., and William J. Petty to William H. Moore, executor of Reuben Moore, dec'd., $570.76 as surety so she can keep two negroes in her possession until the day of the sale of Marshall Petty's personal property. The sheriff had taken the children because of a law suit.

(Note by this compiler: All papers in Package No. 1 were listed.

The same method was considered for Package No. 2 but serious consideration resulted in the decision to abstract only those papers bearing a date earlier than 1860. All papers in Package No. 2 were assorted by dates: (1) Those before Jan. 1, 1860; (2) those dated Jan. 1, 1860 to Dec. 31, 1869; (3) those dated after Jan. 1, 1870. The loose papers before 1860 are presented below. The papers in the other two packages have been studied and used only in those instances where family relationships or residences provided genealogical information.)

8 Aug., 1836. F. T. Lightfoot letter to Sheriff of Culpeper re suit Archibald Tutt vs Martin Slaughter shows that Martin Slaughter died testate between 1 June, 1835, and date of this letter. William Green was appointed administrator because Richard H. Field, executor had refused to act.

30 May, 1849. Summons. John Vaughan, John S. Petty, John Foushee, Samuel Major as witnesses in case of Reuben Rosson's administrator vs Benjamin Rosson. Indebtedness.

22 May, 1846. Letter from recommendation for Mr. Thomas to be appointed Commissioner. Signature illegible.

8 May, 1846. Letter recommending George T. Thomas for commissioner in Chancery to succeed John C. Green. Reuben J. Clark.

No date. List of attorneys who recommended George T. Thomas for commissioner. Fredericksburg and Falmouth: John M. Forbes, John M. Herndon, William H. Fitzhugh, William Little, E. Conway, C. Herndon, J. L. Marye, Jr. Madison: A. R. Blakey, Thomas J. Humphries, Thomas Welch, Theophilus(?) Smoot. (illegible): James F. Strother, H. G. Moffett, J. G. Turner, Jr., Robert H. Spindle. Also: Edward Spillman, George Pannill, Jr., John S. Pendleton, P. Lightfoot, H. Shackelford, J. C. Gibson, John Rixey.

5 June, 1857. Lawson Wheatley, administrator of Philagathus Roberts, dec'd., vs John P. Kelly. Suit had been decided in Culpeper, 17 Nov., 1849, appealed and decision made 13 Jan., 1857. Decision made to close the case after certain sales and adjustments be made.

1 Jan., 1858. Summons. Thomas Miles to answer Thomas O. Flint. Indebtedness.

17 June, 1858. John P. Duvall and Ann F. Duvall vs Samuel J. Tebbs. The answer of Samuel J. Tebbs in his own right and as administrator of W. W. Tebbs, dec'd., and as administrator of Foushee Tebbs, dec'd., and as trustee of William Carr, Sr., dec'd., was presented. Decree of the Court as to the original third, which the late Betsy Tebbs was directly entitled for her life by the provision of the will of the late William Carr, Sr., of the funds received by Defendants Samuel J. Tebbs as Trustee under the decree of the Circuit Superior Court of Law and Chancery for Spotsylvania Co., entered on the 20th day of May, 1836, in the case of

Tebbs and Chapman in the bill and proceedings specified the complainant Ann F. Duvall and the defendants Mary F. Spence and Samuel J. Tebbs who are the three children of said Betsy Tebbs who survived the said Betsy are now severally entitled to the same absolutely and that as to the two-thirds of said trust fund to which the said Betsy Tebbs became entitled for her life by virtue of the provisions of said will upon the death of William Carr, Jr., and John Carr, sons of the testator, William Carr, Sr., her seven children generally as well those who died in the lifetime of said Betsy Tebbs as those who survived the said Betsy became entitled to the same, and that the administrators of those children of said Betsy who so died in her lifetime are now entitled to with said surviving children of said Betsy to said two-thirds......

21 June, 1858. Fiduciary Bond of Fayette Mauzy and John C. Green. $3,000. Fayette Mauzy had been elected Clerk of County Court of Culpeper.

19 July, 1852. Fiduciary Bond of Fayette Mauzy, John C. Green, George T. Thomas, Thomas A. Foushee and Alexander Lawrence. $3,000. Fayette Mauzy had been elected Clerk of the County Court of Culpeper.

3 March, 1846. Rappahannock Court House. Letter endorsing appointment of George T. Thomas as Court Commissioner. Signed by attorneys: James F. Strother, H. G. Moffett, J. G. Menefee, Zachariah Turner, Jr., R. H. Spindle.

6 April, 1846. Belle-plaine. Similar letter from Thomas N. Welch.

18 April, 1846. Letter to Judge R. H. Field re recommendations enclosed and others to follow for his appointment as Commissioner. Signed by George T. Thomas.

4 April, 1848. Summons. Caleb Shackelford to testify in Case of Commonwealth vs William G. Allen.

10 April, 1849. Same.

8 June, 1847. Summons. William G. Allen to answer re selling whiskey without a license.

No date. J. C. Green, attorney for the Commonwealth. Wit. Caleb Shackelford. Brief of case against William G. Allen. Case was continued even in Oct., 1848.

11 April, 1846. Letter of Theophilus Smoot endorsing George T. Thomas for Commissioner of the Court.

15 April, 1846. Warrenton. Edward M. Spilman endorsing appointment of George T. Thomas, as above.

16 Oct., 1859. Nelson and Grinnan vs Lucian D. Winston. Indebtedness. (Lewis P. Nelson and James S. Grinnan.)

1 Jan., 1861. Summons. Daniel Farrer to answer Frances Norman, executrix of Thomas Norman, dec'd., over a matter begun in Court 1 May, 1835.

19 March, 1846. John C. Green of Culpeper Court House to Judge Richard H. Field recommending appointment of J. W. Bell as Commissioner of the Court.

No date. Letter from William S. Early to Judge Field (as above). Other signers: A. B. Blakey, Thomas J. Humphreys.

6 June, 1857. Editor of "Warrenton Whig," Fauquier Co., certified that the notice of Case of Duvall vs Tebbs had appeared in the paper 4 consecutive weeks, beginning 4 Oct., 1856.

No date. A paper in the Case of Duvall vs Tebbs which gives full names of each plaintiff and each defendant and residences of the latter. See above for settlement paper, 1858. John P. Duvall and Ann F. Duvall, his wife vs Samuel J. Tebbs in his own right and as Administrator of Willoughby W. Tebbs and as Administrator of Foushee Tebbs and as Trustee of William Carr, Sr., dec'd., Fauquier Co. Charles B. Tebbs in his own right and as Administrator of Thomas F. Tebbs, dec'd., Loudoun Co. Mary F. Spence, Fauquier Co.; Thomas F. Tebbs, Prince William Co.; Louisa H. D. Rowell, Loudoun Co.; Foushee C. Tebbs, Loudoun Co.; Elizabeth P. Tebbs, _____ __; Sally T. Tebbs, Loudoun Co.; Ann L. Tebbs, Fauquier Co.; Margaret F. Tebbs, N. R.; Willoughby M. Tebbs, _____ __; John W. Tebbs, Albemarle Co.; Thomas Triplett, Fauquier Co.; William Byrne, Fauquier Co.

3 Nov., 1855. Resignation of John S. Shackelford as Commissioner in Chancery.

9 Nov., 1853. Culpeper. Marriage contract between Maria G. Slaughter and William B. Slaughter. She filed a petition 14 Nov., 1860, to have Fayette M. Latham appointed Trustee in the place of John C. Green, dec'd., original Trustee. Her petition was granted but nothing in this file indicates the name under which she had made the Marriage Contract as she used her married name in 1860.

20 June, 1857. Thomas B. Nalle vs Coleman Beckham. Judgment $3000.00. March Term 1867. Presentation of credits for payments made 1858, 1859, 1861, 1862 to cover interest at 6%. No payment on the principal.

Oct., 1855. Daniel Fulvy(?) vs Orange and Alexandria Railroad Co. re indebtedness on 1853 adjudication.

March, 1846. Orange Court House. Col. J. C. Gibson's endorsement of George T. Thomas for Commissioner of the Court.

20 Feb., 1854. Payments to begin by Thomas G. Gibson on shares of stock in the Fredericksburg and Valley Plank Road Co. 15 May, 1858. Notification of suit for indebtedness. Case dragged on with notation June 1, 1866, of death of the defendant.

April, 1846. Philip Lightfoot's endorsement of appointment of George T. Thomas as Commissioner of the Court.

1852-1857. Report of Advancements made to Mary Lucelia Hunt and Daniel Hunt in account with the estate of William Rixey, dec'd. Total $15,568.94. (Account is itemized.)

21 July, 1845. William H. Moore, executor of Reuben Moore, dec'd., and Thornton F. Petty bond to James William and Zacheriah Petty. Suit over non-payment.

2 March, 1850. Thornton F. Petty and George E. Marshall bond to Abraham Curtis.

2 Feb., 1850. Thornton F. Petty and George E. Marshall bond to Coleman C. Beckham.

12 Aug., 1837. John Gordon and Frederick Fishback bond to Margaret R. Gordon, Sarah Gordon and Joseph F. Gordon because of court decision.

2 Feb., 1850. Thornton F. Petty and George E. Marshall bond to Samuel Shadrack in case re Shadrack vs Petty.

2 Feb., 1850. Thornton F. Petty and George E. Marshall bond to Charles William Ashby in case of Ashby vs Petty.

23 Dec., 1848. Gabriel Gray and William L. Anderson bond to William Green, administrator of Robert R. Stringfellow, dec'd., in case of Gray vs Green's Administrator.

2 Feb., 1850. Thornton F. Petty and George E. Marshall bond to Leroy Cooper in case of Cooper vs Petty.

1 Jan., 1851. Joseph W. Roberts and Garland T. Wheatley bond to John P. Kelly in case of Kelly vs Roberts.

31 Jan., 1835. Thomas L. Moore and Edward Digges bond to Richard Thompson in case of Thompson vs Moore.

7 Aug., 1844. George Towles and Robert Bowers bond to Sarah H. Towles. George Towles was administrator of William Towles, dec'd., in case of Towles vs Towles.

7 Aug., 1844. George Towles and Robert Bowers bond to John W. Towles in case of Towles vs Towles.

18 Sept., 1848. Elijah Cheek and John Brady bond to John Covington and Robert C. Covington in case of Covington vs Cheek.

7 Aug., 1844. George Towles and Robert Bowers bond to Judith Towles in case of Towles vs Towles.

2 Feb., 1850. Thornton F. Petty and George E. Marshall bond to Thomas O. Flint, and Henry Hill, Jr., late Merchants and Partners trading under the name and style of Henry Hill (or Hite), Jr., in case of Hite(?) Jr. vs Petty.

2 Feb., 1850. Thornton F. Petty and George E. Marshall bond to Fountain F. Henry in case of Henry vs Petty.

2 Feb., 1850. Thornton F. Petty and George E. Marshall bond to Philip Lightfoot in case of Lightfoot vs Petty.

1 July, 1837. Judgment for John Hoomes Freeman and wife against Reuben Moore, administrator of John Grinnan, dec'd.

1 Sept., 1837. Reuben Moore, administrator of John Grinnan, dec'd., and William H. Moore bond to John Hoomes Freeman and wife in same case.

7 Aug., 1844. George Towles, administrator of William Towles, and Robert Bowers bond to John W. Towles in his own right and as administrator of Joseph Towles in case of Towles vs Towles.

7 Aug., 1844. George Towles, administrator of William Towles, and Robert Bowers bond to Arthur Towles in case of Towles vs Towles.

7 Aug., 1844. George Towles, administrator of William Towles, and Robert Bowers bond to James M. Towles in case of Towles vs Towles.

21 July, 1845. William H. Moore, executor of Reuben Moore, dec'd., and Thornton F. Petty bond to Elizabeth, administratrix of Marshall Petty, dec'd., in case of Petty vs Moore.

7 Aug., 1844. George Towles, administrator of William Towles, dec'd., and Robert Bowers bond to Samuel Decamp, administrator of Mildred Decamp, dec'd.

7 Aug., 1844. George Towles, administrator of William Towles, dec'd., and Robert Bowers bond to John W. Towles, administrator of Joseph Towles in suit settlement.

18 June, 1844. William B. Ross, executor of George Ross, dec'd., and Henry Shackelford bond to William Green, administrator of John Thompson, dec'd., in settlement of suit.

2 March, 1842. Summons. John S. Barbour, Eliza A. Barbour, Sally Barbour, John S. Barbour, Jr., James Barbour, Jr., Calhoun Barbour, Eliza Barbour, Alfred M. Barbour and Edwin Barbour to answer John W. Stubblefield. Note: John S. Barbour, Jr., not found.

31 Jan., 1835. Thomas L. Moore and Darnall Smith bond to Richard Thompson, Nathaniel Gray, William Blackwell and Samuel Johnson in suit of Thompson et al vs Moore.

2 Feb., 1850. Thornton F. Petty and George E. Marshall bond to William Green in case of Green vs Petty.

8 Jan., 1842. Charles Pinckard and Fayette Mauzy bond to John H. Freeman in case of Freeman vs Pinckard.

2 July, 1838. Isaac Winston, Walter C. Winston and John Slaughter bond to Thomas Walden, executor of Jane Thornton, dec'd., to settle suit.

21 March, 1844. George Towles and Robert Bowers bond to Robert Saunders to settle a suit.

5 Aug., 1841. James H. Fitzgerald and Murray Forbes bond to Isaac Winston, administrator of John Thornton, dec'd. James H. Fitzgerald is guardian to Mary F. Thornton, now Mary F. Clifton, one of the distributees of the estate of the said John Thornton, dec'd. Thomas Walden is executor of Jane Thornton and others.

20 Aug., 1841. Isaac Winston and Walter C. Winston bond to Mary F. Thornton.

26 Nov., 1842. Richard E. Tutt and Albert Tutt bond to Edwin Bowen.

11 June, 1837. Reuben Moore, Sr., and William H. Moore bond to Henry Dogan and wife. Reuben Moore is executor of John Hilton.

1 Jan., 1857. John Jameson and Eliza T. C. Jameson his wife, John W. Jameson, Eliza F. Jameson Corbin, D. Jameson, Philip G. Jameson, John C. Major, executor of William Major, dec'd., trustee, and John W. Bell, administrator of William Emison, dec'd., trustee bond to James Colvin.

20 Aug., 1841. Isaac Winston and Walter C. Winston bond to Elizabeth Thornton.

2 Feb., 1850. Thornton F. Petty and George E. Marshall bond to Foushee and Moore.

17 Dec., 1856. William Rixey and Charles W. Rixey bond to William Green.

2 Feb., 1850. Thornton F. Petty and George E. Marshall bond to John Guinn.

2 Feb., 1850. Thornton F. Petty and George E. Marshall bond to Wesley Hill.

11 Jan., 1837. Reuben Moore and William H. Moore bond to Henry Hilton.

1 Jan., 1827. Reuben G. Ward conveyed land by deed of trust for the payment of the balance due on a bond of $5,000, given by said Ward to

Francis J. Thompson. In 1869, a suit was instituted to subject the aforesaid land to sale as part of bond remained unsold. Suit was James W. Green, administrator of Francis J. Thompson, dec'd., vs Robert G. Ward, Robert C. Newby, executor of William P. Newby, dec'd., and in his own right, Richard N. Newby, Sarah A. Newby, Ellen Newby, Alpheus P. Rudasil, and Louisa, his wife, F. Addison Newby, Elizabeth Newby, and James G. Field, administrator of Richard H. Field, dec'd. In 1869, the court believed Alpheus P. Rudasil was then a non-resident.

28 Oct., 1848. Summons. Richard J. Rixey, Jacob S. Eggborn and John W. Hume to answer for non-attendance as Jurors.

25 March, 1846. John Pendleton's letter to Judge Richard H. Field recommending appointment of George Thomas as Court Commissioner.

13 June, 1838. In the case of Marius Hansbrough, Alexander K. Hansbrough and others against James Hansbrough and Peter Hansbrough, executors of Peter Hansbrough, dec'd., and in their own right, James M. Bell and others, it was shown that one of the defendants, William Hansbrough had died and his executor was Richard H. Field who was Judge of Superior Court in Culpeper area and wanted case transferred to Circuit Superior Court in Spotsylvania Co.

14 July, 1837. Peter Hansbrough and James Hansbrough, executors of Peter Hansbrough, dec'd., and William H. Hansbrough bond to Alexander H. Hansbrough because of adjudication of a law suit.

15 Oct., 1860. Further action in case of Hooe and others vs Hansbrough and others in which the decree was made, 1 July, 1852.

1 March, 1854. Indenture between William A. Hill, J. Frances Hill, his wife, Edward T. Hill and Lucy F. Hill, his wife, William Cowherd and Sarah Ann Cowherd, his wife, Henry Hill and F. E. Hill, his wife, Thomas O. Flint and Elisa W. Flint, his wife, Thomas Hill, Jr., and Elizabeth Hill, his wife, William H. Twyman and F. H. Twyman, his wife, of the one part and John H. Rixey of the other part. Attached are statements from Justices that the respective wives signed willingly. Elizabeth Hill was of Culpeper Co. Frances H. Twyman, J. Frances Hill, Lucy F. Hill were of Madison Co. Sarah Ann Cowherd was of Orange Co.

Oct., 1848. Grand Jury presentment John J. Settle to a slave belonging to Mrs. Ann C. Freeman without her written consent.

11 Aug., 1849. Deposition of William G. Fishback in the case of E. Williams vs Alfred L. Ashby.

July, 1851. Testimony and Judge's statements in case of Charles Jones' case.

PACKAGE No. 3

Guardians' and Administrators' Bonds before 1860.

4 Jan., 1854. Thomas Hill, Jr., Langdon C. Major, A. P. Hill, Thomas Hill. $12,000. Thomas Hill, Jr., guardian for Joseph E. Ficklin.

25 July, 1851. Jane F. Jones, William H. Brown, Jr., Presley M. Rixey, John T. Jones, William R. Jones, John H. Rixey. $12,000. Jane F. Jones, guardian for Henry B. Jones, Philip M. Jones, Charles S. Jones, Powhatan E. Jones and Epps E. Jones, infants of Charles Jones, dec'd.

3 Jan., 1854. John H. Rixey and Richard S. Rixey. $5,000. John H. Rixey, guardian of Eugene A. Rixey.

14 June, 1852. Henry M. Lewis, Samuel Rixey. $800. Henry M. Lewis, administrator of Lucinda Rixey, dec'd.

19 Nov., 1854. Lewis P. Nelson, George Nelson, Gustavus S. Ficklin, John H. Rixey, Perry J. Eggborn. $45,000. Lewis P. Nelson, guardian for George Eggborn Nelson and James Jacob Nelson, orphans of Arthur B. Nelson, dec'd.

5 Nov., 1853. Granville J. Kelly, John P. Kelly. $1500. Granville J. Kelly, guardian for Robert Granville Coleman and David J. Coleman.

5 June, 1854. William F. Botts, Benjamin F. Settle. $2000. William F. Botts, administrator of Ann C. Freeman, dec'd.

27 Oct., 1851. Samuel A. Daniel. $20,000. Executor of William S. Daniel, dec'd.

22 June, 1832. Woodford Taylor, William Tannahill, Vincent Corder. $12,000. Woodford Taylor, administrator of Thornton Taylor, dec'd.

9 June, 1856. James Bowen, Robert A. Bowers. $100. James Bowen, guardian of Ann Elizabeth Crigler.

5 June, 1846. John Glassell, John P. Kelly, Alexander Laurence. $25,000. John Glassell, administrator of Margaret C. Glassell, dec'd.

4 Nov., 1847. Joseph O. Stewart, William A. G. Stewart. $3,000. Joseph O. Stewart, guardian of Harriett S. Kuth, orphan of James Kuth.

2 Nov., 1847. John R. Colvin, Alfred B. Lewis. $2,500. John R. Colvin, administrator of James A. Colvin, dec'd.

4 June, 1838. Thomas Beazley, Charles Beazley. $500. Thomas Beazley, administrator of Alice Beazley, dec'd.

9 June, 1852. Zacheriah S. Petty, William Crittenden. $10,000. Zacheriah S. Petty, administrator of James Crittenden, dec'd.

10 June, 1852. William Walker, George N. Thrift, William Simms of Madison. $10,000. William Walker, administrator of John Walker, dec'd.

12 Nov., 1853. John C. Green, William Green. $1,600. John C. Green, administrator of Carter C. Portus, dec'd.

7 June, 1850. Sarah Wheatley, Henry Miller, John Miller and Benjamin F. Miller. $12,000. Sarah Wheatley, administratrix of George ? J. Wheatley.

9 June, 1856. John T. Wright, Benjamin H. Shackelford. $400. John T. Wright, administrator of John Wright, Sr., dec'd.

__ June, 1842. Henry Hill, Jr., Thomas Hill. $300. Henry Hill, Jr., executor of George Johnson.

7 June, 1847. Anthony W. Griffin, Alexander Lawrence. $2,000. Anthony W. Griffin, administrator of Edward Green, dec'd.

29 Oct., 1850. George Ficklen, Thomas Hill, Jr. $8,000. George Fickley, executor of Rebecca Brown, dec'd.

11 June, 1852. Octavus Jeffries, George Jeffries, Thomas Hill, Jr. $5,000. Octavus Jeffries, executor of Alice Wood, dec'd.

15 June, 1852. William S. Anderson, George D. Gray, Richard W. Anderson, John R. Anderson. $16,000. William S. Anderson and George D. Gray, administrators of Gabriel Gray, dec'd.

17 Dec., 1837. Reuben Gaines, Fountain F. Henry. $500. Reuben Gaines, administrator of Elizabeth Dogan, dec'd., late of Illinois.

9 Nov., 1857. James M. Griffin, John Connor, Robert S. Thomas. $10,000. James M. Griffin, administrator of Thomas J. Griffin, dec'd.

4 June, 1849. Joseph J. Halsey, Jeremiah Morton. $20,000. Joseph J. Halsey, guardian of John Thomas Morton Wharton and Susan Walker Wharton, orphans of Thomas Wharton, dec'd. Includes letter - Raccoon Ford. 1 June, 1849, to Hon. Richard H. Field, from Lucinda Wharton, widow of Dr. Thomas Wharton, requesting appointment of Joseph J. Halsey.

__ Nov., 1854. George Nelson, power of attorney to Thomas O. Flint to sign guardianship bond for Lewis P. Nelson.

28 May, 1852. George N. Thrift of Madison Co., power of attorney to Robert G. Wark, clerk of Circuit Court of Culpeper Co.

1 Nov., 1849. John W. Bell, John S. Barbour, Jr., James Barbour. $4,000. John W. Bell, curator of estate of William Emison, dec'd.

9 Nov., 1857. John N. Griffin, John Scott, Robert C. Covington. $10,000. John N. Griffin, administrator of Thomas J. Griffin, dec'd.

11 June, 1855. John C. Green, James W. Green. $1,000. John C. Green, guardian of James E. Wayland.

25 July, 1851. Jane Jones, William H. Browning, Presley M. Rixey, John T. Jones, William R. Jones, John H. Rixey. $30,000. Jane Jones, administratrix of Charles Jones, dec'd.

5 June, 1854. Felix S. Huffman, Benjamin Matthews. $6,000. Felix Huffman, administrator of Nancy Green, dec'd.

15 Nov., 1851. George Jeffries, John C. Green. $5,000. George Jeffries, curator of estate of Alice Wood, dec'd., during the minority of Octavus Jeffries, executor named in the will of the said Alice Wood, dec'd.

8 Nov., 1853. Fayette M. Latham, Zachariah S. Petty, Thomas A. Foushee. $6,000. Fayette M. Latham, guardian for John Abner Petty, Charles M. Petty, James F. Petty, infant children of Charles M. Petty, dec'd.

21 July, 1851. George Jeffries, Enoch Jeffries, Joseph N. Armstrong. $5,000. George Jeffries, curator of estate of Alice Wood, dec'd.

7 June, 1837. Thomas Hill, Ambrose P. Hill, George Ficklin, Henry Hill. $40,000. Thomas Hill, administrator of Edward B. Hill, dec'd.

14 June, 1837. Ambrose Jeffries, Waller R. Asher, Fountain F. Henry. $500. Ambrose Jeffries, administrator of Susan Jeffries, dec'd.

8 June, 1837. Thomas W. Cowne, Henry Fox, William Helm (by his attorney, J. D. Latham). $4,000. Thomas W. Cowne, administrator of Elizabeth Cowne, dec'd., formerly Elizabeth Taliaferro, dau. of Christopher Taliaferro and first wife of Augustine Cowne, dec'd. Included: Power of Attorney from William Helm of Fauquier Co. to Jeremiah D. Latham of Culpeper Co. and stated that Christopher Taliaferro formerly lived in King William Co.

21 July, 1858. Jeremiah Hudson, Robert Hudson. $7,000. Jeremiah Hudson, guardian for Mary J. Colvin, Susan V. Colvin, Gabriel C. Colvin, William Colvin and John Colvin.

7 Nov., 1853. Franklin M. Young, James M. Button. $28,000. Both as executors of John M. Young, dec'd.

7 Nov., 1857. James G. Field, Thomas O. Flint. $1,500. James G. Field, guardian of ___ Field infant orphan of Albert Field. (Given name of ward unknown to the Court.)

13 Nov., 1855. Benjamin H. Shackelford, Henry Shackelford. $700. Benjamin H. Shackelford, administrator for Joshua Buttus, dec'd.

No date - no signature. Appears to be handwriting of Judge Richard

H. Field as a memorandum. (Difficult to read so there may be errors in this transcript.-DFW) "Persons who would be heirs-at-law and distributees of Alice Wood, if she had died intestate: Lewis Wood, Culpeper; John Wood, Fauquier; George W. Forrest and June, his wife, Culpeper; Latney M. Wood, Missouri; Walter B. Smoot(?) and Letha, his wife, Missouri; Columbia Jeffries, George L. Jeffries, Maria Jeffries, Hill Jeffries, infant children of George Jeffries.

13 Nov., 1855. Benjamin H. Shackelford, Henry Shackelford. $700. Benjamin H. Shackelford, administrator of Thomas Brown, dec'd.

13 Nov., 1855. Benjamin H. Shackelford, Henry Shackelford. $700. Benjamin H. Shackelford, administrator of John Brown, dec'd.

10 June, 1857. William A. Hill, Edwin F. Hill. $2,000. William A. Hill, administrator of Frances Field, dec'd.

4 June, 1857. Reuben K. Long, Benjamin Farish. $3,000. Reuben K. Long, administrator of William B. Long, dec'd.

3 Nov., 1857. William W. Lewis, John Lewis, Simeon B. Lewis, Joseph D. Brown, Robert C. Covington, John R. Colvin, James M. Duncan. $60,000. William W. Lewis, executor of Thomas C. Brown, dec'd.

5 June, 1854. French Strother, Jr., John C. Green, Samuel W. Somerville. $15,000. French Strother, Jr., administrator of Mary D. Petty, dec'd.

22 Oct., 1831. Ezekiel Haines, John Popham. $1,000. Ezekiel Haines, administrator of John Haines.

4 June, 1855. Reuben T. Thom. $200,000 as executor of John Thom, dec'd.

4 June, 1855. William Alexander Thom. $200,000 as executor of John Thom, dec'd.

4 June, 1855. John Catesby Thom. $200,000 as executor of John Thom, dec'd.

5 Nov., 1831. Isaac Winston, Walter C. Winston. $10,000. Isaac Winston, executor of James M. T. Winston, dec'd.

11 June, 1853. James H. Freeman, William F. Botts. $1,000. James H. Freeman, administrator of Ann C. Freeman, dec'd.

8 June, 1853. John C. Green, William Green. $18,000. John C. Green, administrator of Joseph B. Redd, dec'd.

5 Nov., 1851. Alexander Lawrence, Edward B. Hill, William Green. $15,000. Alexander Lawrence, administrator of Mary Lawrence, dec'd.

7 Nov., 1853. Martha E. Walker, Thomas G. Gibson. $8,000. Martha E. Walker as guardian for her infant children, Thomas G. Walker, Lucy W. Walker, John Walker and William Walker. She signed as "Elizabeth Walker."

6 June, 1853. Ambrose P. Hill, Thomas Hill. $2,000. Ambrose P. Hill, executor of Francis Field, dec'd.

8 Nov., 1853. Felix Huffman, Benjamin (X) Matthews. $6,000. Felix Huffman as curator on estate of Nancy Green, dec'd.

6 June, 1832. Charles Allen, Archibald Freeman. $500. Charles Allen as administrator of Thornton Taylor, dec'd.

14 Nov., 1853. James G. Field, Thomas Hill, Jr. $800. James G. Field as administrator of Mary Dulaney, dec'd.

9 June, 1852. John Glassell, John C. Green. $6,000. John Glassell, administrator of Margaret C. Glassell, dec'd.

5 Nov., 1834. William Green, Martin Slaughter. $1,000. William Green as administrator of Mary Stevens, dec'd.

24 July, 1844. John Glassell, John P. Kelly and Alexander Lawrence. $25,000. John Glassell as administrator of Margaret C. Glassell, dec'd.

7 June, 1839. Isabella McNeale, John B. McNeale. $50. Isabella McNeale, administratrix of John McNeale, dec'd.

28 Oct., 1841. Ambrose P. Hill, Thomas Hill, William A. Hill. $20,000. Ambrose P. Hill as administrator of James Colvin, dec'd.

14 June, 1850. John F. Bell, John Wharton, James Barbour. $8,000. John W. Bell as administrator of William Emison, dec'd.

5 June, 1851. George W. Rowles, John F. Rowles, Perry J. Eggborn. $3,000. George W. Rowles as administrator of Samuel Rowles, dec'd.

17 June, 1852. James Bickers, James Barbour. $100. James Bickers as administrator of William McCoy, dec'd.

8 June, 1852. William Simms of Madison Co. gave power of attorney to Robert G. Ward, clerk of the Circuit Court of Culpeper Co. to sign as security on bond of William Walker as administrator of John Walker, dec'd.

3 June, 1851. John F. Rowles gave power of attorney to Thomas Hill re sign as security for George W. Rowles. Wit.: B. H. Shackelford, Samuel Shadrach.

3 June, 1851. Judith Rowles renounced right to administer estate of her late husband, Samuel Rowles, dec'd. Wit.: John T(?). Jones, Susan A. Rowles.

7 Nov., 1854. Gustavus S. Ficklin power of attorney to Thomas O. Flint re sign as security on guardian bond of Lewis P. Nelson. Wit.: F. M. Latham, James A. Rudasil.

PACKAGE No. 4

This is a package of fiduciary bonds similar to those noted in this section but all are dated 1860 or later and have not been abstracted by this compiler.

PACKAGE No. 5

11 March, 1859. Note from J. N. Armstrong to Capt. Wm. Rixey for $223.81. Suit after 1870.

13 Sept., 1849. Note from Wm. H. Hill to James Bickers for $28.61. Suit after 1870.

(A badly torn manuscript). Rule of practise of the Circuit Superior Court of Culpeper adopted 4th November, 1835.
"The Causes upon the court docket shall be called and disposed of in the order of their arrangement by the Clerk - but untill the second day of the ____ causes at the first calling may lie open, for instance ____ ___ that day and afterwards they may be passed by ma____ consent, until the second calling.
The causes of each day they passed shall not be called until after the subsequent causes of each day's docket shall have been called - then said causes so passed shall be called again according to their priority on the docket and upon such second calling must be tried or continued. If it appear upon the first or second calling of a cause that the parties or either of them be unprepared for a trial, having used due diligence, the court will, if deemed expedient, at the instance of both or either party, continue the case to a subsequent day of the term at the costs of the party in default if either be, or if both be unprepared, without costs. A cause so continued shall have precedence over the cause set for that day by the Clerk unless otherwise ordered and when called shall be finally disposed of for the term by trial, dismissal, non suit, or continuance."

A Printed Circular - badly worn and torn.
RULES OF COURT
Adopted by the County Court of Culpeper County, on the 17th day of May, 1853.

1. The Court will meet at 11 o'clock A.M., unless some other hour be named for a particular day: and will sit till 4 P.M., unless the business ready for action be sooner done.
2. The Bell is to be rung precisely at the hour appointed for the Court's meeting.
3. The Sheriff shall preserve silence and order, not by general calls of "Silence," or "Order," but by going to any person who audibly talks, or

otherwise makes a noise or violates good order, and in a low voice desiring him to be silent or keep order.

4. If such person repeat the noise or disorder on the same day, the Sheriff shall report him to the Court; who will repress the evil by admonition, reprimand, fine, or imprisonment.

5. Smoking or wearing the hat in Court, shall be deemed disorder.

6. No person shall stand between the bar and the Court or Jury, when a lawyer or other person is addressing them in order.

7. No lawyer shall be heard by the Court, unless he be standing in the bar. Other persons, on their own business, may address the Court from the floor or from the bar; but not from the witness' bench, or Jury-bench or the Court's platform.

8. Not more than two speeches will be heard on either side of a civil cause or question.

9. No speech or argument at all will be heard on a motion for a continuance.

10. Upon any matter or question to be decided, the party making the motion or holding the affirmative shall begin; be answered by the opposite party; and reply if he chooses; which shall close the discussion.

11. The Court will stop a party from speaking on whose side its opinion is made up.

12. The Presiding Justice shall enforce the foregoing rules, without consulting the associates, unless he deem their concurrence needful or proper. But any one of them may have the Court's opinion taken on the case.

13. If the Sheriff does not properly preserve order, not only in regard to the 5th, 6th and 7th rules, but by prohibiting all things tending to disturb the Court he shall be admonished, and (if proper) be fined by the Court.

14. The Chancery Docket will be called through at April and December Terms in every year; and the appeal Docket at July and October Terms in every year.

15. The absence of counsel, unless occasioned by sickness or other equally good cause, shall not be regarded as good cause for delay; and the opposite counsel may at his pleasure have the case tried or continued. Nor shall any continuance or non-suit entered in consequence of counsel's absence, be set aside without good cause shewn to the court.

         Teste,
         F. MAUZY, Clerk.

7 Aug., 1866. Summons. Charles E. Hume to answer James P. Hume.

10 Nov., 1865. Demand draft by J. R. Smoot on Messrs. Harvey and Williams of Richmond, Virginia.

3 Dec., 1869. Executor's Account on Estate of Eliza Gaines, dec'd. Made by William H. Gaines.

Suit of Roberts vs Wheatley. Plea of Joseph W. Roberts in his own right was administrator of his father Philagathus Roberts, dec'd., who died in 1844 or 1846, intestate, leaving the following children, heirs:

Joseph W. Roberts; Meredith H. Roberts; Helen M. Roberts married William Linn; Francis A. Roberts married John F. Banks; ____ Roberts married T. Rasher and died without issue and intestate during the life of her father. Boaneges Roberts died unmarried and without issue during the life of his father, having first made his will, bequeathing all his estate to his brother, Joseph W. Roberts.

5 April, 1860. Demand note. Elizabeth Mitchell and Henry H. Mitchell to Samuel Shadrach.

3 Sept., 1857. Promissory note. Elizabeth Mitchell and James W. Mitchell to William A. Willis.

25 May, 1858. Bill due James G. Field from John P. Mitchell.

23 March, 1857. Demand Note. John P. Mitchell and Elizabeth Mitchell to James W. Mitchell.

4 Nov., 1858. Demand Note. John P. Mitchell to Samuel Shadrach.

10 May, 1858. Demand Note. John P. Mitchell and Elizabeth Mitchell to James W. Mitchell.

25 May, 1858. Demand Note. John P. Mitchell to Samuel Shadrach.

1 Feb., 1860. Demand Note. John P. Mitchell, security E. Y. Mitchell, to James W. Mitchell.

9 June, 1858. Demand Note. J. P. Mitchell to James W. Mitchell.

1858. Account of Mrs. Elizabeth Mitchell to Dr. R. K. Long.

15 Sept., 1858. Letter from Crab Orchard, Wythe Co., Virginia, signed by J. P. Mitchell who is practicing medicine there.

(Many more Mitchell papers but they are of no genealogical nor historical value and are not included here.)

24 July, 1869. Papers in Suit of John H. Eggborn vs Benjamin M. Yates, administrator of O. H. Yates. Indebtedness.

1866-1869. R. S. Stringfellow in account with M. S. Stringfellow, trustee.

1 Jan., 1861. Farish Guinn's account with Foushee and Fry.

1860, 1861, 1862. Daniel G. Freeman, Dr. to S. A. Freeman.

1861-1866. Papers in suit for indebtedness of Lewis Y. Field to James G. Field.

21 July, 1856. Promissory note of Lewis Y. Field to E. B. Hitt. (Many other Field notes of this period.)

1859-1866. One package of vouchers for money paid by M. S. Stringfellow as trustee for R. S. Stringfellow.

1867. Decree in case of Gordon's executor vs Gordon et al indicated that John H. Gordon had died and left the following heirs: Alexander Y. Gordon and Lucy A., his wife, in right of the said Lucy; Susan A. Ragland; Wellington, Nannie, Fanny and Martinetta Gordon, infant children of John G. Gordon, dec'd.; Albert S. Gordon; Benjamin F. Smith and Harriet E., his wife, in right of the said Harriet E.; Church G. Gordon, dec'd., left infants, Bettie Gordon and Susan Gordon.

14 Feb., 1868. Order for a rehearing of the case of Thomas Hill vs William Cowherd and Sarah E., his wife, William H. Twyman and Frances H., his wife, Thomas O. Flint and Eliza W., his wife, Maria T. Hill, Thomas B. Wetmore and Octavia T., his wife, Elwin F. Hill, Louisa V. Hill, William A. Hill in his own right and as executor of Ambrose P. Hill, dec'd., James H. Hill and his guardian, Fayette Mauzy. Decree had been rendered 14 Nov., 1867.

1861 and following years. Account of Daniel G. Freeman, dec'd., by Thomas O. Flint, curator.

June, 1868. Walter O'Bannon, executor of Joel Hitt, dec'd., obtained a judgment against William J. Lillard, Silas B. Lillard and William H. Browning with interest from 14 Oct., 1862. Suit appeared again in 1876 when Walter O'Bannon had died and Benjamin Pulliam became administrator of Joel Hitt and William H. Browning had died.

PACKAGE No. 6

A law suit in Chancery, Hill, administrator vs Hill et al, relates to property owned previous to 1857 in Culpeper Co., and requests notification in 1875 to some of the defendants. Although this request does not designate relationships of the parties, the names will give clues for the searcher.

Plaintiffs: Henry Hill, as administrator of Henry Hill, dec'd., and in his own right sues in behalf of himself and all other heirs and legatees of Thomas Hill, dec'd., who shall come in and contribute to the expenses of the Suit.

Defendants: E. B. Hill, executor of Thomas Hill, dec'd.; Mildred A. Hill; Admisah Shipe (member of a partnership to which E. B. Hill, trustee, had sold real estate); *Carter A. Saunders in his own right and as guardian of Eva B. Hill; *Lucy R. Saunders; *Eva B. Hill; F. M. Latham, administrator of F. T. Hill, dec'd.; B. F. Pulliam, committee administrator of John W. Hill, dec'd.; *Thomas J. Hill, Edward B. Hill, Jr., Fanny Hill, Elisa Hill, and the other heirs of Jno. W. Hill, dec'd., whose names are unknown. James G. Field, administrator of Thomas T. Hill, dec'd.;

*Thomas R. Hill, James B. Day, Georgia P. Day, Gillie M. Hill, Eveline Hill, *Edward L. Hill, Clarence Hill. B. F. Pulliam, committee administrator of A. P. Hill, dec'd.; *Kate G. Forsyth, *Russell Hill, *Lucy Lee Hill.

The object of the suit was to set aside a deed from E. B. Hill, trustee under power of attorney from the heirs of Thomas Hill, dec'd., dated 26 Nov., 1857. (Deed Book 18, p. 62)

*Non-residents of Virginia in 1875 or when suit was filed, soon after 1875.

1 Jan., 1860. Promissory Note from William R. Vaugham, Hampton, Virginia, to Samuel Cumming.

Another late suit, filed in 1875, gives some relationships of earlier date.

Payne et al vs Sibert et al.

Plaintiffs: Daniel J. Payne and his assignee, J. C. Gibson.

Defendants: James H. Sibert and Elizabeth J. Sibert, his wife, and relict of Albert W. Payne who died before 1857; George S. M. Payne in his own right and as trustee of Jane M. Carson, Mary Emily Gee, Albert W. Payne, George A. Payne and Josepha G. Stewart; Jane M. Carson; Mary Emily Gee; Albert W. Payne; George A. Payne; and Josepha G. Stewart.

The suit was over land in Culpeper County near Brandy on the Great Southern Railroad Company and adjoining the lands of J. C. Gibson and Mary G., his wife; of Alvin Jameson; of James H. Jameson, dec'd.; of Robert L. Stringfellow; of Daniel Wine and others. This land had been left by Albert W. Payne, Sr., to his widow, Elizabeth J. Payne, now the wife of James H. Sibert. This land had been sold in 1857 and some payments were questioned.

PACKAGE 1880-1900.

3 Aug., 1889. A Deed which gives information on people and residences in 1840's and 1850's and is quoted in its entirety.

This deed made the 22 day of September, 1859 between Eliza A. Walden, Fannie E. Walden, Milton Ritenour and Jaqueline C. his wife, Thomas P. Walden and Isaiah C. Perry Executor of Pierce Perry deceased of the first part and Paul Yates of the second part. Witnesseth that the said parties of the first part in consideration of one dollar in hand paid and nine hundred and fifty dollars with interest thereon from the 22nd day of September 1856 secured to be paid by the party of the second part do grant with special warranty unto the said Paul Yates a certain tavern house and lot in the town of Woodville; also a certain other lot of land adjoining the town of Woodville supposed to contain three acres being the same real estate conveyed by Thomas Walden to Pierce Perry in trust for the said Eliza A. Walden and her children by deed dated 19th day of July 1843 and recorded in the County of Rappahannock.

Signatures: Eliza A. Walden, Fannie E. Walden, Milton Ritenour, Jacqueline P. Ritenour, Thomas P. Walden, Isaiah C. Perry.

These signatures were certified as follows: Eliza A. Walden and

Fannie E. Walden in Culpeper Co. 25 Oct., 1859. Milton Ritenour in Madison Co. 2 Dec., 1859. Jaqueline C. Ritenour, the wife of Milton Ritenour, Madison Co. 2 Dec., 1859. Thomas P. Walden, Monroe Co., Missouri, 16 Jan., 1860. Isaiah C. Perry, Culpeper Co., 8 Feb., 1860.

The deed and the five certificates were recorded in Rappahannock Co., 13 March, 1860, and a copy of all was made and sent to Culpeper Co. in connection with a Court Suit in 1889.

Court papers as late as 1890 include exhibits as early as 1848 in the case of administrator of Samuel Shadrach vs James Barbour over a note for $110.20 which Barbour made to Samuel Shadrach in connection with a blacksmith shop which they had rented jointly, 16 Dec., 1848, and Barbour's note for $100 to Samuel Shadrach, 7 Oct., 1852.

CULPEPER COUNTY, VIRGINIA

COURT SUITS

Suit of George Allan vs Peter Hansbrough and
William G. Allan, administrator of James Allan, dec'd.,
William Hansbrough, Charles Allan, dec'd.,
George F. Strother and Polly Johnston.

Will of James Allan of Culpeper Co.
Dated 1 Aug., 1814. Proven 20 March, 1815.
Legatees: Owned land in Orange Co. Erasmus Chapman, dau. Polly Johnson, son George Allan, wife-not named. At death of wife "equally divided among all my children as well those by my present wife as my daughter Polly and my son George above mentioned."
Executors: Peter Hansbrough, Jr., bro. William G. Allan.
Wit.: Armistead Long, George Fitzhugh, Jr., George S. Thom.

George Allan vs Peter Hansbrough and William G. Allan,
administrator of James Allan, dec'd., and
William Hansbrough and Polly Johnston. Aug., 1836.

Note: "Peter Hansbrough of Coleshill" Summons - included Charles Allan and George F. Strother as well as others named above. James Allan had purchased land, 27 Feb., 1797, from William Chapman and Benjamin Chapman, recorded in Orange Co., 346 acres.

Account of the Estate of Major James Allan, dec'd.,
by P. Hansbrough, administrator. 1 Sept., 1824.

George Allan of Romney, Hampshire Co., William G. Allan of Culpeper Co., Charles Allan of Fauquier Co., William Hansbrough of Culpeper Co., George F. Strother now of Pettis Co., Missouri, Polly Johnson res. of Kentucky, Widow Elizabeth Allan, dec'd by William Hansbrough, filed a statement that he was not a Security. "It was old William Hansbrough called 'old Indian' who is dead."

Account of Estate. 17 July, 1820, by Peter Hansbrough
on Estate of James Allan, dec'd.

Same 16 Feb., 1826. 1815 William G. Allan lived in Stevensburg, Culpeper Co. 1815 George Allan lived in Maryland. 3 Jan., 1797, contract James Allan of Culpeper Co. and Erasmus Chapman of Rowan Co., North Carolina. William Johnson received his share, 17 Oct., 1832. (Note: Probably in right of his wife, Polly (Allan) Johnson - or as her son.)
1836. William Hansbrough made affidavit that he was not the one who was security for the administrators of James Allan, dec'd. "that the William Hansbrough who did subscribe the bond was William Hansbrough, dec'd., who died in Stevensburg many years ago commonly called "the old Indian."

16 Aug., 1836. Peter Hansbrough stated he believed Elizabeth Allan, widow of James, removed to Campbell Co. with her several children by James Allan. He has received no proof of her death. (Note: At no place is there any proof that there were children by James Allan and his 2nd wife, Elizabeth (____).)

Hiram B. Crump and wife vs William Rixey

Hiram B. Crump property sold under execution. 24 Jan., 1839. Account. Deposition of Thomas R. Rixey, who became a clerk in store of William Rixey, Oct., 1836. He deposed that amounts charged to Crump and wife were correct. He was son of William Rixey. Margarett S. Crump was wife of Hiram B. Crump on 5 Nov., 1838. A deposition of Lewis Wood, 11 June, 1841. He calls the defendant "Capt. William Rixey."

Hiram B. Crump had been allotted, in right of his wife Margaret S., negroes, horse, furniture from estate of the late William Green. 24 Aug., 1837, Crump turned over this property in trust to William Rixey for use of Crump's wife during her life-time. John Gordon was appointed Trustee while case vs Rixey was in progress.

Various bills and receipts are in the file.

No. 51 Moore's Executors vs Gaines

Indebtedness. Fredericksburg, 14 Dec., 1799. Received from Mr. Reuben Moore in account with Mr. Robert Patton in December last fifty-two pounds five shillings and six pence in full of debt ____ by Bernard Moore's estate to William Cunningham.
Signed: Daniel Grinnan.

Reuben Moore vs Reuben Gaines

Deposition 13 Nov., 1815 of Thomas S. Holloway of lawful age, taken at the house of Benjamin Shackelford in the Town of Fairfax. The deponent lived with Reuben Moore from 1st Oct., 1796 to 1 Jan., 1798, and knew Moore made shoes for some of Gaines' children, etc. Deposition John Helton, 19 July, 1817, made before Jeremiah Strother. Capt. Reuben Gaines - addressed as such.

1775-1777. Account of Amount Due to the Estate of Archibald Campbell, dec'd., by the Estate of Barnett Moore, dec'd. (All items were medicines for family or slaves.)

Deposition 16 March, 1818, by William Mitchell in Culpeper Co.

Note of Reuben Moore. 7 Jan., 1790, to Duncan Campbell of Orange Co.

Pages from Account Book of Reuben Moore, 1780-1800, in account with Capt. Reuben Gaines.

Note of Bernard Moore of Orange to John Glassell. 14£ 4s current money 6 March, 1773. Wit. William Wiatt.

Deposition 1 Jan., 1818, by James Sim in Culpeper Co.

Affidavit 2 Jan., 1818, of William Mason at house of Jeremiah Strother in Town of Fairfax, Culpeper Co.

Deposition of John Walker _____ 1774, a Mr. Campbell, then in the business of John Glassell, gave the deponent for collection a bond Bernard Moore payable to the said John Glaskell. When Courts were reopened after the War, Bernard Moore was dead and Joseph Spencer was executor or administrator of his estate. Spencer had given estate to widow and child and widow had married Reuben Moore and Reuben Gaines had married the only child.

27 Jan., 1831. Slaves, listed by name, sold from Estate of John Sampson, dec'd. Sold by John Massey for Reuben Moore, late Sheriff of Culpeper Co. as advertised in Madison Co. Moore had been administrator of Sampson's estate.

9 Nov., 1839. Separate answer of Nancy W. Singleton to complaint of William Brooke, Jr. She states she has life interest in certain slaves with reversion to her children: Minor W. Singleton, defendant, and Mary, Reuben, Esther, Jane and James Singleton. Slaves were not her dower from dec'd. husband, Joshua Singleton, but came to her through last will of her father (not named), probated in court of Fauquier. Slaves: Benjamin, Elizabeth, William, Washington, Tarlton, Albert and Hannah Noonan.

William Brooke, Jr., vs Minor W. Singleton
Albert R. Singleton, administrator of Joshua Singleton, dec'd.,
and Nancy W. Singleton, widow of said Joshua.

Nancy W. Singleton and Minor W. Singleton did not reside in area that Albert R. Singleton did. Another summons for them showed Rappahannock Co. but report was that Minor W. Singleton lived in Missouri and Nancy W. in Culpeper.

Papers in Suit of Garnett vs Barnes. May, 1828.

Statement by Robert Garnett and Rhoda, his wife: Martin Barnes, late of Madison Co. was husband of Rhoda at time of his death. She refused part designated in Barnes' will and took the part allotted by law. The executors named refused to act and administrators appointed were William Slaughter, Jr., and John Massey.

Rhoda was dau. of John Sampson, dec'd., whose will probated in Culpeper Co. Mary Sampson, widow of John and mother of Rhoda made a nuncupative will, probated in Madison Co., leaving all to Rhoda.

The following persons are interested in the will of Martin Barnes: Nancy Breedlove and her husband, Churchill Breedlove; John Barnes and his children; Elinor Ship and her children; William Bradley; Elizabeth Oder; Paulsey Kirtley and Thompson Kirtley; William Weatherell and Jane, his wife; Henry Barnes, Sr., and Henry Barnes, Jr., his son. They did not know names of children of John Barnes nor Ellinor Ship as they "in some foreign State."

The following persons were interested in the Estate of John Sampson, dec'd., so closely connected with Estate of Martin Barnes: Lucy Berry, wife of Aaron Berry; Thomas Sampson; Delia Dickens, wife of William Dickens; Jemima Hughes, wife of John Hughes; Mary Hughes, wife of William Hughes; Ann Burdine; Barsheba Clark, wife of Reubin Clarke; Frances Berry, wife of Elisha Berry; Joseph Sampson; Elizabeth Rinder. Elisha and Frances Berry are dead and left Merry Berry, Philomil Berry and Judith Fincham. Others dead: Elizabeth Rinder, William Sampson, William Dickins, Thomas Sampson with estates administered in Madison Co.; also Oridgal Burdine.

Summons for Superior Court of Chancery, Fredericksburg.

Nun-cupative Will of Mary Sampson.
Dated 11 Aug., 1824. Proven 28 Oct., 1824, Madison Co.
Legatee: Daughter Rhoda Barnes.
Wit.: Thomas Chapman, Strother Lillard, Gabriel Lillard.
Administrator: John Hume, Sheriff.

The file contains estate accounts of all administrators through Jan., 1830 - about 25 pages.

Inventory of Estate of Martin Barnes, dec'd. Recorded 28 June, 1827, Madison Co. Total value of slaves, $3,015.00.

Will of Martin Barnes.
Dated 6 June, 1821. Proven 29 Oct., 1824, Madison Co.
Legatees: Wife Rhoda Barnes; sister Nancy Breedlove; Churchill Breedlove, grandson of my sister, Nancy Breedlove; brother Armistead Barnes; Henry Barnes and his "little dau. Harriot" (relationship of Henry not stated); Lenard Wetherall, son of William Weatherall (relationship not stated); sister Nelly Ship "now living in the State of Kentucky;" brother John Barnes; (At death of wife legatees become children of bro. John Barnes and of sis. Nelly Ship.); sister Elizabeth Oder "now in Kentucky."
Executors: Lenard Barnes, William Chapman and Thomas Shirley.
Wit.: Thomas Shirley, William H. Wetherall, Zacharias Shirley.

Another will of Martin Barnes.
Dated __ ___, 1824. Recorded 29 Oct., 1824, Madison Co.
Court designed the 1821 "last will" and 1824 "last testament."
Legatees: Wife Rhoda Barnes; cousin Henry Barnes and his son, Henry Barnes; sister Elenor Ship; brother John Barnes; William Bradley, son of Smith Bradley (relationship not stated); sister Elizabeth Order; cousin Paulsey Kirtley of Kentucky; cousin Thomson Kirtley of Kentucky; Jane Weatherall, wife of William (relationship not stated); sister Nancy Breedlove. At wife's death, part lent her to be divided equally among children of sister, Elenor Ship and bro. John Barnes.
Executors: Leonard Barnes, Thomas Shirley, William Chapman, Thomas Clore.
Wit.: Strother Lillard.

13 June, 1828. Notice in the "Political Arena" for 2 months in case

of Garnett vs Moore, executor of John Sampson, et al. Statement that Delia Dickens, William Hughes and Mary, his wife, John Hughes and Jemima, his wife, John Barnes and his children and Eleanor Ship and her children did not appear as defendants and are not inhabitants of Virginia. Also, copy for paper, signed by John Hume, stated that Ann Burdine was not living in Virginia.

Inventory of John Sampson, 23 Nov., 1825, by Leonard Barnes, Thomas Chapman, Thomas Clore, Culpeper Co. Recorded 19 Feb., 1828. Total $3,415.

Deed of Lucy Berry and Aaron Berry to Martin Barnes, 14 July, 1820, shows Lucy was dau. of John Sampson, dec'd. Outside contains a note made by Richard H. Field 9 Feb., 1827 that this Aaron Berry was the son of Capt. Aaron Berry, dec'd.

In settlement of case no new heirs were mentioned except "Rhoda Berry and Elisha Berry." Settled 1 July, 1832. (Note: Frances may have been 1st wife of Elisha Berry and Rhoda his 2nd wife - or were they children?)

James Clark's answer 23 July, 1832. Barsheba Clark has died and he and she were executors of Reuben Clark, dec'd.

William Sampson of Culpeper Co. Power of Attorney to brother Thomas Sampson of Madison Co. to get his share of legacy from his father, John Sampson. Dated 25 March, 1791. Wit. Benjamin Lillard and Martin Barnes.
19 June, 1811, Thomas Sampson assigned this paper and all rights to Reuben Booton.

15 April, 1830. Lucy Berry notified Robert Garnett that deposition of William Nalle would be taken at Fairfax in Culpeper Co.

Public Notice in the Culpeper Gazette, 9 March, 1832 for 2 months named as defendants: Reuben Moore, administrator of John Sampson, dec'd.; William Slaughter, Jr., and John Massey, administrators of Martin Barnes, dec'd.; John Hume, administrator of Mary Sampson, dec'd.; Robert Thomas, administrator of Thomas Sampson, dec'd.; William Dickins, dec'd ; William Sampson, dec'd.; Elizabeth Kinder, dec'd.; Original Burdine, dec'd.; Judith Fincham, dec'd.; Samuel Slaughter, administrator of Aaron Berry, dec'd.; Lucy Berry; Delila Dickins; William Hughes and Mary, his wife; John Hughes and Jamima, his wife; James Clarke, executor of Reuben Clarke, dec'd.; Anthony Twyman, administrator of Barsheba Clarke, dec'd.; Andrew Smith, administrator of Nancy Breedlove, dec'd.; Churchell Breedlove; Richard I. Tutt, administrator of Mary Berry, dec'd., and Philemore Berry, dec'd.; John Barnes and his children; John Massey, administrator of Eleanor Ship, dec'd.; children of Eleanor Ship; Elizabeth Oder (she had not been located).

25 April, 1811. John Hughes, Jr., was of Kentucky when he conveyed to Martin Barnes, his right in estate of John Sampson, dec'd. He had purchased this right from Thomas Sampson.

27 March, 1788. William Hughes of Culpeper gave Power of Attorney to Martin Barnes of Culpeper Co. re legacy to Hughes from John Sampson, dec'd. Wit.: Benjamin Lillard, Wm. Bradley, Aaron Berrey. Filed Culpeper 6 May, 1829.

27 Jan., 1829. Churchill Breedlove resided Rockingham Co. when he answered the suit.

1 package of receipts given to John Massey before Oct., 1832.

Answer of Samuel Slaughter that in 1778 John Sampson died and his will was probated in Culpeper Co.

Indenture 23 Jan., 1804. Mary Sampson to Martin Barnes.

Account of Estate of Martin Barnes, dec'd. 27 Dec., 1827.

Deposition of Williamson Nalle. Filed 11 May, 1830. Taken in the Town of Fairfax, Culpeper Co.

Affidavit of Gabriel Smith.

Affidavit of Simeon Bates re conveyance, 1817 to Martin Barnes by Morgan and Frances Sisk(?).

Decree 8 Nov., 1831.

A Memorandum states that Joseph Sampson, Nancy Breedlove and Churchill Breedlove lived in Rockingham Co. 10 Aug., 1812.

Affidavit of Ambrose Ship of Green Co., Kentucky, 29 July, 1830. States he married 18 June, 1789 by Rev. William Mason to Elender Barns, full sister to Martin Barnes, late of Madison Co., Virginia. Elender was dead by 1830. Their children: Salley Ship m. Henry Moore; Rhoda Ship m. William Sanderfer; Easter Ship d. spinster; Judith Ship m. John Brockman; Nelley Ship m. Robert Craig; Martin Ship; Polley Ship m. Riley Chaney; Betsey Ship d. spinster; Thornton Ship; Ambrose Ship; Allen Ship; Nicey(?) Ship, a minor. Elender (Barnes) Ship d. 21 Nov., 1828.

Estate Account of Martin Barnes, dec'd. 26 Dec., 1825. Filed Madison Co., 25 Jan., 1827.

22 July, 1833. Pinkard vs Freeman

Deposition of John Massey taken at the tavern house of Howard Wright in the Town of Madison re land sold at auction. Details of bill of this case. Further depositions taken, 14 March, 1834 by Gabriel Jones, Reuben Rosson, James Collins, John Collins. Answer of Charles Pinckard, 3 Aug., 1833. Decree rendered 4 Nov., 1841. John H. Freeman vs Charles Pinckard.

Robert Garnett and Rhoda, his wife, vs Reuben Moore.
18 May, 1830

Reuben Moore, administrator of John Sampson, dec'd.; William Slaughter, Jr., and John Massey, administrators of Martin Barnes, dec'd.; John Hume of Madison Co., administrator of Mary Sampson, dec'd.; Robert Thomas of Madison Co., administrator of estates of Thomas Sampson, dec'd., William Dickins, dec'd., William Sampson, dec'd., Elizabeth Rinder, dec'd., and Original Burdine, dec'd.; Aaron Berry and Lucy, his wife; Delia Dickins; William Hughes and Mary, his wife; John Hughes and Jemima, his wife; Reuben Clarke and Barsheba, his wife; Joseph Sampson; Nancy Breedlove; Churchill Breedlove; Merry Berry; Philomel Berry; Judith Fincham; John Barnes and his children and Eleanor Ship and her children - defendants.

Suit abated as to Aaron Berry and Judith Fincham by their deaths. Samuel Slaughter, administrator of Aaron Berry, dec'd, Robert Thomas of Madison Co., administrator of Judith Fincham.

Court orders for settlement of this case. Deposition of John Massey 12 May, 1830, in this case. Deposition of Belfield Cave 27 April, 1829, referring to papers relating to this case as early as 1788.

Articles of agreement, 10 Aug., 1829, between Joseph Sampson and Robert Garnett.

Account report, William Slaughter, Jr., administrator of Martin Barnes, dec'd.

Clerk's report with dates of court records in this case. 5 May, 1828 court report.

3 May, 1839. Decree after case appealed - Freeman vs Pinckard.

13 June, 1839. Plaintiff is listed as John Holmes Freeman. Commissioner's Report.

24 Oct., 1840. Freeman vs Pinckard. Depositions of Reuben Rosson, Mordecai Yager, John S. Petty, James Collins.

12 May, 1841. Itemized account. John H. Freeman Dr. to Charles Pinckard Dec. 1827 through 1839. Pinckard's notice to Freeman that deposition of A. H. Hansbrough to be taken.

11 Sept., 1841. Freeman vs Pinckard. Depositions of John Day, Cornelius Tanner, Thomas F. Petty and Gabriel Freeman.

14 Aug., 1841. Freeman vs Pinckard. Deposition of John Fennell.

16 Aug., 1841. Ibid. Depositions of George Green and W. C. Allen.

21 Aug., 1841. Depositions of Samuel Shadrack and Thomas Jeffries.

18 June, 1778. Copy of will of John Sampson, filed in case of Garnett vs Barnes. Proven 20 July, 1778.

Legatees: Wife Mary Sampson. Children: William Sampson, Joseph

Sampson, Thomas Sampson, Rhoda Sampson. Having formerly given to Eliza-Rinder, wife of Lewis; Bathsheba Clerk, wife of Reuben; Ann Burdyne, wife of Reginal; Delilah Dicken, wife of William; Lucy Berry, wife of Aaron; Franky Berry, wife of Elisha.

Executors: Wife May, Reuben Clerk, Reginal Burdyne and friend Henry Lewis.

Wit.: Geo. Wetherall, Mich (X) Yeager, Joseph (X) Campbell.

Answer of John Hume, administrator of Estate of Mary Sampson. Madison Co. 9 Feb., 1829.

8 May, 1829. Garnett vs Moore. Decree.

Not dated. Garnett vs Barnes. Judge Browne's analysis and order.

11 May, 1830. Garnett vs Barnes. Answer of Lucy Berry.

May, 1828. Garnett vs Moore. Statement by Commissioner that defendants Delia Dickens, William Hughes and Mary his wife, John Hughes and Jemima his wife, John Barnes and his children, Eleanor Ship and her children not inhabitants of Virginia.

23 May, 1834. Freeman vs Pinckard. Deposition of Presley N. Smith.

7 March, 1834. Freeman vs Pinckard. Depositions of C. C. Beckham, John Thompson, William G. Allen, Thornton F. Petty, Joel Inskeep.

Asher vs Nalle's administrator

Waller R. Asher of Culpeper Co. vs Anne Nalle, administratrix of Jessee Nalle, dec'd. 1836. Relates to 1835 suit of Anne Nalle, administratrix of Jessee Nalle vs Waller R. Asher, Robert G. Ward and William Slaughter, Jr.

Booton vs Fitzpatrick

10 June, 1836. Henry M. Lipscomb had been guardian of Jane S. Wood, who had married William Booton and Edward C. Fitzpatrick was administrator of estate of Henry M. Lipscomb.

Henry M. Lipscomb's estate was decreed to owe William Booton and wife, Jane, the principal with interest from 31 Dec., 1813.

Jane S. Wood in 1811 was orphan of Thomas Wood, dec'd., whose executor was James Wood.

28 Oct., 1813. Guardian bond of John Walker, Richard C. Booton surety, for Jane Wood and Mary Wood, orphans of Thomas Wood, dec'd.

The case in Superior Court, 15 May, 1828. Plaintiffs: William Booton and Jane S., his wife. Defendants: 1. Edward C. Fitzpatrick, administrator of Henry M. Lipscomb, dec'd. 2. John Walker, security for Fitzpatrick and guardian of Jane S. Booton, and administrator of Henry M.

Lipscomb, dec'd. 3. Richard C. Booton. 4. William Madison. 5. Henry Tinsley. 6. Benajah Rice. 7. William Tinsley. 8. William Wright and Polly, his wife. 9. Lucy M. Lipscomb. 10. William Lipscomb. 11. Jane Lipscomb.

John Walker, referred to as Capt. Walker. In 1833 Edward C. Fitzpatrick, William Wright and Polly, his wife, were not residents of Virginia.

Deposition 1836 of Mrs. Lucy M. Lipscomb, sister of Jane S. Booton. Jane Wood, now Booton, lived in Fredericksburg with Henry M. Lipscomb, March, 1811, moved with him to Raccoon Ford in Orange Co. and stayed until late 1813. Mrs. Lucy M. Lipscomb was wife of Stapleton C. Lipscomb and lived in Madison Co. Jane was about 12 and 13 years old in 1811-13.

In public notice 1835. Defendants included Nos. 1, 2, 8, 9, 10, 11, and added Hiram Booton, Joseph Bohannon, Joseph Bohannon.

Non-residents of the Commonwealth: Edmund C. Fitzpatrick, William Wright and Polly, his wife, and Lucy M. Lipscomb.

10 July, 1811. John Walker, administrator of E. Wood, dec'd., paid Stapleton Lipscomb, one of the Legatees. Receipt signed by Henry M. Lipscomb, guardian for heirs of James Woods, dec'd.

Deposition of Humphrey Hume of Culpeper, 1836, by Justice of the Peace, Thornton F. Petty.

1806. Henry Tinsley was guardian of Jane S. Wood, making a report through 1809.

Inventory and Appraisal of Estate of Henry M. Lipscomb, dec'd. Recorded 27 July, 1815, Madison Co. Made by William Twyman, William Tinsley, Winfield Wright, James Barnett.

26 March, 1811. Guardian's bond. Henry M. Lipscomb for Jane S. Wood, orphan of Thomas Wood. Co-signed by John Alcock and John Walker.

Will of Elizabeth Wood of Madison Co.
Dated 4 March, 1803. Proven 23 June, 1803.
Legatees: "heirs of my son, Thomas Wood, dec'd." -- mentions legacy left her by her father but does not name him.

Original filing of William Booton and his wife Jane S. formerly Jane S. Wood, Bill of complaint, Oct. 1828, gives following statements.

Thomas Wood, father of Jane S. left a widow, Rebecca and children: Sally, Lucy, Patsey, Jane S. and Polly.

Sally Wood m. Henry M. Lipscomb. When he died he left the children William Lipscomb and Jane Lipscomb.

Hiram Bohannon m. widow of Henry M. Lipscomb and she died after having one child, Joseph Bohannon.

Lucy M. Wood m. Stapleton A. Lipscomb who has since died but Lucy survives.

Patsey Wood has never married.

Jane S. Wood m. William Booton.

Polly Wood m. William Wright and now resides in Missouri.

Administrators of Estate of Thomas Wood were Rebecca Wood, the widow, and William Smith, who has died.

Henry Tinsley m. Rebecca (___) Wood, widow of Thomas; rem. to Kentucky.

Executors of William Smith, dec'd., were Camp Porter and John Alcock.

Henry M. Lipscomb became administrator of Thomas Wood, dec'd., after death of William Smith.

Jane S. (Wood) Booton was legatee of her grandfather, Joseph Wood, and grandmother, Elizabeth Wood.

John Alcock was administrator of Joseph Wood, dec'd., and made a report in 1805. Joseph Wood, dec'd., was of Madison Co.

John Walker was administrator of Elizabeth Wood, dec'd., of Madison Co. and made a report in 1807.

Henry Tinsley and Rebecca (___) Wood Tinsley, and William Smith, administering estate of Thomas Wood, made a report in Madison Co., 1807.

Benajah Rice was non-resident of Virginia in 1828.

Henry M. Lipscomb died about 1 Jan., 1815.

Thomas Wood, son of Joseph and Elizabeth, died after his father but before his mother.

Elizabeth (___) Wood, widow of Joseph, died before 10 July, 1811.

Answer of John Walker is in this file.

Account Sales of Henry M. Lipscomb, dec'd., 29 May, 1815.

Account of Administrator of Estate of Henry M. Lipscomb, dec'd., by Edward C. Fitzpatrick, executor. Recorded 28 Oct., 1824, covering 1816-1819 and 1815 through 1817.

Fiduciary Bond. 23 June, 1803. From John Walker, Jr., administrator of Elizabeth Wood, dec'd. and his security William Madison to Justices of the Peace Henry(?) Walker, Daniel Field, Daniel James and Elliot Rucker - Madison Co.

A deposition of Willis Tinsley, Madison Co., 23 Sept., 1836.

Fiduciary Bond. 25 May, 1815. Madison Co. Edward C. Fitzpatrick, administrator of Henry M. Lipscomb with John Walker, his security, to Justices of the Peace Daniel Field, William Mallory, Thomas Shirley, Robert Beale and Michael Wallace.

Francis Lightfoot was guardian of Joseph Bohannon in 1836.

Received of Henry Tinsly his bond for Eighty-two pound and 12s which when paid will be in full of all demands against him for money due Jane Wood and Mary Wood, orphans of Thomas Wood, dec'd., by him as guardian, also in full of amount due Wood heirs by J. Field, which he collected, also in full of debt due by William Smith, dec'd., for a balance due the heirs of T. Wood, dec'd., Smith administrator, also the amount of a Richmond Lot due by said Smith deceased to Henry Tinsley which he relinquished all his rights and interest in the debt to Thos. Wood heirs and has no claim against them on no account whatever. Signed: 27 April, 1811. Henry M. Lipscomb.

Record of Joseph Alcock, executor of John Alcock, dec'd., who was executor of Joseph Wood, Sr., dec'd., two hundred and thirteen pounds Interest and principal of a Legacy left Thos. Wood, dec'd., by said Joseph Wood, Sr., dec'd., and by the demise of said Thos. Wood reverts to his heirs namely Sarah E. Wood now S. E. Lipscomb, Lucy M. Wood now L. M. Lipscomb, wife of S. C. Lipscomb, Martha Wood, Jane S. Wood and Mary C. Wood, all of which are grandchildren to Joseph Wood, Sen., dec'd.

9 July, 1811. Henry M. Lipscomb, guardian for the single heirs of Thomas Wood, namely Martha, Jane and William Wood. Wit. James Kidwell.

Perry vs Beckham's administrator.

Deposition of Garnett Corbin. 3 Nov., 1832, in Fredericksburg in case of Pierce Perry vs Wm. Major, executor of Isaiah Corbin.
Answer of William Major, 13 May, 1832.
Garnett Corbin was son of Isaiah Corbin, dec'd., and Pierce Perry had married Nelly Corbin, dau. of Isaiah Corbin, dec'd.
Isaiah Corbin made a Deed of Gift, 27 March, 1821, to Garnett Corbin.
Widow of Isaiah Corbin, dec'd., was Lydia Corbin.
Deposition of Archibald Tutt, Culpeper Co., 1 June, 1833.
Isaiah Corbin held land under the will of his father, William Corbin, dated 10 Nov., 1789 and proven 19 June, 1797.
The children of William Corbin as named in Dec., 1829: Mrs. Catharine Gaunt, Isaiah Corbin and others.
1830. Garnett Corbin resided in Stafford Co.
Administrator's Account, receipts, summons, depositions, but no further information of a genealogical nature.

Virginia to Missouri. Dr. Samuel Gibbs Rixey, b. 25 May, 1827, son of Richard Rixey III of Fauquier County, Virginia, and Penelope (Gibbs) Rixey, his second wife, removed to Missouri and lived in Platte County when his first son, Richard Hughes Rixey, was born. His four marriages are given Rixey, pp. 107-108.

Brooke vs Singleton

Answer of Albert R. Singleton, administrator of Joshua Singleton, to William Brooke, Jr., complainant. In 1838, Albert R. Singleton as administrator had paid to James A. Irvin, attorney of Minor W. Singleton, $150.00 on account as part of Minor's share in estate of Joshua Singleton, dec'd.
William Brooke, Jr., vs Minor W. Singleton, Albert R. Singleton,

administrator of Joshua Singleton, dec'd., and Nancy W. Singleton.

Minor W. Singleton was "absent from the Commonwealth" Jan., 1840.

In 1822 Minor W. Singleton created indebtedness to William Brooke, Jr. Suit was continued from 1827 for a decade or more because Singleton failed to appear. Summons for Singleton was sent to Rappahannock Co. but report was he was not found there and it was thought he had gone West.

Wm. Brooke, Jr., 1838, to Hon. Richard H. Field, Judge of the Superior Court of Law and Chancery at Culpeper Co. This states that Minor W. Singleton, a non-resident of Virginia was son of Joshua Singleton, dec'd., whose administrator was Albert R. Singleton. Joshua's widow was Nancy W. Singleton.

Barnes vs Barnes, 22 Dec., 1825.

Rhoda Barnes vs William Slaughter, Jr., and John Massey, administrators of Martin Barnes, dec'd.

Madison Co. Court. She sued for her dower right. By 25 Jan., 1827, she had intermarried with Robert Garnett. Contains surveyor's description and map of the dower property in Madison Co.

Appraisal of Estate of John Sampson, dec'd., 18 May, 1830, which was ordered by Chancery Court of Fredericksburg. 7/12 and 6/9 of 1/12 allotted to Martin Barnes' administrator.

Inventory of Estate of John Sampson, dec'd., is included.

Copy of Deed - 23 Feb., 1809: Reuben Clark, Sheba Clark wife of Reuben, James Clark, William Clark and John Clark of Madison Co. to Martin Barnes of said county - rights in estate of John Sampson, dec'd., devised to Mary Sampson, his wife.

Wit.: William Sims, Sr., Isaac Smith, William Anderson for Reuben Clark and Bathsheba Clark.

Wit.: P. Lightfoot and Wm. Chapman for James Clark, William Clark and John Clark.

1830. Statement of amounts due heirs of estate of Martin Barnes, dec'd. Henry Barnes, Jr., William Bradly, Ellinor Ship, John Barnes, widow. Defendants were John Barnes and his children, Eleanor Ship and her children, Elizabeth Oder, Paulsey Kirtley, Thomas Kirtley, William Bradley, Jane Witherall, Henry Barnes, Sr., Henry Barnes, Jr., Ann Breedlove, Reuben Moore as administrator of estate of John Sampson, dec'd., John Hume as administrator of estate of Mary Sampson, dec'd., John Massey and William Slaughter, Jr., as administrators of Martin Barnes, dec'd.

3 Jan., 1827. When summoned to answer Robert Garnett and Rhoda, his wife, late Rhoda Barnes.

6 Sept., 1828. Summons - Joseph Sampson, Nancy Breedlove and Churchill Breedlove to answer Robert Garnett and Rhoda, his wife.

25 March, 1829. Summons served on Joseph Sampson in Rockingham Co. Ann Breedlove was served in Rockingham Co.

26 Oct., 1829. Deposition of Aaron Berry, Jr., of Culpeper Co.

26 Sept., 1813. Elizabeth Render of Madison Co. Power of Attorney to Madison Barnes of same county to sue for her share of estate of her father, John Sampson, dec'd. Wit.: William Bates, Joshua Mackcolester.

25 April, 1811. Bond of Thomas Sampson of Orange Co. to John Hughs, Jr., of Linkhorn County and State of Kentucky re: int. in estate of his father, John Sampson, dec'd.

25 March, 1788. Power of Attorney William Dicken of Culpeper Co. to Christopher Dicken of Culpeper Co. to collect his 1/12 part of estate of John Sampson. Wit.: Daniel Dicken, Benjamin Lillard, Benjamin Dicken. Recorded in Madison Co. 28 Nov., 1811.

Christopher Dicken assigned it to Thomas Sampson 25 Sept., 1789.

Thomas Sampson assigned to John Hughs of Lincoln Co., Kentucky, 13 June, 1811. Wit.: Reuben Booton, Mary (X) Booton.

John Hughs assigned to Martin Barns, 22 June, 1811. Wit.: Jno. Wright, Wm. Kemper.

Garnett vs Barnes

8 Aug., 1828. Summons. Lucy Berry, widow of Aaron Berry, dec'd., to answer Robert Garnett and Rhoda, his wife.

20 Nov., 1815. Aaron Berry had died more than 3 months before and court ordered an inventory of his estate.

8 May, 1786. Deed in trust or Power of Attorney, John Hughs of Culpeper Co. to Capt. Aaron Berry "all that legacy or remainder of estate willed to me and my heirs by John Sampson, dec'd." Wit.: Benjamin Lillard, David Yowell. Recorded Madison Co., 28 Nov., 1811.

Freeman vs Pinckard

Deposition of Thomas Marr 29 Oct., 1834. "About that time my youngest brother was about removing to Florida. John Pinckard, the son of Charles Pinckard, had made arrangements to go with him. Some few days after the sale day of the land I saw Mr. John Pickard in Fauquier, who informed me his father had purchased the land of Freeman and that he was on his way to his Uncle Samuel Fisher's......."

A notice re affidavits to be taken given to John Hoomes Freeman by Charles Pinckard, 23 Oct., 1834. Same dated 27 May, 1834; 18 July, 1833; 7 March, 1834.

Deposition of Jeremiah Strother, 21 Jan., 1833, in his home in Culpeper Co.

Public Sale of Freeman land was advertised in the "Political Area," Fredericksburg, 23, 27, 30 Nov., 1827, and 7, 14 Dec. This land had been purchased from the heirs of Asher and of Hudson.

Deposition of John Clark, in Spotsylvania Co., 7 June, 1834.

Depositions of Francis J. Thompson, George W. Jameson, William G. Allen and Waller B. Asher, Culpeper Co., 6 Nov., 1833.

The land had been conveyed in trust by Freeman to Thomas W. Lightfoot for a debt due John Massey.

Depositions of Reuben Hudson, William S. Daniel, Benjamin Wharton, 31 May, 1834.

Depositions of Daniel Brown, Russell Vaughan and Daniel Rosson, Culpeper Co., May, 1834.

Depositions of Reuben Moore, Waller R. Asher, John Collins, June, 1834.

Deposition of William Robertson, June, 1834.

Deposition of Johuze Tongue, Fauquier Co., and of Samuel Fisher, William Horner, 7 May, 1834.

Suit was over forced sale of Freeman's property "Summer Duck" including the saw mill and question of Charles Pinckard having been a by-bidder for the family. It was in Superior Court in 1841.

23 March, 1822. Deed of Trust from John Hoomes Freeman of Culpeper Co. to Archibald Freeman of same to pay John's indebtedness to William A. Knox, Daniel Grinnan, John and Francis J. Thompson, Garland Thompson, Hugh N. Thompson, Gabriel Freeman, Robert G. Ward, Thomas Chew, William A. McConchie, William Wallace, Jr., Thornton Foushee.

2 June, 1834. Depositions of Cornelius Tanner.

Vaughan vs Jones and Baughan vs Jones

List of sales of property of Mrs. Eve Vaughan, also given on many papers as Baughan.

Copies of wills, deeds, herein are in proper books in Court House.

Children of Jeremiah Baughan, dec'd., were: Frances, Juliett Ann, Jane, Mary, Almond Burgess Vaughan, Albert Vaughan and widow of Jeremiah was Molly. Joel Vaughan had wife, Fanny, and sons, Jefferson and Mordecai Vaughan.

Copy of the Will of Mordecai Baughan.

Dated 19 June, 1792. Proven 17 Sept., 1792.

Legatees: Widow Eve Baughan. Children: Henry Baughan, Sarah Baughan, Susanna Baughan, Lystra Baughan, Jeremiah Baughan, Mordecai Baughan, Moses Baughan and Catherine Baughan, Simeon Baughan, Joel Baughan.

Executors: Wife Eve Baughan, John Brown.

Wit.: Vincent Baughan, William Wall, James Davis.

In case included of Gerard Popham vs Robert Jones, depositions were taken in Rappahannock Co. in Sept., 1838, from Thomas C. Brown, Joel Hitt, Henry Vaughan and wife Jael.

An heir of Mordecai Vaughan was his dau. Sarah who m. Michael Aylor. When this suit occurred Michael and Sarah were dead and their children were listed as follows: (probably inhabitants of Virginia) Henry Aylor, William Aylor, L____ Aylor, James Aylor, Lucy Powell wife of Hezekiah Powell and formerly Lucy Aylor.

Lystra Baughan and Margaret or "Peggy" his wife were dead and left heirs - Berryman Baughan and Margaret his wife, John Baughan and Margaret his wife, Joseph Henry Baughan, Newby(?) James Baughan and Ann his wife, Sarah Baughan, Susannah M____, Jane who married A. P____ (?Parrot).

Fanny Baughan was guardian of Jefferson Baughan and Mordecai Baughan infant children of Joel Baughan, dec'd. These infants were grandchildren of Eve Baughan and Mordecai Baughan, both dec'd.

Eve Baughan's will dated 5 June, 1829; proven 18 May, 1835. Wit.:

Daniel Brown, Frances H. Brown, Mary Ann Allen.

Answer of Robert Jones and his wife, Suzan, formerly Susan Baughan, dau. of Mordecai Baughan, to Gerard Popham who was executor of Moses Baughan, dec'd.

Robert Jones was defendant in his own right and as administrator of Mordecai Baughan and Eve Baughan.

A plaintiff listed as Nancy Wilhoite must have been Susanna Baughan, dau. of Mordecai and Eve.

William Ashby vs Alexander H. Hansbrough
in his own right and as Trustee of James B. Clayton.
3 Nov., 1834

3 June, 1831. Indenture between James B. Clayton, of the first part, John S. Pendleton and William S. Field of the second part and William Ashby of the third part involving Alexander H. Hansbrough. Wit.: G. W. Jameson, Thomas W. Wharton, Thomas C. Freeman.

    Depositions of Fountain F. Henry, 1831.

    Depositions of Beverly Henry, 1831.

    Depositions of James B. Clayton, 1831.

    Decree rendered June, 1836.

    10 June, 1835. Petition of Alexander H. Hansbrough.

    7 June, 1836. Depositions of Thomas M. Howard and William Green.

    7 Nov., 1836. Commissioners' Report.

    9 June, 1835. Depositions of Edward Green, John Thompson, Philip Lightfoot.

    1 Nov., 1834. Separate answer of A. H. Hansbrough.

    Bill of Particulars. May, 1834.

    26 Oct., 1829. Trust Deed. James B. Clayton to Alexander H. Hansbrough.

    12 June, 1835. Depositions of Thomas D. Hansbrough and F. Mauzy.

    16 June, 1835. Depositions of James W. Smoot, William G. Allen and Marius Hansbrough. (His signature very interesting). He and A. H. Hansbrough worked in a store belonging to one of them.

    11 June, 1835. Deposition of James B. Clayton.

    31 Oct., 1835. Deposition of John J.(?) Pendleton and James Pendleton.

    June, 1835. Supplemental answer of A. H. Hansbrough.

Barnett's administrator vs Stone et al.

27 Dec., 1835. Summons. James Richards and Winifred, his wife, to answer Benjamin N. Barnett, executor of Judith A. Barnett, dec'd.

Printed notice, 18 March, 1837. Messrs. William Stone and Agnes B., his wife; William Brown, Trustee of Agnes B. Stone, late Agnes B. Benson; Stephen McCormick and Elizabeth, his wife; Benjamin F. Richards and Dulcebella, his wife; James R. Benson; Willis Benson (the latter an infant, by James R. Benson, his guardian ad litem, appointed by the court) and Berry Benson:

Take Note that on the 29th day of April, 1837, ... etc. indicating depositions to be taken of Miss Mary Benson at her mother's house in Fredericksburg, Benjamin Watson, James G. Watson and Sally his wife, John Jackson and Lindsay Pollard, Alexander Wharton - signed by Plaintiff, Benjamin N. Barnett, administrator of Judith A. Barnett, dec'd.

The answer of William Stone and Agness, his wife, stated that Judith A. Barnett, dec'd., was formerly Judith A. Benson. Agnes B. Stone was a sister to Judith A. (Benson) Barnett.

A partition of the disputed land had been made in 1827. Their answer was notarized in Bourbon County, Kentucky, 27 July, 1836.

Plat and division of Benson's Land, 1827, on Richard's Road and Rapidan River is in this docket.

Depositions by Benj. Watson, James Pollard.

Copy of Deed, 1 May, 1830, between Benjamin H. Barnett and Judith A., his wife, of Spotsylvania Co. to William Browne of Fredericksburg of same county and Agness B. Stone of Culpeper Co.

Rental agreement between Agness Stone and Joseph Hall. 11 Oct., 1826.

The heirs-at-law of Judith A. Barnett (formerly Benson) are Agnes B. Stone, wife of William Stone; Elizabeth McCormick, wife of Stephen McCormick; Winifred Richards, wife of James Richards - all of whom were sisters of Julia A. (Benson) Barnett. Enock Berry Benson - a brother. Another brother was Willis Benson who had died and left children: Dulcibella C. Richards, wife of Benjamin F. Richards, James R. Benson and Willis Benson. Judith A. (Benson) Barnett had never had any children.

17 April, 1837. Deposition of Alexander Wharton, Culpeper Co., who had worked on the disputed land.

21 April, 1837. Deposition of James G. Watson.

27 Aug., 1836. Deposition of William Browne taken in Spotsylvania Co.

Deposition of Richard Bullard, Jr., same date and place; of Richard W. Bullard, same.

Copy of Deed, 1830, Benjamin Barnett and wife Judith A. Barnett to William Browne.

Major vs Harrison

1837. William Major and William Emison were trustees for John Jameson.

Fiduciary Bond of Philip Harrison of Richmond, Virginia, and John M. Herndon of Fredericksburg, Virginia, to William Major and William Emison.

10 May, 1837. Deposition of Henry Shackelford of Rappahannock Co.

John Jameson owned land in Western Virginia, in Culpeper Co., in Kentucky and in Ohio, a house and lot in the Town of Fairfax, Culpeper Co., which he was occupying and which had been occupied by his father, the late Col. John Jameson.

Moore vs Jeffries

Administrator's Account and Estate Division of John Hilton, dec'd. Legatees: Widow Susannah Hilton and 7 children: William Hilton, Henry Dogan, Robert Hilton, Ann Hilton, Henry Hilton, George Hilton, Susan

Hilton. Made by Garland Thompson, John Colvin, Jeremiah Strother.

Reuben Moore was executor of John Hilton, dec'd., and James Garnett, Jr., was guardian of Susan Hilton, dau. of John Hilton, dec'd., in Aug., 1827, where Reuben Moore gave bond in this suit. James Garnett, Jr., m. Ann Hilton before 6 April, 1836, dau. of John Hilton, dec'd. Ambrose Jeffries m. Susan Hilton, dau. of John Hilton, dec'd., before 6 April, 1836.

John McNeale was Executor for John Jameson, dec'd., who had a son John Jameson, and John Hilton, dec'd., had been a Trustee for John McNeale.

Included is a copy of will of John Hilton, dated 7 Sept., 1820. Proven 18 Dec., 1820.

Hudson vs Marshall's Heirs.

Thomas Marshall of Fauquier Co. power of attorney to son John Marshall of same county to sell to Robert Hudson of Culpeper Co. land "conveyed to me by a deed from John M. Patton dated September the seventh one thousand eight hundred and thirty five."

Deed, 1835, Thomas Marshall of Fauquier Co. to Robert Hudson of Culpeper Co.

Separate answer of Mary Marshall, Fielding L. Marshall, Anne L. Marshall, Margaret Marshall and Thomas Marshall, infant children of Thomas Marshall, dec'd., by Alexander J. Marshall, their guardian, to Robert Hudson, plaintiff. Filed 17 Oct., 1836.

Answer of Alexander Taliaferro who had married Agness ____, one of the defendants by their attorney, Samuel Chilton. No date.

Answer of William B. Archer and Mary, his wife, by their attorney, Samuel Chilton. No date.

William Green was attorney for the plaintiff.

Suit filed 3 Nov., 1835. Robert Hudson against John Marshall heir-at-law and administrator of Thomas Marshall, dec'd., Agness H. Marshall, Mary Marshall, Fielding L. Marshall, Ann L. Marshall, Margaret Marshall, and Thomas Marshall, heirs-at-law of Thomas Marshall, dec'd.

Deposition of John Marshall. 9 Aug., 1837, Warrenton, Fauquier Co. Other routine papers and decree are in this docket.

Cheek vs Seddon's Heirs
and
Browning vs Cheek

In same packet. Recorded in Book 2 Folio 182.

Original Indenture 20 June, 1791, between James Williams of Culpeper Co. and John Strother, juner - land granted to Robert Green, dec'd., from the Proprietor and by him devised to his son, Moses Green, now dec'd., by will recorded in Orange Co.

John Strother, Jr., assigned it to George Watters, 22 April, 1793. Wit.: John Coghill, Elias Waters.

George Waters assigned it to James Clark, June 15, 1803. Wit.: George P. Thompson, John McNeale, Reubin Samuel.

James Clark assigned to George Waters, 2 Nov., 1804.
George Watters assigned to John Strother and William Pendleton, 1812.
John Strother assigned to French Strother. Date illegible.
French Strother assigned to Wm. Pendleton, 18 Nov., 1816.
Wm. Pendleton assigned to Wm. W. and Charles D. Browning, 3 May, 1822.
Wm. W. Browning and Chas. D. Browning assigned it to Elijah Cheek, 3 May, 1822. Included notation of suit of William W. Browning and Charles D. Browning vs Elijah Cheek, June 1835, including a note of 1822, made to them by Elijah Cheek.

Deposition of Zepkaniah Turner made at the home of Samuel DeCamp in Town of Woodville and County of Rappahannock, 4 March, 1837, for suit of Elijah Cheek, plaintiff and defendants were Philip Alexander, Arthur Morson and John Moncure, Executors of Thomas Siddon, dec'd.

Deposition of George Eggborn of lawful age at house of Samuel DeCamp in town of Woodville, Rappahannock Co., 4 Nov., 1837.

Wall vs Balthrop

Suit of Wall vs Balthrop over a patent right Case was begun in 1811 and ended in 1839.

Schedule of patent of improvement in the Double Shovel Plough made by John Ballthorpe.

Memorandum from John Lewis to John Armistead dated 9 Dec., 1828.

In 1837, Armistead Wall, plaintiff, was dead and Enoch Jameson was executor. John Balthrope one of the defendants was dead and Sally Balthorpe was administratrix.

Case removed to Chancery Court, 22 May, 1838.

12 Sept., 1835. Deposition of John Lewis taken at his house in Prince William Co.

John Lewis had filed in Washington for a patent.

Thom vs Hansbrough

19 May, 1832. Reuben T. Thom and William H. Hansbrough, executors of George S. Thom, dec'd. vs Mary Long, John Slaughter, Thomas C. Hansbrough, Larkin G. Nalle and Judith Nalle.

Sale of negroes. Nalle to George S. Thom.

Mary Long and John Slaughter were administratrix and administrator of estate of William B. Long, dec'd.

Oxley vs Emison

William Emison, administrator of John Cummings, dec'd., who d. 10 Oct., 1826, intestate, made answer to the charges re estate of the deceased.

28 Sept., 1829. Chancery Court in Spotsylvania. Plaintiffs: Thomas Oxley and wife Elizabeth. Defendants: William Emison, administrator of John Cummins, dec'd., Samuel Beale and Rebecca his wife, Robert Cummins,

John Cummins, George Roach and Sarah his wife, William Penquito(?) and Jane his wife, Margaret Cummins. No defendants were residents of Virginia, Nov., 1826, except William Emison and Margaret Cummins.

Margaret Cummins, administratrix, was widow of John Cummins.

Reference to a suit in Fauquier Co., Jan., 1821, Thomas Oxley vs Samuel Beale.

One report states that Robert Cummins, George Roach, William Penquite lived in Ohio.

Johnston vs Hansbrough et al.

13 Nov., 1834. Chancery Court. Plaintiff: Benjamin Johnston. Defendants: James Hansbrough and Peter Hansbrough, executors of Peter Hansbrough, dec'd., and James M. Bell.

James M. Bell was a legatee in the right of his wife, Amelia Bell.

Debits and credits of account of estate of Peter Hansbrough, dec'd., are listed from 1822 through 1838.

Also given as Benj. Johnson of King George Co. Case related to the sale of "Belvidere."

Original sketch of platte of Belvidere.

Copy of Will of Peter Hansbrough, dated 4 Oct., 1821; proven 21 Oct., 1822, Culpeper Co.

Kelly vs Cole, executor of Kelly.

Daniel Cole, executor of estate of Thomas Kelly, dec'd., filed report May 15, 1827 through 1828.

Account of Sales of estate of Thomas Kelly, dec'd.

Polly Kelly vs Daniel Cole, executor of Thomas Kelly, dec'd.

Mary "Polly" Kelly was widow and relict of Thomas Kelly.

Copy of will of Thomas Kelly, dated 25 Aug., 1823; proven 18 June, 1827.

Daniel Cole had married Mary Ann Kelly, dau. of Thomas Kelly, dec'd.

In 1831 Thomas Kelly, Jr., had the following children: James Kelly, Richard Kelly, Susan Kelly, Mary Kelly and Whitfield Kelly; all were infants and their father was guardian.

Other legatees: George Kelly, Daniel Threlkeld in right of his wife, Elizabeth Threlkeld, William Kelly, Joseph Kelly.

William Kelly was a minor.

Thomas Kelly and George Kelly did not live in Virginia.

Mary "Polly" Kelly m. (2) James Emmons, March, 1833. Final decree 19 June, 1835.

Court Suit, Chancery 3 June, 1834. Daniel Cole in his own right and as executor of Thomas Kelly, deceased, and Mary Ann his wife vs Daniel Threlkeld and Elizabeth his wife, Polly Kelly, Joseph Kelly, William Kelly, George Kelly and Thomas Kelly and the infant children of Thomas Kelly (as above) whose guardian was John C. Major.

Court Suit 1839

Alfred L. Ashby, administrator of John Jones, dec'd., vs John Slaughter, administrator, and Mary S. Long, administratrix of William B. Long, dec'd. Suit began in 1832 when John Jones was alive.

Court Suit 1839

John S. Barbour, administrator of James Byrne, dec'd., Eliza A. Barbour, wife of John S. and infants of them: Sally Barbour, John S. Barbour, Jr., James Barbour, Calhoun Barbour, Eliza A. Barbour, Jr., Alfred M. Barbour and Edwin Barbour.

James Byrne left an only child, Eliza A. Barbour and a widow, Sally, who married Mordecai Barbour, father of John S. Barbour and Sally Barbour has since died.

Will of James Byrne was recorded in Prince George County.

In 1839, Mordecai Barbour and his last wife, Sally Barbour, relict of James Byrne, had died.

Copy of Will of James Byrne, dated 22 July, 1817, of town of Petersburg.

Trust deeds, depositions, decrees of suits for indebtedness by various parties are included.

WORKS PROGRESS ADMINISTRATION
OF
VIRGINIA HISTORICAL INVENTORY

This write-up is a part of the Virginia W. P. A. Historical Inventory Project sponsored by the Virginia Conservation Commission under the direction of its Division of History. Credit to both the Commission and W. P. A. is requested for publication in whole or in part. Unless otherwise stated, this information has not been checked for accuracy by the sponsor.

Most of the leaflets in these files are descriptions of old homes in the County, noting the ownership back many generations and describing the building and its furnishings when they have historical value.

This compiler has extracted data from the leaflets on cemeteries and family Bibles, using only the information on people born in 1800 or before.

BIBLE RECORDS

Benjamin Crisler was born the 15th of December in the year 1783 - and departed this life the 5th day of November 1847.

The Crisler Family Bible, owned in 1937 by Mrs. Harry Berry, Culpeper.

***

Bradford Dawson was born March 11th, 1787.
K___ Dawson was born February 18, 1793.

Dawson Family Bible, owned in 1938 by Mrs. Fox.

***

William Crittenden died in the 77th yr. of his age on the __ day of October, 1854.
Catherine, wife of Wm. C. Crittenden died on the 24th day of July, 1868 in the 70th year of her age.

Petty Bible, owned in 1938, by Mrs. C. H. Smith, 605 North Main St., Culpeper, and Miss Georgie Petty.

***

George Routt, father of Wm. Pope Routt, was married to Winny Pope about 1780. He was killed by Indians in going to Kentucky after the close of the American Revolution in which he served as Captain of Company.
William Pope Routt and Margaret Mitchell were married Oct. 12th, 1812.

Died on 15th of Aug., 1862 in the 79th year of his age.

Routt Family Bible owned in 1938 by Mrs. C. H. Smith, Miss Georgie Petty and Mrs. Snead.

***

Charles Rixey, husband of Lucinda Rixey, departed this life June 6th 1846, age 62 yrs.
Lucinda Rixey, wife of Charles Rixey, departed this life Nov. 19, 1851, aged 63 yrs.

***

EARLY TOMBSTONES

John Armstrong
Born in Byton in the County
Derham, England
Died May 23, 1831
Aged 85 years

Remember me as you pass by
As you are now, so once was I
As I am now so you must be
Prepare for death and follow me.

Armstrong Cemetery: About two miles NE of Rixeyville on Rte 29, west side of road.

***

Sacred to the memory of
Major Amistead Brown
who died Sept. 4, 1858
Aged 71. A Christian.

The architect of his own fortune
And virtue and ornament of manliness.

Mary A. R. Brown
Consort of
Major Armistead Brown
who died Aug. 1, 1852
Aged 52 yrs.

Brown Cemetery: 1.4 miles southeast of Slate Mills, west side of Rte 604.

***

Thomas C. Brown
Born Nov. 10, 1789
Died Oct. 26, 1857

Francis H. Brown
Born March 5, 1812
Died May 28, 1852

Brown Cemetery: 1 mile northwest of Reva on Rte 636; thence 2 miles in same direction to gate. It is said that Daniel Brown, a soldier in the Revolutionary War, is buried in it.

***

In memory of our dear Mother
Mary, wife of
Richard Payne
Born July 30, 1780
Died Dec. 19, 1840

In memory of our dear Father
Richard Payne
Born Dec. 18, 1763
Died March 31, 1843

Bleak Hill Cemetery: 1.5 miles north of Alanthus on Rte 625 and Rte 631 on west side of the latter.

***

James Bickers
Aug. 18, 1789
Mar. 4, 1870
"God is love."

Catherine Crump
wife of
James Bickers
Sept.   1803
Aug. 28, 1869
"The Lord is my Shepherd."

Bickers Cemetery: 6.5 miles southwest of Culpeper Courthouse.

***

Cumberland George
born
April 15, 1797 in
Fauquier Co., Va.
died
Aug. 23, 1863
at Culpeper, Va.

Elizabeth Churchill George
Born 1795
In Stafford County, Va.
Died June 9, 1861 in
Culpeper Co., Virginia

Bell Cemetery: .4 mile northeast of Culpeper on Rte 15 on north side of road.

***

Our Aunt Nancy Hitt
Sister of Betsy Strother
died 1874 aged 88 years
She hath done what she could.

Our Grandmother Betsy
wife of
John Strother
Died 1876 age 92 yrs.
The righteous are sure
of their reward.

Mary R. Bickers
Died Dec. 25, 1876
Aged 76 years.

Alexander Bickers
Died Aug. 4, 1875
Aged 83 years.

Bethel Baptist Church Graveyard: 8 miles west of Culpeper on Rte 29; thence north .3 mile on Rte 609 on west side of road.

***

Daniel Colvin
Virginia
Pvt. Va. Rgt.
Rev. War
1790

Colvin Graveyard at "Mt. Airy": 4.5 miles west of Culpeper on Rte 3; thence south 1.5 miles on Rte 635 to house. Graveyard 100 yards south of house.

***

In Memory of
Mitcham Corbin
Son of William &

(Mitcham Corbin, cont.)

Sarah Corbin
Born Jan. 25, 1789
Died Oct. 11, 1860
Therefore be ye also ready
For in such an hour as ye
Know not the Son of Man
cometh.

In Memory of
Ann Corbin
Consort of
M. Corbin and daughter
of John and Elizabeth Bywaters
Born Oct. 14, 1795
Died Dec. 13, 1859
The body rests beneath the sod
The soul forever dwells with God.
If you are not prepared to die
You cannot meet with her on high.

Elizabeth Corbin
Born December 12, 1798
Died December 25, 1852
An affectionate wife
A tender mother
A kind mistress
A loving neighbor.

Corbin Cemetery: 1.5 miles north of Rixeyville, on Rte 29; thence 3 miles on Rte 611; thence west on private road to house, across field to cemetery.

***

William Crigler
Born June 28, 1778
Died Feby. 28th, 1855

Catherine
Wife of William Crigler
Born Aug. 10th, 1783
Died Aug. 28, 1850

Crigler Cemetery: 6.7 miles northwest of Culpeper, on Rte 3; thence north on Rte 634, 2.8 miles to Fant Place; thence east 1 mile across fields to farm of Jesse Settle; thence north 300 feet to cemetery.

***

Coons Cemetery: .4 mil south of Rixeyville; turn east on Rte 640 for 2 miles then turn south through gate.

There is a monument in the cemetery upon which the following names and dates are inscribed. This was erected because the stones used for each grave are only field stone and bear no inscription.

Note by D. F. W.: There are 11 names but shown here are only those born before 1800.

		Born	Died
1.	John Dillard		June 10, 1808
2.	Ann Dillard	1750	May 15, 1815
3.	William Coons, Sr.	Jan. 23, 1773	Mar. 19, 1842

***

William S. Daniel
Born ___ __ 1782
Died October 12, 1857 (Given in Bible as 1851 - at age 70)

Ann G. Daniel
Born ___ __ 1785
Died March 21, 1842 (Given in Bible as 1847, aged 65)

Daniel Cemetery: 1.8 miles west of Winston on Rte 610; thence right 2.9 miles east of Viewtown on Rte 642.

***

To the memory of
Eleanor
wife of
Birket Davenport
who departed this life
the 6th day of
May, 1790
Aged 38 years
Had issue three daughters
Susannah, Elizabeth and Eleanor

To the memory of
Susannah
the wife of
Philip Rootes Thompson
who in the zenith of life fell a
victim to a cancer in the breast,
the most painful of all diseases.
After it had baffled the utmost
efforts of human skill, she died
on the ninth day of December,
1798, aged 50 years.

Passion and pride were to her soul unknown
Convinced that nature only is our own

Susannah Thompson (cont.)
        So unaffected, so composed in mind
        So firm yet so strong yet so refined
        Heaven as its purest gold by torture tried
        The saint sustained it but the woman died.

Davenport-Thompson Cemetery: 1 mile northeast of Calatapa on Rte 669, turn south.

***

    In memory of   In memory of
    George Eggborn   Harriet Eggborn
       Died   wife of
    Sept. 4, 1848   George Eggborn
    Age 51 years   Died
                         Feb. 25, 1854

Eggborn Graveyard: 1 mile north of Culpeper on Rte 29; thence northwest 6.5 miles on Rte 49; thence south .4 mile of Rte 634; thence onto private road to the house. Graveyard in garden west of house.

***

No. 92.   Elizabeth wife of
                   George Bowyer
           Born in Rappahannock Co., Va.
                 March 9, 1799
              Died at Culpeper, Va.
                July 22, 1892

     Blessed are the dead who die in the Lord.

No. 204.   John Glassell
                    son of
           Andrew and Elizabeth Glassell
              Born Oct. 29, 1780
              Died Sept. 30, 1850.

No. 205.   Sacred to the memory of
               Mrs. Susan C. Wrenn
              who departed this life
                Nov. 23, 1852
                Age 117 years

No. 227.   Sacred to the memory of
              Philip Thornton, M. D.
               Born in Virginia
                June 25, 1788
              Died March 3, 1853
              in Washington, D. C.

No. 237.   Isaac Hiter
                     A servant of God
                     Died Jan. 14, 1886
                        Aged 104 years
                     A consistent member of
                   the Culpeper Baptist Church
                          for 62 years

No. 329.   Lucy, wife of William Ashby
                        Born April 8, 1790
                        Died Oct. 5, 1860

No. 544.   To the memory of Emily
                   Wife of Col. Pickett Withers
                        Died Jan. 25, 1865
                         Aged 73 years

No. 545.   To the memory of
                      Col. Pickett Withers
                       Died Jan. 25, 1865
                         Aged 73 years

Fairview Cemetery: 1 mile west of Culpeper on the north side of Rte 3.

***

Ann C.
wife of
George Freeman
who died July 4, 1851
Aged 60 yrs. 3 mo. & 2 days.

Colonel George Freeman
Died July 29, 1841
Aged 56 yrs. 8 mos. & 29 days.

Freeman Cemetery: 2.2 miles N. of Rixeyville on Rte 29; thence east .3 mile on private road.

***

Fannie Field	Anne P. Kelly
Died April 23, 1859	wife of John P. Kelly
In the 79th year of	Died Oct. 24, 1856
her age.	In the 60th year of
	her age.

Old Field Cemetery: 1.4 miles south of Remington on Rte 651; thence west 1 mile to Kelly's Ford; thence south .5 mile on Rte 620. East side of road.

***

John Farish
Born 1777
Died 1850

Ann Piper
wife of William
Robertson
Born 1778
Died 1814

Farish Cemetery: 1 mile northeast of Mitchell's on Rte 522; thence southeast on Rte 655; thence on Rte 647, 1.8 miles to entrance of Clairmont; thence on private road northeast .2 mile to house, thence west .2 mile to graveyard.

***

George son of
Fielding and Elizabeth Ficklin
Born Nov. 2, 1792
Died Oct. 15, 1852

Sacred to the
Memory of
Frances Ficklin
daughter of William Kennon, Ky.
wife of
George Ficklin
Born Nov. 4, 1796
Died Oct. 20, 1840

Sacred to the
Memory of
Evelina L. Ficklin
daughter of
Thomas Spindle, Va.
wife of
George Ficklin
Born July 25th, 1802
Died Jan. 12th, 1837

Ficklin Cemetery: West of Eggbornville 2.3 miles on Rte 49 turn north on Rte 627 for .9 mile on west side of road.

***

John Guinn
Born 1785
Died 1852

Guinn Cemetery: 2 miles N.E. of Winston on Rte 49; thence west of Rte 49 about 300 yards.

***

145

Tabitha Garnett
Died April 18, 1793
Aged 86 years 9 mo. & 5 da.

Mary Garnett
Born 1757
Died 1841
Aged 84 yrs. 2 mo. & 22 da.

Reuben Garnett
Born July 27, 1753
Died June 16, 1839
Aged 86 yrs. 11 mo. 19 da.

In memory of
Edmund Garnett
Born April 25, 1765
Died Sept. 11, 1826

Garnett Cemetery: 10 miles south of Culpeper on Rte 15; thence left on Rte 648; thence 8 miles to end of Mt.; thence 1.2 miles to cemetery.

***

Sacred to the memory of
Jeremiah Hall
Who departed this life
at Culpeper Courthouse
on the 24th day of Sept., 1840.
Aged 72

He was an affectionate husband
Kind father and sincere friend
Who passed through a long life
Without leaving an enemy behind.

Hall Graveyard: 2.2 miles southeast of Winston on Rte 617; thence north 1.8 miles on Rte 655; thence northeast 1 mile on Rte 656; thence .8 mile on private road.

***

In memory of
Thomas Hall, Sr.
Who departed this
life July 26, 1804
in his 58th year

In memory of
Elizabeth Hall
wife of
Thomas Hall, Sr.
Who departed this
life 2nd of Feby. 1817
in her 70th year

The sorrowing children of
Jeremiah Hall
have erected this monument
to the memory of their Uncle,
Thomas Hall
who departed this life
at Oakland, Culpeper County,
Virginia
on the 7th day of May, 1840
Aged 69 years

Fear not them which kill the body but not the soul,
Rather fear him which is able to
Destroy both soul and body in hell.

In Memory of
Our Mother
Judy Hall
who died March 14, 1849
in the 84th year of her age.

In her last moments she gladly committed
her spirit to the hands of her Redeemer
"Who had done all things well for her"
and entered as we believe into that rest
which remaineth for the people of God.

In memory of
Burgess Dayton Hall
only son of
Thomas and Elizabeth Hall
of Culpeper County, Va.,
Who departed this life
Oct. 11, 1833
Age 34 years and 19 days.

Sacred to the memory of
Mary G. Tongue
Who departed this life
February 15, 1833
In the 36th year of her age.
She was the daughter of
Jeremiah and Judy Hall
Who have erected this monument.

Sacred to the memory of
Elizabeth C. Norris
Who departed this life
May 7th, 1825
In the 26th year of her age.

In memory of
Jane Russell
Who died on the
20th day of June, 1828
Age 90 years

"Many were the days of her pilgrimage
And full of sorrow,
But they that sow in tears,
Shall reap in joy."

Hall Graveyard: 2.2 miles southeast of Winston on Rte 617; thence north 1.8 miles on Rte 655; thence northeast 1 mile on Rte 656; thence .8 mile on private road.

***

To the memory of
Mary Jameson
The beloved wife of
David Jameson
Who departed this life
The second day of July, 1802
In the 30th year of her life
Much regretted
By all her acquaintance
This monument is erected

Jameson Cemetery: 2 miles north of Culpeper on old Rte 49 on west side of road.

***

In memory of our Mother
Who fell asleep in Jesus
October 27, 1861
Aged 74 years
Erected by her children
B. H., S. E., J. A. and John R. Spillman

Thomas J. Sudduth
Born Oct. 30, 1789
Died Jan. 18, 1888

Mary Young
Consort of Benj. Young
Born Oct. 22, 1769
Died Sept. 23, 1809
May she rest in peace

Jeffersonton Baptist Churchyard: 15 miles N.E. of Culpeper, 100 yards E. of Jeffersonton on the south side of Rte 29.

***

Sacred to the
Memory of
Gabriel Jones
who died the 10th
July, 1835
in the 67th year
of his age.

In memory of
Kitty W. Thompson
who departed this life
Jan. 21, 1819
Aged 28 years

Kinloch Cemetery: 2 miles south of Culpeper, east side of Rte 15.

***

Mary Lewis
Wife of William Lewis
Who was born Feb. 4, 1767
Departed this life Oct. 18, 1828

Lewis Cemetery: 3 miles west of Culpeper on Rte 29; thence 1.6 miles northwest on Rte 642; thence private road 2 miles west to cemetery.

***

Capt. Reuben Gaines
Born 1765
Died 1847

Lucy Barbour Moore
Born June 26, 1771
Died October 8, 1837

Locust Hill Cemetery: 2 miles SW of Culpeper on Rte 29; thence south on private road .7 mile to cemetery.

***

1.   In Memory of General Edward Stevens who died Aug. the 17th 1820 at his seat in the county of Culpeper in the 76th year of his age.
This gallant officer and upright man had served his country with reputation in the field and senate of his native state. He took an active part and had a principal share in the War of the Revolution and acquired great distinction at the Battles of Great Bridge, Brandywine and Germantown, Camden, Guilford Courthouse and seige of Yorktown and although zealous in the case of American freedom, his conduct was not marked with the least degree of malevolence or party spirit. Those who honestly differed from him in opinion he always treated with singular

tenderness. In strict integrity, honest patriotism and immovable courage, he was surpassed by none, and had few equals.

2.   Sacred to the Memory of
Gilly Stevens
Widow of General Edward Stevens
and daughter of Robert Coleman, Esquire
Who died Dec. 4th 1820 at her
residence in Culpeper County
in the 74th year of her age

Such was the benevolence of this lady that she was never known to speak ill of her neighbor.

Possessing an ample fortune she used the bounties of Providence in dispensing blessing to the poor and destitute.

She was a devoted wife, affectionate mother, an indulgent and humane mistress, a kind neighbor and pious Christian.

It is believed that when her pure spirit left this for a better world, she had no enemy on earth and all who knew her lamented her departure.

3.   Sacred to the memory of
John Stevens
son of General Edward and Gilly Stevens
Who died February 8th, 1820
at his seat in the County of Culpeper
in the 55th year of his age.

He was an affectionate husband, indulgent master, a kind neighbor, and an honest upright man.

His death was much lamented by an extensive circle of friends and relatives.

4.   Sacred to the memory of
Edward Stevens, Jr.,
son of General Edward and Gilly Stevens
Who died March 14, 1795 in the
County of Culpeper in the 22nd year
of his age.

His polite and easy behavior insured distinction in every society. The warmth of his heart gained the affection of his friends. His sincerity their confidence and esteem.

Few persons ever died more lamented by their friends and neighbors. To his family and near relatives his death was a stroke most severe.

5.   Sacred to the memory of
Elizabeth Stevens
daughter of General Edward and Gilly Stevens
Who died in the year 1780 age 2 years.

6. Sacred to the memory of Mary Stevens, daughter of William Williams and wife of John Stevens who departed this life on the 11th day of May 1828 in the sixty-third year of her age, beloved and regretted for her exemplary piety and benevolence.

88.	Henry Miller
Born Nov. 1, 1796
Died Apr. 17, 1862

90.	Elizabeth, daughter of
William & Catherine Crigler
and wife of Henry Miller
Born Jan. 12, 1800
Died July 20, 1852

158.	In memory of
John Thompson
Born June 27, 1787
Died June 17, 1840
and his wife
Elizabeth Fleming
Born May 25, 1798
Died June 26, 1862
They also which sleep in Jesus
Will God bring with him.

   Masonic Cemetery: ½ mile N of Culpeper on Rte 685, east side of road.

***

Sacred to the memory of
Daniel Moffett
Who was born
January 30th 1765
and died
Sept. 2nd 1839

   Moffett Cemetery: 10.3 miles NW of Culpeper Court House; .5 mile E of Estes on Rte 49; thence ¼ mile E of house.

***

Martin Nalle
Died Dec. 2, 1843
Aged 66 years

Elizabeth M. Nalle
Died July 3, 1826
In her 42nd year

   Nalle Cemetery: 4 miles S of Stevensburg on Rte 663; thence W 100 yards to house. Graveyard adjacent to yard on north.

***

In memory of
John Puller
Born 27th August 1714
Married 23 April 1772
Departed this life
5th of March 1818

Think oh man as you pass by
As thou are now so once was I
As I am now so you must be
Prepare for death and follow me.

In memory of
Ann Puller
consort of
John Puller, dec'd.
Who departed this life
April 21st A. D. 1829
In the 80th year of her age.

"So death teach us to number our days that we may apply our hearts unto wisdom."

Puller Graveyard: 1 mile E of Amissville on Rte 211; thence N 100 yards.

***

Presley Rixey
Born Aug. 24, 1780
Died   1821

Rixey Graveyard: .7 mile W of Rixeyville on Rte 640; thence across field for ¼ mile.

***

John Read, Jr.
Born the 10th of September 1789
Died the 10th of November 1855

Sacred to the memory of
Mrs. Loy Read
consort of John Read, Jr.
Born in Fauquier Co. July, 1797
Died April 9, 1848

Read Cemetery: ¼ mile south of Jeffersonton on Rte 29; thence W across a field 150 yards.

***

Margaret Ann Glassell
wife of Wm. E. Glassell
and daughter of
James and Mary Somerville
Born Dec. 1800
Died Mar. 9, 1832

Mary E.
wife of
David E. Briggs
Died 1852
In her 80th year

Mary Somerville
Born Jan. 22, 1778
Died Feb. 14, 1845

James Somerville
Born in Glasgow, Scotland
Nov. 1774
Died Feb. 14, 1858

Family Cemetery at "Somer Villa" 3.2 miles SE of Winston on Rte 49; thence 1.5 miles E on Rte 647; thence .3 mile S on private road.

***

Mary Stringfellow
Died 1844
In the 65th year of her age

Robert Stringfellow
Died 1857
In the 85th year of his age.

Stringfellow Graveyard: 1 mile NE of Mitchell's on Rte 652; thence 21.7 miles SE of Rte 655; thence E on Rte 647 1.8 miles S by private road.

***

Here lies the body of
Martha Spilman, Deceased
September the 7th, 1771.

Spilman Graveyard: 9.5 miles NE of Culpeper Court House; 2.5 miles NE of Rixeyville on Rte 29; thence E 1.5 miles of Rte 624; thence N (left) on private road to house; thence .5 mile through field to cemetery.

***

In Memory of
Edward E. Tutt
son of
Richard Tutt and Mildred Tutt
who departed this life
Feb. 28th, 1771.

In Memory of
Mildred Tutt,
dau. of Lewis Tutt and Mary Connor
and consort of Richard I. Tutt
Who departed this life
May 15, 1837
Aged 61 yrs 2 mos 19 days

Tutt Graveyard: 6 miles NE of Culpeper on Rte 3; thence S 6 miles on Rte 634; thence SE .5 mile on private road to house; thence 500 yards W to cemetery.

***

No inscriptions on tombstones but the family Bible in the possession of Mr. Enoch Lewis in 1937 indicates that the following people, among others, are buried there:

William Wallis
Born Jan. 6, 1759
Died Mar. 19, 1831

Mildred Walker Wallis
Born Mar. 1, 1772
Died Aug. 6, 1794

Wallis Cemetery: 2.7 miles W of Culpeper on Rte 29; turn N on Rte 642 for 1.7 miles; turn W through gate.

***

Sacred to the memory of
Alice Grimes
relict of
William C. Williams
who was born in the county of
Gloucester
January 18, 1774
and departed this life
August 14, 1842

Williams Graveyard: .5 mile E of Culpeper on Rte 15; thence S .3 mile on private road to graveyard.

***

Sacred to the Memory of
John Wigginton, Senior
Who departed this life
Trusting in Jesus
April 27th 1825
Aged 84 years

Sacred to the Memory of
Elizabeth
wife of John Wigginton, Senior
Who departed this life
In the full assurance
Of faith in Jesus Christ
July 15th 1824

William W. Jones
Born August 20, 1783
Died March 11, 1835

Pencil notes by a descendant state that he was the son of Gabriel Jones.

Wigginton Cemetery: 1.7 miles N of Lakota on Rte 29; thence S about 100 yards to cemetery.

※※※

To the memory of
Thornton Wheatley
Born Nov. 5, 1793
Died May 3, 1852

Wheatley Cemetery: 4 miles NW of Rixeyville on Rte 640; thence SW .5 mile on Rte 627; thence .5 mile S on private road to house; thence ¼ mile E of house to graveyard.

※※※

Thomas Yancey 1752-1826
Sarah Mitchell 1778-1854
Parents of Charles L. Yancey 1801-1867

Major Yancey
Died 1849
In the 71st year of his age

Charles Yancey
Eighteenth Century
Married
Caroline Powers 1740
Parents of Kaleia, Ann, William,
Thomas, Charles Major, James II

※※※

Inscriptions from tombstones in the old Major graveyard located on a farm now owned by Mrs. Robert Settle (1959) east of the road between Amissville and Viewtown and about two miles south of Amissville. This farm is part of the farm formerly owned by William Major of Fairview and called "the Major Quarter."

(Note by the compiler: When the W. P. A. compiled the information on cemeteries in Culpeper Co., this cemetery was in the County of Rappahannock. Inscriptions of tombstones of those who were born before 1800 are included here because this graveyard was in Culpeper County when it was used first.)

John Corbin
Father of
Elizabeth T. Major
Died June 16, 1813
In the 66 year
of his age

Frances
wife of
John Corbin
Died
May 1, 1814

William Major, Sr.
Died March 19, 1847
in the 73d year
of his age

Our Mother
Elizabeth T.
Consort of
William Major, Sr.,
Died March 16, 1869
Aged 89 years 2 months
and 24 days
"A sinner who trusted
for redemption in Jesus only"

The Mortal Remains
of
Frances H. Larue
Who departed this life
on the 21st day of August
Anno Domini 1836
in the 55th year of her age
So affectionate a wife
So tender a mother
The memory of whose
Genius and Virtue
The grave can ne'er smother

These and later inscriptions in this graveyard are to be found in a typed copy of "The Majors of Virginia and Their Connections," by Julian N. Major, Sr., which was presented to the Culpeper Town and County Library in 1959 by Col. William Nalle of "Fox Hill," who wrote the Foreword and added three pages of inscriptions read in 1935 by him and members of his family.

INDEX

A

ABBETT
  Harwood 50
  Joseph 50
  Roger 15, 62
  William 50
ABBOTT
  Ann 85
  Ann (____) 27
  Richard 92
ABELL, Peter 25
ACRE, William 60
ACREE, Will. 70
ADAMS
  Henrietta 85
  Robert 4, 5
AHART, Abram 73
ALCOCK
  John 124, 125, 126
  Joseph 126
  Robert 18, 25, 30, 34
ALDERS, Francis 85
ALEXANDER
  George 57
  James 19
  Philip 133
  William 58
ALFORD, Elizabeth
  (____) 15
ALLAN
  Charles 116
  Elizabeth (____) 116, 117
  George 116
  James 116, 117
  James M. 92
  William 32
  William G. 116
ALLASON, Will. 70
ALLEN
  Benjamin 18
  Caty (____) 21
  Charles 109
  George 78
  James 85
  Joseph 37
  Judith (Peyton) 4
  Mary (____) 33

ALLEN (cont.)
  Mary Ann 130
  Thomas 21, 36, 52, 85
  Vincent 46, 54, 64
  W. C. 122
  William 10, 33, 35, 40, 49
  William G. 99, 123, 128, 130
AMISS
  Ann 85
  Ann (____) 66
  Philip 66
  Timothy 31
ANDERSON
  Augustin 67
  Eliza. 85
  George 53
  Isaac 56
  James 85
  John R. 106
  Richard W. 106
  Sarah (____) 56
  William 127
  William L. 101
  William S. 106
APPERSON
  Betty 80
  Francis 52, 79, 80
  John 82
  Nancy Kay 79
ARCHER
  James 20, 21, 34, 84
  John 31
  Mary (____) 132
  William B. 132
ARMISTEAD
  Bowles 57, 62
  Elizabeth 57
  John 57, 133
  Mary Ann (____) 57
  Mary Bowles 57
  Peter Fontaine 57
  William 57
ARMSTRONG
  J. N. 110
  John 137
  Joseph N. 107
ARNOLD
  James 45, 50, 51

ARNOLD (cont.)
  Margaret 11
  Nicholas 11, 12
ASCHER, John 31
ASHBY
  Alfred L. 90, 104, 135
  Alfred S. 91
  Charles William 101
  Lucy (____) 143
  William 95, 130, 143
ASHER
  Jeremiah 4, 32
  Peter Russell 4
  Waller B. 128
  Waller R. 107, 123, 129
  William 23
ASHFORD
  John 51
  Samuel 39
  Thompson 55
ASHLEY, John 8
ATKINS
  Ann 9
  Sharper 8, 9
ATTWOOD, James 4
ATWOOD
  Catharine (____) 44
  William 4
AUBERTHNOT, Thomas 51
AUTRAIN, Caleb 84
AVERY, Charles 64
AYLOR
  Henry 129
  Jacob 65
  James 129
  L___ 129
  Lucy 129
  Michael 129
  William 129

B

BACK, Henry 82
BAILEY, Washington 91, 96
BAILLEY
  Ann 31
  John 31

BAILS, Molly (___) 70
BAKER
  David 26, 30
  Henry 26, 45
  James 70
  John 30
  Nancy 45
  Thomas 5
BALL
  Burgess 77
  Frances 51
  Joseph 51
  Joseph, Jr. 51
  William 2, 8, 9, 13,
    14, 16, 29, 33, 34,
    44, 49, 51, 53, 58,
    71, 76, 77, 84
BALLARD
  Curtis 68
  Morman 11
BALLENGER
  Edward 31, 32
  Frances 31
  John 31
  Mary 31
  Susanna 31
BALLTHORPE, John 133
BALTHORPE, Sally 133
BANBEVER (See VAN BE-
  BER)
  John 31
BANKS
  Adam 50, 65, 68
  Henry 23
  John 23
  John F. 112
  Lynn 10
  Thomas 32
BARBEE, John 40, 42,
  43
BARBER
  Ambrose 32
  William 71
  William R. 92
BARBEY, John 67
BARBOUR
  Alfred M. 102, 135
  Ambrose 14, 22, 25,
    29, 37, 41, 51, 59,
    68 79
  Betty 14
  Calhoun 102, 135

BARBOUR (cont.)
  Edwin 102, 135
  Eliza 102
  Eliza A. 102, 135
  Eliza A., Jr. 135
  Frances 68
  James 3, 14, 16, 18,
    36, 68, 69, 77, 90,
    106, 109, 115, 135
  James, Jr. 9, 15, 102
  John S. 102, 135
  John S., Jr. 102, 106,
    135
  Mary 14, 68
  Mordecai 67, 68, 135
  Philip 14, 68
  Richard 14
  Sally 102, 135
  Sally (___) 135
  Sarah 68
  Sarah (___) 68, 77
  Thomas 14, 68
BARKER, James 28, 29
BARLER
  Adam 5
  Joshua 73
BARLOW
  Adam 61
  Adam N. 15
  Henry 38
BARNES
  Armitead 119
  Harriot 119
  Henry 119
  Henry, Jr. 118, 127
  Henry, Sr. 118
  John 75, 118, 120,
    122, 123, 127, 199
  Leonard 37, 85, 120
  Martin 118, 119, 120,
    121, 122, 127
  Rhoda 119, 127
  Rhoda (___) 119
BARNETT
  Benjamin M. 130
  Benjamin N. 131
  James 124
  John 64
  Judith A. 130, 131
BARNHYTH, Leonard 11
BARNS
  Elender 121

BARNS (cont.)
  Leonard 62
  Martin 128
BARON, Mary 37
BARRACLE, John 27
BARRAN, William 5
BARROW
  John 85
  Margaret 8
BASYE
  Elijah 85
  Ethelbert 85
  Joseph 79, 85
BATES
  Simeon 120
  William 3, 127
  William, Jr. 67
BAUGHAN
  Ann (___) 129
  Berryman 129
  Catherine 129
  Eve (___) 129, 130
  Fanny 129
  Henry 129
  Jane 129
  Jefferson 129
  Jeremiah 129
  Joel 129
  John 129
  Joseph Henry 129
  Lystra 129
  Margaret (___) 129
  Mordecai 11, 129, 130
  Moses 129, 130
  Newby James 129
  Sarah 129
  Simeon 129
  Stephen 60
  Susan 130
  Susanna 129, 130
  Susannah M. 129
  Vincent 129
BAXTER
  Alexander 4
  Will 31, 32
BEALE
  Rebecca (___) 133
  Reuben 35, 42
  Robert 125
  Samuel 133, 134
BEALL, Alpheus 41

BEAZLEY
  Alice 105
  Charles 105
  Thomas 105
BECK, Lucy (___) 68
BECKHAM
  Abner 85
  C. C. 123
  Coleman 100
  Coleman C. 101
  Elijah 85
  Kemp 90
BEEN, Richard 10
BELFIELD, Joseph 1, 13
BELL
  Alpheus 41
  Amelia (___) 134
  J. W. 100
  James M. 104, 134
  John 31
  John F. 109
  John M. 63
  John W. 103, 106
  William 33
BENGER, Eve (___) 70
BENSON
  Agnes B. 130
  Berry 130
  Enock Berry 131
  James R. 130, 131
  Judith A. 131
  Mary 131
  Willis 130, 131
BERRY
  A. 74, 76
  Aaron 24, 28, 38, 41, 54, 85, 112, 119, 120, 121, 123, 128
  Aaron, Jr. 127
  Abrey 38
  Acary 28
  Acre 74
  Acrey 32, 38
  Aere 31
  Airey 58
  Anna (___) 74
  Anthony 28, 32
  Aron 32
  E. 74
  Elijah 28, 32, 38, 41
  Elisha 24, 28, 31, 32, 119, 120, 123

BERRY (cont.)
  Elizabeth (___) 18
  Frances (___) 119
  Franky (___) 24, 123
  Jemima(-h) 28, 38
  John 28, 29, 32, 34, 38
  John S. 92
  Leonard 38
  Lucey (___) 24
  Lucy 123
  Lucy (___) 119, 120, 122, 123, 128
  Malchia(-h) 28, 32, 34, 38
  Mary 38, 120
  Mary (___) 74
  Merry 119, 122
  Philemore 120
  Philomil 119, 122
  Rhoda 120
  Sary 38
BICKERS
  ___ 97
  Alexander 139
  James 90, 94, 109, 110, 138
  Mary R. 139
BIGBIE, Archibald 51
BIRD, Mark 92
BIRK, Francis 70
BLACKBURN, Robert 11
BLACKWELL
  Benjamin 33
  Catey 33
  Catharine 85
  Elizabeth 33
  James 50, 52
  Joseph 33, 39
  Lucy 33
  Thomas 64
  William 102
BLAKE, John 7
BLAKEY
  A. B. 100
  A. R. 98
  Churchill 40
  Jane (___) 40
  John 40, 42
  John, Jr. 42

BLANKINBEEKER (BLANKEN-BAKER, BLANKENBEEK-ER, BLACKINBEEKER)
  ___ 38
  Ann Barbara 12
  Ann Margaret 12
  Balthasar 12
  Christeenah 35
  Christopher 7, 12, 35, 38
  Elizabeth 12
  Elizabeth (___) 82
  Ephraim 35
  Henry 32, 35
  Jacob 35, 37, 67
  John 35
  Jonas 35
  Lewis 35, 77
  Michael 82
  Samuel 67
  Zachariah 10
BLEDSOE
  Elizabeth (___) 57
  James 67
  William 1
BLUFORD, Simeon 32
BLUNT
  Betty 9
  Charles 9, 10
  Eloner 9
  Francis 9
  Mary (___) 9
  Sarah 9
BOALS
  James R. 85
  Kate R. 85
BOBO
  Absolom 38
  Amay (___) 58
BOGGESS, Joseph 2, 4
BOHANNON
  Am. 83, 84
  Ambrose 31, 34, 35, 66
  Ann (___) 34
  Ellick 68
  Elliott 34, 35, 71
  James 65
  John 34
  Joseph 124, 125
BOLEY, Elizabeth (___) 32

BOON(-E), Hezekiah 34, 51
BOOTEN (BOOTON)
  Ambrose 14, 65, 78
  Elenor (___) 18
  Hiram 124
  Jane S. (___) 124
  Judah 65
  Lewis 35, 65
  Mary 128
  Reuben 120, 128
  Richard C. 123, 124
  William 65, 66, 83, 123, 125
BOTTS, William F. 105, 108
BOULLEY, John 33
BOURN(-E)
  Andrew 76, 78
  Betsey 24
  Betsy 59
  George 11, 13, 24, 25, 59, 71
  Jane (___) 76
  John 13, 24, 76
  Lucey 24, 59
  Polly 76
  Salley 24
  Sarah 59
  William 76
BOWEN
  Edwin 103
  George 16
  James 105
  Robert T. 92
  William 77
  William A. 94
BOWERS
  Robert 101, 102, 103
  Robert A. 105
  Thomas 85
BOWIN, Francis 18
BOWMER, William 40
BOWYER
  Elizabeth (___) 142
  George 142
BOYD, James 14
BRADFORD
  Alexander 84
  Daniel 33
  Enoch 33
  John 4, 27, 33, 37, 42, 44, 46, 84, 85

BRADFORD (cont.)
  Mary 38
BRADLEY
  Absolom 40, 77
  Augustin 70
  Elizabeth (___) 70
  Lawrence 70
  Smith 119
  William 11, 32, 33, 118, 119, 121, 127
BRADY, John 101
BRAGG, William 18
BRANHAM
  James 29, 39, 62, 63, 65, 84, 85
  Robert 84
BRASFIELD, Sally (___) 71
BREEDING, Richard 9
BREEDLOVE
  Ann 127
  Churchill 118, 119, 120, 121, 122, 127
  Nancy 120, 122
  Nancy (___) 118, 119, 121
BRIAND
  Benjamin 36
  Bruenton 36
  Sarrah (___) 36
  Wilfre 36
BRIGGS, David E. 152
BROADUS (BROADES, BROADDUS)
  James 52, 66
  Milley 36
  Richard 36
  Sarah (___) 65
  Thomas 85
  William 34, 53, 68, 80
BROCKMAN, John 121
BROILE
  Matthias 15
  Michael 15
BROOCE, Christeene (___) 74
BROOKE
  Lawrence 57
  William 83
  William, Jr. 118, 126, 127

BROOKING
  Charles 29, 33, 50, 52
  John 50
  Robert 42, 50
  Samuel 42
  William 50
BROOKS
  James 13, 17
  Richard 5, 70
  Susanna 24
  William 73
BROWN
  A. M. 93
  Ann 33, 52
  Ann (___) 18
  Anne (___) 13
  Armistead 137
  Coleman 33
  Daniel 6, 19, 33, 34, 48, 53, 83, 128, 130
  Dixon 70
  Elizabeth 52
  Elizabeth (___) 33, 52
  Evan 57, 64
  Frances H. 130
  Frances H. (___) 138
  George 52
  Gideon 64
  Henry 52
  Hezekiah 13, 33, 52, 63
  James 52, 53, 64
  James F. 95
  James K. 93
  John 11, 30, 33, 37, 41, 43, 48, 59, 64, 66, 108, 129
  Joseph D. 92, 108
  Lettice (___) 37
  Mary 33
  Mary A. R. 137
  N. 66
  Nathaniel 11
  Nelly 13
  Pamaly (___) 92
  Pollard 35
  Rebecca 106
  Richard 33
  Robert 35, 83, 84
  Sarah 52
  Sarah (___) 64

BROWN (cont.)
  Susanna (___) 35
  Thomas 33, 34, 35,
    39, 43, 45, 64, 65,
    85, 108
  Thomas, Sr. 42
  Thomas C. 108, 129,
    138
  William 33, 70, 130
  William Ambrose 70
  William C. 66
  William H., Jr. 105
  William M. 93
BROWNE, William 131
BROWNING
  Caleb 4
  Charles 39, 52, 54,
    63, 72, 83
  Charles D. 133
  Edmond 12
  Frances 68
  Francis 68, 70, 71
  Jacob 17
  James 4, 27, 29, 43,
    44, 46, 55, 76,
    82, 83
  James, Jr. 43, 44
  John 45, 85
  Mary 74
  Nicholas 70
  Shadrach 37, 85
  William 37, 39
  William H. 107, 113
  William W. 133
BROYLE(-S)
  Dortha (___) 17
  Elizabeth 77
  John 32, 33, 58
  Margaret 77
  Margaret (___) 77
  Michael 77
  Moses 61, 73
  Nancy 77
  Rosanna 77
  Susanna 77
  Zachary 82
  Zachy 75
BRUCE
  Charles 8, 9, 13
  James 23
BRYAN
  James 50

BRYAN (cont.)
  Joseah 45
  Thomas 12
BRYAND, Thomas 36
BRYANT
  Mark 37, 45
  Thomas 13, 39
BUCHANAN, ___ 9
BUFORD
  Abraham 67
  James 67
  John 10, 67
  Simeon 67
  William 67
BUKUS, James 97
BULLARD
  Richard, Jr. 131
  Richard W. 131
BULLER
  John 16
  Mary 17
BULLITT
  ___ 9
  Cuthbert 47
BUMGARDNER, Adam 30
BUMGARNER
  Frederick 11
  Joel 11, 12
BURBRIDGE
  Esther (___) 57
  Hannah (___) 57
BURDINE
  Ann 119, 120
  Ann (___) 24
  Betty (___) 25
  John 31, 32
  Oridgal 119
  Original 120, 122
  Reginal 5, 24, 31
BURDITT, Frederick 5
BURDYNE
  Agnes 61
  Amos 61
  Ann (___) 123
  Benjamin 61
  Betty 61
  Betty (___) 61
  Catherine 61
  Catherine (___) 61
  John 61, 62
  Nancy 61
  Reginal 123

BURDYNE (cont.)
  Sarah 61
  Susanner 61
BURK
  Alexander 2
  Ann (___) 43
  John 5
  Mary 18
  Mitchell 26
  Robert 27
  Susannah (___) 64
BURNLEY, John 85
BURROUGHS, Jesse S. 95
BURTON
  Edmond 67
  William 67
BUSH
  Alex. 71
  Edward 15, 18, 21, 71
  Enoch 15
  Frances (___) 40
  Hezekiah 54
  Margaret 15
  Maximilian 15
  William 15
BUSHOP, Francis 9
BUTLER
  James 22
  John 2, 11, 12, 22,
    62
  Margret (___) 5
  Peter 7
  Susanna 22
  Thomas 22
  Walter 7, 12
  William 45
BUTT
  Alender 54
  Alender (___) 54
  Eleanor 85
  Elizabeth 54
  John 54
  Rose 54
  Samuel 54
  Thomas 54
  William 55
BUTTEN, Susannah 50
BUTTON
  James M. 107
  John 58
  Sarah (___) 44
BUTTS, William 54

BUTTUS, Joshua 107
BYRNE
  James 135
  Sally 135
  William 100
BYWATERS
  Elizabeth (___) 140
  John 140
  Robert 61
  Seena (___) 61
  Thomas 60, 70
  Winifred (___) 57

C

CADWALLADER, John 41
CALVERT
  Anna 76
  Cealius 76
  Delilah 76
  Elizabeth 76
  George 27, 43, 51, 54, 76
  George, Jr. 51
  George, Sr. 41
  Gettah 76
  Hannah 76
  Helen (___) 76
  John 29, 41, 51, 54, 76, 83
  Mary 51
  Peggy (___) 57
  R. S. 85
  Rall. 85
  Sarah 76
CAMBLE
  Isbell 14
  Owing 51
CAMBWELL, Elisabeth 37
CAMMEL, Joseph 75
CAMP
  Ambrose 21
  John 26, 29, 63
  Thomas 3, 11, 18, 26, 29
  William 16, 85
CAMPBELL
  Dr. 9
  Mr. 118
  Archibald 13, 25, 117
  Colen 51
  Daniel 32

CAMPBELL (cont.)
  Duncan 117
  Elias 3, 31, 32, 38
  Elizabeth (___) 66
  Isaac 27
  James 22
  John 31, 32, 38
  Joseph 123
  Margaret 31
  Margaret (___) 31
  Mary Elling 27
  Will 33
CANNADA, Catharine 53
CANNADY (CANADY, CANADAY)
  James 85
  Leeroy 48, 73, 75, 80
  Sarah (___) 49
  Thomas 50
CANNON
  John 85
  William 40
CAPPORT, Fredick 69
CARNAGEE (CANAGGEE, CARNAGGIE)
  David 43, 44, 45, 46
  Elender 43
  James 56
CARDER
  Ankay 26
  George 71
  James 17
  John 58
CARPENTER
  Andras 78
  Andrew 20, 38, 44
  Ann Barbara 44
  John 7, 43, 44
  Mary (___) 17
  Michael 44
  William 44
CARR
  Elizabeth (___) 53
  John 99
  Walter 53
  William, Jr. 99
  William, Sr. 98, 99, 100
CARSON, Jane M. 114
CARTER
  Charles 31, 39
  John 48, 51

CARTER (cont.)
  John Beverly 64
  Lunsford 80
  Susannah 62
  Thomas 10, 71
CARTY, William 25
CASPER, Peter 66
CASTALAS, Robert 85
CASTLE, Hawkins 70
CATLETT
  Alice 44
  George 44
  Kemp 44, 70, 73
  Lawrence 18, 25, 44, 49, 73
  Mary 44
  Mary (___) 44
  Nancey 44
  Sally 73
  Sarah 44
  Thomas 44, 73
CAVE
  Belfield 1, 13, 74, 122
  Ben 16
  Benjamin 1, 12, 79
  Elizabeth (___) 1
  John 12, 16, 32, 47
  William 11
CHADWELL, William 54
CHAMPE
  Mary (___) 54
  William 30, 41, 54
CHANEY, Riley 121
CHAPMAN
  Benjamin 116
  Erasmus 116
  Jno. 71
  John 41
  Thomas 32, 45, 112, 120
  Will 31
  William 10, 22, 25, 31, 61, 66, 68, 116, 119, 127
CHAVIERI, Shadrach 20
CHAVUE, Shadrach 28
CHEEK
  Elijah 101, 133
  Elisha 41
  Elizabeth 85
CHELF, Philip 58

CHEW
  John 47
  Thomas 129
CHICK, Francis 86
CHILD
  Ann 1
  Elizabeth 1
  Isable 1
  James 1
  Miner (____) 1
  William 1
CHILES
  Henry 53
  Susannah (____) 52
CHILTON
  Richard 37, 83
  Samuel 132
CHISHAM, Nancy (____) 24
CHISM
  Gabriel 63
  Richard 11
CHOWNING, William 79, 80
CHRISLER
  Elias 82
  George 82
  Henry 31, 32
CHRISMOND, R. E. 97
CHRISTIAL, George 10
CHRISTIAN, Edmund 90
CHRISTLER
  Adam 17
  Catharine 17
  David 17
  George 17
  Henry 17
  Leonard 17
  Michael 17
  Thebolt 17, 18
CHRISTOPHER
  Molten 68
  Morton 31, 69
CLAGETT, Henry 95
CLARK(-E)
  Ambrose 68, 75
  Ann 36
  Ann (____) 52
  Barsheba 120
  Barsheba (____) 119, 122
  Bathsheba (____) 127

CLARK(-E) (cont.)
  Elizabeth 4, 75
  Fanny 75
  George 68, 94, 97
  James 38, 48, 74, 75, 120, 127, 132, 133
  Joannah 75
  John 31, 75, 94, 95, 127, 128
  John N. 94
  Joseph 68, 75
  Larkin 68
  Lucy 75
  Mary 16
  Mary (____) 75, 84
  Molly 75
  Nancy 75
  Oliver 26, 39, 84
  Reuben 62, 68, 75, 119, 120, 122, 127
  Reuben J. 98
  Rhoda 75
  Robert 68
  Sarah 68
  Sucky 75
  Teasly Oliver 16
  Thomas 75
  William 48, 68, 75, 77, 79, 127
CLATERBUCK, William 32
CLAYTON
  Ann (____) 66
  George 6
  James B. 130
  Philip 1, 6, 66, 70
  Sam 82
  Samuel 2, 3, 5, 6, 23, 29, 35, 66
  Samuel, Jr. 2, 6, 11, 13, 16
  Samuel, Sr. 13, 18
CLERK
  Bathsheba (____) 24, 123
  George 63
  Reuben 24, 123
CLIFT
  Jemima 50
  William 50, 62
CLIFTON (CLIFFTON)
  Charles 15, 27, 37, 76

CLIFTON (cont.)
  Frances 15
  Mary 37
  Mary F. (____) 103
  Thomas 9, 13
CLINCH
  Barbary 19
  Gean 19
  Jacob 5, 19, 20
  Ledia 19
  Mary 19
  Rachel 19
CLORE
  Anne 57
  Elizabeth 13
  Frances 57
  George 57
  John 32, 57, 58, 60, 66, 68, 82, 83
  Katherine (____) 57
  Margaret 17
  Michael 32, 57, 58
  Milley 57
  Thomas 119, 120
CLUNT, Peggy (____) 70
COCHRAN(-E) (See COCKRANE)
COCK, Charles 23
COCKE, John C. 29, 41
COCKRANE
  Andrew 31
  Eleanor 77
  Elizabeth 77, 81
  John 77, 81
  Mary 77, 81
  Patrick 77, 79, 81
COFER, Joel 84
COFFER, Ambrose 67
COGHILL, John 132
COLBERT
  Patsy (____) 91
  William 91
COLE
  Daniel 134
  John 92
COLEMAN
  Ambrose 16, 21, 22, 47, 48, 62
  David J. 105
  Elizabeth 2
  Robert 11, 13, 18, 25, 47, 51, 82, 149

COLEMAN (cont.)
  Robert, Jr. 23, 31,
    32, 49, 71, 76, 84
  Robert Granville 105
  Thomas 9, 39
  Wyatt 9
  Wyatt 32
COLENS, Thomas 36
COLLINGS
  Francis 36
  James 36
  Jemimah 80
  John 36
  Margaret 36
  Mary 36
  Mary (____) 36
  Tandy 36
  Thomas 36
COLLINS
  Ann 34
  James 10, 34, 43,
    121, 122
  John 121, 129
  Marget 34
  Robert 5
  William 16, 22, 24,
    86
COLVIN
  Daniel 66, 139
  Gabriel C. 107
  James 103, 109
  James A. 105
  John 79, 81, 82, 107,
    132
  John R. 105, 108
  Mary J. 107
  Mason 16
  Mayson 3
  Sarah (____) 79
  Susan V. 107
  William 107
COMPTON
  Henrietta 86
  James 31
  Mary 77
  Sarah (____) 63
  Walter 73
  Zachariah 17, 77
CONN
  Sally (____) 65
  Thomas 4

CONNER
  Elizabeth 11
  John 11
  Lewis 42, 68, 73, 74,
    82, 84
  Mary 11
  Philemon 11, 12
  Rachel (____) 11
CONNOR, John 106
CONWAY, E. 98
COOK
  Caty 48
  Peter 32
  Sarah 37
COOLEY, Richard 82
COON, Joseph 61
COONES
  Elizabeth (____) 60
  Henry 50, 60
  Jacob 50, 56, 58, 60
  Joseph, Jr. 52, 56
  Mary (____) 60
COONS
  Joseph 5, 44
  Joseph, Jr. 44
  William, Sr. 141
  Winfield S. 90
COONZE, Joseph 61
COOPER
  Abraham 70, 71, 86
  Henreter 39
  John 33, 71
  Judith 54
  Layton 41
  Leroy 101
COPER, Grizzel (____)
    49
COPHER, George 67
COPPAGE, John 60
CORBIN
  Ann (____) 140
  Betsey 66
  Catherine 66
  Charles 66
  David 5, 19
  Elizabeth (____) 19,
    140
  Eliza F. (Jameson)
    103
  Frances (____) 66,
    155
  Francis 47

CORBIN (cont.)
  Garnett 126
  Harry 66
  Isaiah 126
  James 90
  Jane (____) 90
  Jean (____) 30
  Jeromiah 4, 79
  Jno. 71
  John 3, 4, 35, 39, 53,
    66, 71, 86, 155
  John, Sr. 66
  Lewis 63
  Lucy 66
  Lydia (____) 126
  M. 140
  Magdely 66
  Mitchum 139
  Nelly 126
  Sarah (____) 140
  William 4, 19, 66, 86,
    126, 139
  William, Sr. 66
CORDELL, George 48, 62
CORDER
  Elizabeth (____) 50
  Vincent 105
CORLEY
  Aquilla 78
  Curtis 78
  Drucylla 78
  Effie (____) 78
  John 78
  Manoah 3, 78
  Richard 78
CORNAGGEY, Ellender 5
CORNAGGIE, David 47
CORNELIUS
  Absolom 40, 61, 79
  Charles 40
  Milley (____) 40
CORTLY, Thomas 57
COTTON
  Edward 63
  Elizabeth 63
  James 63
  Jonathon 63
  Polly 63
COURTS
  Charles 43
  Elizabeth (____) 70
  John 43

COURTS (cont.)
  Mary 73
  Mary (___) 43
  Walter Hanson 43
  William 43, 45, 61, 73
COVINGTON
  Ann 47
  Elizabeth 49
  Frances 54
  Francis 45, 49, 53, 75
  Jael (___) 47
  John 101
  Lucy 49
  Margaret 86
  Richard 49
  Robert 41, 49, 54
  Robert C. 101, 106, 108
  Thomas 47
  William 49, 51, 52, 53, 54, 75
COWHERD
  Elisabeth 40
  Jonathan 3, 9, 14, 40, 67, 81
  Sarah Ann (___) 104
  Sarah E. (___) 113
  William 104, 113
COWNE
  Augustine 107
  Elizabeth (___) 107
  Robert 66, 72
  Sarah Watkins 66
  Thomas W. 107
COX
  Philip 17
  William 38
CRAIG
  Elijah 50
  John 10, 11, 13, 14, 72
  Robert 121
CRAIN
  James 60
  Jemimey 46
  William 51
CRANE, Amos 44, 60
CRASS, James 1
CRAWFORD
  Aaron 30

CRAWFORD (cont.)
  Betsey 30
  Charles 30
  Daniel 30
  David Strother 30
  George 30
  Gideon 34, 36
  Hannah 30
  John 30
  Lucey 30
  Mary 53
  Maryann 30
  Moses 30
  Nancey 30
  Oliver 34
  Peter 30
  Reuben 30
  Rosanna 30, 53
  Sarah (___) 30
  William 17, 30, 33, 36, 53
CREAL, Charles 31
CREMORE, Henry 31
CRIGLER
  Ann Elizabeth 105
  Catherine 140
  Catherine (___) 150
  Christopher 45, 58, 67, 76
  Jemima 82
  John 52
  Nicholas 75
  Nicholas, Jr. 82
  Ruben 32, 75, 77, 78, 82
  William 140, 150
CRIM
  Jacob 33
  John 5
  Margot 73
  Thurmon 4
  Ursley (___) 30
CRISLER (CHRISTLER)
  Benjamin 136
  George 53
  Henry 53
  Joseph 53
CRITTENDEN
  Mrs. 4
  Ann (___) 45
  C. T. 96
  Catherine 136

CRITTENDEN (cont.)
  Charles T. 96
  James 105
  John 27
  William 105, 136
  William C. 136
CROSS
  James 28
  Richard 9
CROSTHWAIT(-E)
  ___ 7
  Mildred 9
  Milley 3
  William 3
CROW
  Dennis 32
  James 32, 71, 74
  John 31, 32
CRUMM, Lewis 86
CRUMP
  Benjamin 51
  Catherine 138
  Hiram B. 117
  Margaret S. 117
CRUSER, Mary 86
CRUTCHER
  Coleman 29
  Hugh 29
  Robert 29
  William 29
CUBBAGE, Thomas 32
CUMMING, Samuel 114
CUMMINGS, John 133
CUMMINS
  John 134
  Margaret 134
CUNNINGHAM, William 31
CUNNINGHAME
  Ann (___) 81
  John 81
CURTIS
  Abraham 101
  Thomas 2

            D

DALTON, William 67
DANIEL
  Ann G. 141
  Elizabeth 6
  Samuel A. 105
  Simeon 51

DANIEL (cont.)
  Susanna 6
  William 70
  William S. 105, 128, 141
DANIELL, William 4
DARNOLD, David 5
DAVENPORT
  Birkett 21, 47, 70, 141
  Briskett 27
  Burkett 16
  Charles 22, 26, 29
  Eleanor 141
  Eleanor (___) 141
  Elizabeth 141
  Martin 9, 26
  Susannah 141
DAVIS
  Ann (___) 53
  Betty 43
  David 43, 44
  Fanny 43
  Isaac 48, 67
  Isaac, Jr. 68
  James 129
  Jessee 43
  Liddy 43
  Richard 43
  Thomas 43
  William 37, 43, 56, 59
DAVISS, Elizabeth (___) 40
DAWNEY (?DOWNEY)
  Alexander 58, 60, 78
DAWSON
  Bradford 136
  K___ 136
DAY
  Amry 4, 71
  Edward 93
  Georgia P. 114
  James B. 114
  John 122
  William 4
DEAL (or DEEL)
  Elisabeth 38
  John 34, 38
  Peter 31, 38

DEATHERAGE (DEATHE-RIDGE)
  George 22
  Mary (___) 22
  Philemon 22
  Robert 22
  Susanna 22
  Thomas 22, 76
  William 22
DECAMP
  Mildred 102
  Samuel 102, 133
DEDMAN, Samuel 67
DEER
  Catharine 35
  Catron (___) 11
  Elisabeth 35
  John 35, 65
  Mary 35
  Moses 35
DEERING
  Anthony 9, 11
  John 14
DELANY (See DULANY)
  John 9
  Joseph 32
  Nancy (___) 67
  William 13, 58
  Zachariah 64
DELP
  Michael 20
  Samuel 32
DELPH
  Conret, Sr. 53
  Henry 53, 82
  Samuel 86
DICKEN(-S)
  Benjamin "Ben" 25, 29, 31, 32, 128
  Charles 29
  Christopher 25, 31, 42, 128
  Daniel 29, 128
  Delia 120, 122, 123
  Delia (___) 119
  Delilah 123
  Delilah (___) 24
  Ephraim 61, 62
  Isaac 29
  John 31, 61
  Joseph 61

DICKEN(-S) (cont.)
  Mary 31, 32
  Richard 25, 31, 42
  Sarah 25
  William 24, 25, 31, 41, 62, 119, 120, 122, 123, 128
  Winifred 28
DICKERSON, Elizabeth (___) 33
DIGGES, Edward 101
DILLARD
  Ann 86, 141
  George 79, 80, 81, 82
  James 79, 81, 82
  John 12, 33, 53, 58, 75, 76, 79, 81, 82, 86, 141
  Major 10, 79
  Mary (___) 57
  Samuel 79, 81, 82
  Sophia 33
  William 10, 42
DILLEN, Thomas 64
DIXON
  John 8
  Roger 9
DOGAN
  Elizabeth 106
  Henry 103, 131
DOGGET(-T)
  Bushrod 3, 12, 22, 26, 52, 55, 58
  George 65, 75
  Reuben 48
  Richard 39
DOORES
  Edgar 90
  Phoebe 90
  William I 90
DORES
  Charles 30
  Elizabeth 30
DOSS, Edward 16
DOUGLASS, Benjar 59
DOWDALL, Mary 86
DOWDY, Thomas 70
DOWELL, Ambrose 67
DOWNEY, Alexander 61, 86
DRISDLE, Sarah (___) 45
DUFF, William 2

DUKE
  John 86
  William 86
DULANY (DULANEY)
  Benjamin 40
  French C. 91
  John 23, 86
  Joseph 23
  Mary 91, 109
  Mary (___) 41
  William 9, 11, 19,
    29, 39, 52, 63,
    67, 71
DULING, Edmund 45
DUNAWAY, Isaac 86
DUNCAN
  Charles 37, 75, 79,
    81, 82
  James 19, 33, 37,
    41, 86
  James M. 108
  John 9, 37
  Joseph 37, 63, 60
  Liza (___) 79
  Lucy (___) 78
  Rawley 37, 70
  Rice 17, 70
  William 19, 37, 39,
    70, 71, 78
  William, Jr. 33
DUNCANSON, James 32, 70
DUNCASON, James 13
DUVAL(-L)
  Ann F. 98, 99
  Ann F. (___) 100
  Henry 48, 74, 80
  James 22, 52, 74, 75
  John P. 98, 100

E

EARLY (or EARLEY)
  Jacob 64
  James 68
  Jane (___) 64
  Jeremiah 64, 65, 67
  Joel 31, 35, 40, 42,
    64, 67, 68
  Joseph 3, 20, 26, 43,
    50, 51, 64
  Joseph, Jr. 26
  Joshua 68

EARLY (cont.)
  Julianer 50
  Mary 50
  Paschal 50, 64
  Whitefield 50
  Whitfield 64
  William 50, 64
  William S. 100
EASLEY, Joseph 42
EASTEN, Richard 9
EASTHAM
  George 22
  Philip 22, 51
  R., Jr. 10, 25
  Robert 12
  Robert, Jr. 22
  Sarah (___) 57
  William 10, 69
EDDINS, Joseph 62
EDGAR, Susanna(-h) 19,
  20
EDGE, Lott. 86
EDINS
  Joseph 67
  Sarah (___) 40
EDMUNDS, William 74
EDWARDS
  Barbary 62
  Barbary (___) 51
  Elizabeth (___) 51
  George 51
  John 13, 28, 51, 54
  Mary 51
  Peggy 86
  Robert 51
  Thomas 74
  Will. 71
EDZARD, William 83
EGGBORN
  Ann 86
  George 91, 133, 142
  Harriet 142
  J. S. 95
  Jacob 86
  Jacob S. 94, 95, 104
  John H. 112
  Perry J. 91, 105, 109
EHART
  Abraham 74
  Abram 73
  Adam Michal 74
  Jacob John 74

EHART (cont.)
  John 74
  Katharine (___) 74
  Michael 74, 75
ELIAGLE, John 5
ELKIN, Benjamin, Jr. 74
ELKINS
  Benjamin 35, 53
  David 10
ELLY, Henry 36, 41, 64
EMBRY, Joseph 94
EMISON, William 95, 103,
  106, 109, 131, 133,
  134
EMMONS, James 134
ENGLISH, James A. 91
EPHRAIM, Job 37
ESTES
  Coleman 29
  Elisabeth 26
  Elizabeth (___) 29
EVANS, William 77
EVE, George 67, 80
EWALD, Charles 69

F

FAIRFAX, George William
  30
FANT, George 66
FARGESON
  Ann 6
  Ann (___) 6
  Benjamin 6
  Elizabeth 6, 13
  Elizabeth (___) 6
  Francis 6
  Samuel 6, 11, 12, 29,
    31, 71
  Susanna 6
FARGISON, William 10
FARISH
  ___ 97
  Benjamin 108
  John 144
  Thomas 63
FARMER
  Daniel 42, 57, 64, 86
  John 42
FARRER, Daniel 100
FAVER(-S)
  Alice 47

FAVER(-S) (cont.)
  Elizabeth (___) 77
  Frances 47, 82
  Henrietta 47
  Isabel(-la) 47, 77, 82
  Isabell (___) 47
  John 49, 76, 80, 82
  John, Sr. 47
  Rosanna 47, 82
  William 25, 47
FENNELL
  John 122
  Jonathan 48, 55
FERGUSON, Samuel 8
FICKLIN (FICKLEN)
  Eliza A. 86
  Elizabeth (___) 144
  Evelina L. (___) 144
  Fielding 86, 144
  Frances (___) 144
  George 106, 107, 144
  Gustavus S. 105, 110
  Joseph E. 105
  Sarah 86
  Susanna (___) 75
FIELD
  ___ 107
  Abner 15
  Abraham 15, 16
  Abram 14
  Albert 93, 107
  Anna 14
  Anna (___) 14
  Anne (___) 41
  Benjamin 40, 59
  Daniel 6, 14, 15, 36, 40, 41, 45, 67, 125
  Dianah 67
  Elianah (___) 15
  Elizabeth 23, 67
  Ezekiel 14
  Fannie 143
  Frances 108
  Francis 109
  George 67, 72, 76
  Hannah (___) 41
  Henry 15, 23, 25, 54
  Henry, Jr. 2, 15, 16, 20, 21, 41, 52, 64, 67, 72, 73
  Henry Wm. S. 67

FIELD (cont.)
  J. 125
  J. Y. 91
  James G. 91, 93, 104, 107, 109, 112, 113
  Jenny 15
  John 14, 15, 29, 50, 67, 71, 76
  Joseph 67
  Judith 23
  Larkin 14, 35, 50
  Lewis Y. 112, 113
  Mary 67
  Mary (___) 67
  Molley 67
  Nancy 67
  R. H. 93, 99
  Reuben 15, 41, 76
  Richard H. 95, 98, 99, 100, 104, 107-8, 120, 127
  Sarah 67
  Sarah (___) 72
  Suze 67
  Thomas 67
  William 2, 3, 14, 15, 23, 30, 41, 42
  William H. 93
  William S. 130
FINCHAM
  John 17
  Judith 120, 122
  Judith (___) 119
FINKS (FINKE)
  John 86
  Mark 9, 31, 75, 78, 82, 84
FINNELL
  Elijah 62, 64
  Frances (___) 62
  John 56, 62, 73
  Reuben 41, 51
FINNEY, James 49
FISHBACK
  Elliott 86
  Frederick 7, 44, 45, 101
  Harmon 49
  Jacob 27, 49
  John 56, 61
  Martin 86
  Mary 44, 86
  William G. 104

FISHER
  Adam 9, 31
  Barbara (___) 9
  Barnett 9, 38
  Daniel 69
  Elias 31
  Lewis 9, 10, 12
  Samuel 128, 129
  Steven 9, 31, 41
FITZGERALD, James H. 103
FITZHUGH
  George, Jr. 116
  George T. 94
  Thomas 91
  William H. 98
FITZPATRICK
  Edmund C. 124
  Edward C. 123, 124, 125
  John 55
FLEMING, William 54
FLESHMAN
  John 52, 67
  Moses 35
  Reuben 35
  Robert 52
FLETCHER
  Dorothy (___) 35
  Francis 36, 41
  John 40, 83, 86
  Nanny (___) 36
  Patterson 10, 40, 47, 58, 63, 83
  Thomas Clark 47
FLINT
  Elisa W. (___) 104
  Eliza W. (___) 113
  John 34
  Richard 34, 55
  Thomas 91
  Thomas O. 90, 92, 97, 98, 102, 104, 106, 107, 110, 113
FLOWRENCE, William 32
FLOYD
  Jane 4, 21
  Jane (___) 1
  Henry 67
  John 1, 4
  Robert 6, 15, 67
FLYNT
  John 24, 37
  Richard 37, 49

FONTAINE, William 57
FORBES
  John M. 98
  Murray 103
FOREACUS, Herekiel 86
FORREST
  George W. 108
  June (___) 108
FORSYTH, Kate G. 114
FOSHEE (FOOSHEE, FOU-
    SHEE)
  Aphia (___) 27
  Benjamin 27
  Charles 27, 62
  Elizabeth 27
  Frances 61
  George 27, 62
  Hannah 27
  James 69
  John 27, 28, 40, 86,
    98
  John W. 94
  Joseph 27
  Philip 61
  Susannah (___) 61
  Thomas A. 93, 99, 107
  Thornton 27, 62, 129
  William 27, 61, 62,
    75
FOSTER, Anthony 67
FOX
  ___ 9
  Anthony 70
  Henry 107
  John 70
  John Peter 70
  Joseph 70
  Mary Ann (___) 70
  Matthias 70
  William A. 93
FRAY
  Aaron 82
  Anne 82
  Elizabeth 82
  Ephraim 82
  John 82, 83
  Marget 82
  Mary 82
  Rebekah 82
FRAZIER, Alexander 10
FREEMAN
  Ann (___) 79

FREEMAN (cont.)
  Ann C. 105, 108
  Ann C. (___) 104,
    143
  Archibald 107, 129
  Daniel G. 112, 113
  Elizabeth 56
  Frances 56
  Gabriel 122, 129
  George 56, 76, 77, 143
  Harris 10, 96
  Hered 70
  Hugh 10
  Ignatius 29
  James 19
  James H. 108
  John 25, 28, 40, 47,
    63, 77
  John H. 103, 121
  John Holmes 122
  John Hoomes 102, 128,
    129
  Mary 56
  Robert 81
  Robert, Jr. 79, 82
  S. A. 112
  Susanna (___) 76
  Thomas 56, 76, 86
  Thomas C. 130
FRENCH, Samuel 9
FRILAS, Henry, Jr. 11
FROGG
  John 3
  Mary (___) 26
FUGATE, Martin 17
FULTON, Mark 41
FULVY, Daniel 100
FUSHEE, John 13

G

GAAR
  John 36
  Lewis 21, 84
  Michael 18, 53, 66,
    69, 71
GAINES (or GAINS)
  Alexander 29
  Ben 34, 35, 39, 55,
    61
  Benjamin 10, 11, 22,
    23, 43

GAINES (cont.)
  Betty 16
  Catharine 29
  Dolly 71
  Doratha 62
  Doratha (___) 62, 63
  Dorothy 16
  Dorothy (___) 16
  Edmond 67
  Edmund 78
  Edwin R. 94
  Eliza 111
  Elizabeth Ann 29
  Esther 29
  Francis 7, 13, 16,
    18, 46, 64, 71
  Francis Thomas 65
  Hannah 29
  Harry 65
  Henry 51, 66, 77, 84
  Humphrey 29
  Isabella 65
  James 16, 23, 29, 35,
    39, 47, 60, 61, 62,
    64, 65, 71
  Joseph 62, 65
  Lucy 16
  Mary (___) 65
  Mildred (___) 34
  Molly 29
  Reuben 106, 118, 148
  Richard 6, 10, 22,
    23, 27, 29, 31, 38,
    62, 82, 86
  Richard Emund 65
  Richard George 60
  Robert 24
  Rowland 54
  Ruth 21
  Salley 16
  Sarah 29, 43
  Sarah (___) 29, 80
  Susanna 16
  William 13, 23, 24,
    25, 27, 29, 32, 43,
    48, 65, 81, 82
  William H. 111
GAITSKILL
  Henry 54
  Mary 54
GAMBILL
  Thomas 26
  William 26, 71

GARNER
  Charles 48
  Elizabeth (____) 56
  Jonas 56
GARNETT
  A. G. 96
  Anthony 4
  Edmund 145
  Eleanor 78
  Eleanor (____) 77
  Elizabeth 96
  Elizabeth (____) 45
  Etheline 96
  Florence C. 96
  James 65
  James, Jr. 132
  Jeremiah C. 96
  John 4, 27, 65
  Mary 145
  Reuben 145
  Rhoda 118
  Rhoda (____) 122, 127, 128
  Robert 4, 55, 58, 78, 118, 120, 122, 127, 128
  Sarah 4
  Tabitha 145
  Thomas 27, 58, 61, 65
GARR
  John 31
  Lewis 32
  Michael 21, 31
GARRARD, William 78
GARRELL
  James 83
  Jeremiah 83
GARRET
  John 31
  Jonathan 32
GARRIOT(-T)
  John 37
  Jonathan 32
  Moses 32
  Thomas 9, 34
GARROTT, John 62
GARWOOD, John 83
GATEWOOD
  John 43
  Peter 13, 25, 27
  Philip 30

GAUNT, Catharine (____) 126
GEE, Mary Emily 114
GEORGE
  Cumberland 138
  Elizabeth Churchill 139
  Elmore 17
  Henry 59, 60, 77
  William 50, 51
GIBBS
  Francis 10, 47
  John 10, 13, 32, 35, 51, 66, 83
  Julius 34
  Mary (____) 10
  Sarah 10
  Zachariah 11, 73
  Zacharias 10, 11, 40
GIBRON, Shackleford 93
GIBSON
  Abfia 42
  Abraham 33, 42
  Ann 42
  J. C. 98, 100, 114
  Mary G. 114
  Thomas G. 100, 109
GILDART, James 13
GILLISON, John 52
GINN, Thomas 64
GINNENS, Joshua 70
GLANDENING, Jno. 17
GLASS, William 1, 13, 38
GLASSELL
  Andrew 31, 62, 142
  Ann (____) 152
  Elizabeth (____) 142
  John 13, 30, 105, 109, 117, 118, 142
  Margaret C. 105, 109
  William E. 152
GLOVE, Michael 82
GOAR, Adam 17
GOLDING, William 4
GOODWIN, Susanna Anne 30
GORDON
  Albert S. 113
  Alexander Y. 113
  Bettie 113
  Church G. 113

GORDON (cont.)
  Churchill 78, 83
  Elizabeth (____) 63
  Fanny 113
  Francis 91, 96
  John 63, 91, 101, 117
  John G. 113
  John H. 113
  Joseph F. 91, 101
  Lucy A. (____) 113
  Margaret R. 91, 101
  Martinetta 113
  Mary 63
  Nannie 113
  Sarah 91, 96, 101
  Susan 113
  Wellington 113
  William 63
GORE, Janet (____) 16
GORREL, Solomon 67
GRAHAM
  Alice (____) 81
  John 81
GRANT, William 72
GRASTY, Ann (____) 24
GRAVES
  Ann (____) 32, 58
  Edward 32, 53, 67
  Isaac 53
  James 8, 22, 33, 34, 35, 37, 71
  John 6, 24, 32, 34, 52, 53, 67, 82
  Lucy 6
  Sarah 34
  Sarah (____) 32
  Thomas 3, 11, 31, 37, 53, 62, 79
  Thomas, Jr. 11, 37
GRAY
  Ann (____) 70
  Dorothy 72
  Gabriel 71, 72, 77, 101, 106
  George 50, 58
  George D. 91, 95, 96, 106
  Jane (____) 21
  John 2, 5, 6, 8, 9, 13, 14, 16, 21, 27, 29, 34, 37, 71, 77
  Mary 70, 72

GRAY (cont.)
  Nathaniel 102
  Peggy 72
  Sallie W. 92
  W. 92
  William 49, 71, 72, 77
GRAYSON
  Frances (___) 74
  James 38
  Will 31
  William 38
GREEN
  Aaron 87
  Ann (___) 59
  Armistead 15
  Betty (___) 21
  Caleb 15
  Duff 2
  Edward 106, 130
  Eleanor Duff 59
  Elizabeth 81
  Frances (___) 74
  Francis Wyatt 56
  Gabriel 75, 80
  George 122
  Henry 59
  J. C. 99
  James 3, 16, 21, 34, 59, 87
  James, Jr. 75
  James W. 92, 104, 107
  John 2, 9, 10, 16, 59
  John C. 92, 98, 99, 100, 106, 107, 108, 109
  Lucy 51
  Mary 15
  Moses 30, 132
  Nancy 107, 109
  Nicholas 28
  Robert 2, 6, 8, 15, 32, 74, 76, 132
  Susanna Elizabeth 74
  Thomas 15
  William 2, 17, 28, 33, 54, 55, 59, 90, 98, 101, 102, 103, 108, 109, 117, 130, 132

GREENLESS
  Elisabeth 28
  James 28
  Jemima 28
  Mary 28
  Peter 28
  Simon 28
  William 28, 30
GREENWOOD
  ___ (___) 23
  Ellenor (___) 15
  John 15
GREGG, Roberts 86
GREGORY
  Abraham 5
  William 4
GRIFFEN (GRIFFIN)
  Ann (___) 68
  Anthony 45
  Anthony W. 106
  Elizabeth (___) 45
  James M. 90, 106
  John N. 106
  Thomas 11, 12, 45, 48
  Thomas J. 106
  Zachariah 45
GRIFFITH
  Able 80
  James 11
  John 51
GRIGORY, Abraham 11
GRIGSBIE, William 51
GRIGSBY, John 13, 55
GRIMSLEY, William 4, 17
GRINNAN
  Daniel 18, 24, 25, 28, 42, 62, 64, 75, 117, 129
  James S. 91, 99
  Jane J. 24
  John 24, 82, 102
GUINN
  Farish 112
  John 103, 144
GULLY, William 41
GUSTINE, Joel 59

H

HABLER, Nanny 16
HACKLEY
  ___ 9

HACKLEY (cont.)
  Fanny (___) 24
  Francis 9, 11, 25
  James 8, 10, 18, 29, 39
  John 8, 44, 77
  Judith 8
  Richard 6, 8, 9, 13, 14
  Samuel 8
HAGAN, James 60
HAINES
  Carlile 51
  Ezekiel 108
  Isaac 51, 87
  Jacob 41, 51
  John 108
HALL
  Burgess Dayton 146
  Elizabeth (___) 145, 146
  Jeremiah 145, 146
  Joseph 131
  Judy 146
  Judy (___) 146
  Thomas 146
  Thomas, Sr. 145
  William 23
HALSEY, Joseph J. 106
HAMMET, William 19
HAMMETT, George 26
HANBACK
  Catharine 60
  Jacob 60, 61
  John 60
  Susanna 60
HANDLEY, Susannah 68
HANES
  Abraham 39
  Carlile 39
  Ezekiel 39
  Isaac 39
  Jacob 39
HANEY, Charles 82
HANIE, John 13
HANSBROUGH
  A. H. 122
  Alexander H. or K. 104, 130
  Bleecher W. 94, 95
  James 104, 134
  Marius 104, 130

HANSBROUGH (cont.)
  Peter 104, 116, 117, 134
  Peter, Jr. 116
  Thomas C. 133
  Thomas D. 130
  William 87, 104, 116
  William H. 104, 133
HANSFORD
  Lucy 10
  Sallis 9
  William 13
HARBISON
  John 11
  Matthew 12
HARDEN, George 68
HARRELL, Mary (___) 65
HARRIS
  James O. 95
  Patty 78
HARRISON
  Benjamin 51
  Frances (___) 80
  James 80
  John 80
  Philip 94, 131
  Reuben 80
  Richard 80
  Thomas 31, 33
HARRISS, Abigale 64, 67
HART, Ephraim 18
HARVEY
  Frances 31
  Francis 32
  Joel 64
  William 35, 65
HARVY, Frank 67
HATLER, Sebasten(-ian or -ine) 2, 11, 18
HAWKINS
  Ann (___) 76
  Ben 54
  Benjamin 87
  Elizabeth (___) 76
  Jane (___) 76
  Mathew 71
  William 3, 9, 13, 22, 27, 33, 63, 77
  William, Jr. 21
HAYNES
  Anne 39
  Ben 31

HAYNES (cont.)
  Benjamin 25, 39, 52
  Carlisle 54
  Ezekiel 41
  Isaac 41
  James 39, 52
  Jasper 31, 36, 39, 42, 52
  Joseph 36, 39, 52
  Mary 39, 52
  Moses 52
  Stephen 31, 39, 52
  William 39, 52
HAYNIE, Anthony 87
HAYWOOD, George 32
HEAD
  Benjamin 12, 76, 79
  George 65
  Grace (___) 76
  Hadley 49, 73, 75, 83
  Henry 47
  James 68
  John Alfred 61
  Mary 83
  Mildred 83
HEADEN, William 97
HEATH, Mildred 87
HELM, William 107
HELTON, John 117
HENDERSON
  ____ 68
  Joseph 58
  Thomas 29
HENDSON, Charles 32
HENING (or HENNING)
  David 5, 7, 18, 24, 27, 35, 48, 64, 71
  Elenor 27
  Elenor (___) 27
  James 27, 35
  Joanna 27
  Nancy 27, 35
  Nelly 35
  Sally 27, 35
  Samuel 7, 11, 20, 23, 27, 35, 54, 71
HENRY
  Beverly 130
  Beverly W. 97
  Brice M. 97

HENRY (cont.)
  Bushrod W. 97
  Elvira 97
  Fountain F. 102, 106, 107, 130
  James O. 97
  Peyton W. 97
HENSELEY (HENSLEY)
  Agness 49
  Elizabeth 32
  Ellener (___) 49
  Joseph 31
  Robert 32, 51, 54
  William 19, 67
HENSHAW, John 66
HENSON
  Catherine (___) 3
  Charles 3, 4, 11, 31, 32
  Elizabeth (___) 3
  James 4
  Will 31
HERMAN, Dr. 70
HERNDON
  C. 98
  Edward 48, 58, 73, 74, 80
  John 47
  John M. 98, 131
  Mary (___) 34, 65
  Susanna (___) 74
  William 31, 32
HICKERSON, William 87
HICKMAN
  David 28
  Edwin 2, 28, 71
  Henry 28, 41
  James 2, 12, 28, 51, 59
HIGGASON
  Benjamin 92, 94
  Catharine (___) 92
  Esther 92, 94
  William 92
HILL
  A. P. 105, 114
  Ambrose P. 107, 109, 113
  Ann 5
  Ann (___) 73
  Anne (___) 74
  Betty 6

HILL (cont.)
  Betty (____) 5
  Charles 5
  Clarence 114
  E. B. 113, 114
  Edward B. 91, 107, 108
  Edward B., Jr. 113
  Edward L. 114
  Edward T. 104
  Edwin F. 108
  Elisa 113
  Elizabeth (____) 104
  Elwin F. 113
  Eva B. 111
  Eveline 114
  F. E. (____) 104
  F. T. 113
  Fanny 113
  George 5
  Gillie M. 114
  H. 69
  Henry 7, 11, 37, 38, 54, 65, 73, 82, 94, 100, 107, 113
  Henry, Jr. 102, 106
  Isabella (____) 36
  J. Frances (____) 104
  James H. 113
  Jenny 36
  John 14, 21, 36, 37, 64
  John W. 113
  Joseph 5
  Leroy 5, 41
  Louisa V. 113
  Lucy F. 104
  Lucy Lee 114
  Lydia 36
  Maria T. 113
  Mary 36
  Mildred A. 113
  Russell 3, 56, 65, 114
  Thomas 91, 96, 105, 106, 107, 109, 113
  Thomas, Jr. 104, 105, 106, 109
  Thomas J. 113
  Thomas R. 114
  Thomas T. 113
  Wesley 103

HILL (cont.)
  William 7, 11, 19, 37, 56, 87
  William A. 104, 108, 109, 113
  William H. 110
HILTON
  Ann 131
  George 131
  Henry 131
  John 103, 131, 132
  Robert 131
  Susan 131-2
  Susannah (____) 131
  William 131
HINNINS, Joshua 1
HISLE, John 75
HITE, Henry, Jr. 101
HITER, Isaac 143
HITT
  Agatha (____) 43
  E. B. 113
  Henry 52
  Joel 113, 129
  John 50
  Joseph 24
  LeeRoy 41
  Nancy 139
  Russell 43
HODWAY, Timothy 4
HOFFMAN, Henry 67
HOG
  James 80
  Mary 80
HOLDAWAY, John 11
HOLDWAY
  Abigail 81
  Ann(-e) 47, 81
  Elizabeth 81
  Phebe 81
  Timothy 11, 13, 47, 81
HOLLENBACK, Daniel 67
HOLLOWAY, Thomas S. 117
HOOE, Bassil 41
HOOFMAN
  Dilman 7
  Elizabeth 7
  Frederick 7
  George 7
  Henry 7
  Jacob 7
  John 7

HOOFMAN (cont.)
  Margaret 7
  Mary 7
  Mary (____) 7
  Michael 7
  Nicholas 7
  Paul 7
  William 7
HOOMES, Christopher 56, 58
HOOTON, Robert 80
HOPPER
  John 5
  Mary Ann (____) 50
  Thomas 81, 87
  William 12, 18
HORD
  Ambrose 48
  James 84
  James, Jr. 59
  John 48
HORNER, William 129
HOUSE, Matthias 52
HOUSTON, William 47
HOWARD, Thomas M. 130
HOWISON, Dr. Thomas 57
HUBBARD, Mary (____) 24
HUDNALL, John 29
HUDSON
  Abner 95
  Elizabeth V. 94
  Enoch M. 94
  Enoch W. 95
  Ezekiel 94, 95, 97
  Ferdinand 94
  Henrietta 4
  James 94
  Jeremiah 107
  John D. 91
  John H. 94
  Reuben 128
  Richard 64
  Robert 107, 132
  William 94
HUFFMAN (HUFMAN, HUPH-MAN)
  Adam 67
  Alice 50
  Alse (____) 49
  Ambrose 67
  Barbary (____) 53
  Catharine 50

HUFFMAN (cont.)
 Elizabeth 50
 Elsibeth 50
 Eve 50
 Felix 109
 Felix S. 107
 Henry 10, 50
 Herman 50
 James 50
 John 7, 49, 50
 Joseph 50
 Margaret (___) 50
 Mary 50
 Michael 32
 Susanna 50
 Thomas 50
 Tilman 50, 83
HUGHES (HUGHS, HUSE)
 Anthony 11, 31, 41,
  45, 52, 53, 75
 Jemima (___) 119,
  120, 122, 123
 John 24, 31, 32, 61,
  119, 120, 122, 123
 John, Jr. 120, 128
 Mary (___) 119, 120,
  122, 123
 Sarah (___) 2
 Thomas 68, 72
 William 17, 24, 27,
  32, 37, 41, 54, 68,
  72, 119, 121, 122,
  123
HUME
 Armistead 87
 Charles 68, 74, 82
 Charles E. 111
 Francis 36, 41, 64
 George 20, 31, 42,
  57, 58, 59, 60,
  64, 82, 83
 George, Jr. 68
 Humphrey 124
 James 61
 James P. 111
 James R. 95
 John 15, 25, 31, 37,
  42, 58, 59, 60,
  66, 67, 74, 77,
  119, 120, 123, 127
 John W. 104
 Joseph 94

HUMPHREY(-S) (HUMPH-
  RIES)
 James 27, 33, 70
 John 87
 Thomas J. 97, 98, 100
HUNT
 Daniel 101
 Hackney 36
 Joshua 83
 Julius M. 95
 Mary Lucelia 101
 Robert 83, 84
HURLEY, Thomas 65
HURT
 James 31, 38, 42,
  74, 76
 Jemima (___) 38
 Sarah (___) 74
 Will 31-2
 William 38, 74

I

INSKEEP
 James W. 90
 Joel 123
IRION, Mr. 70
IRVIN, James A. 126
IRWIN, Francis 58, 83
ISBELL, Jacon 17
ISH, Christian 83
ISRAEL, Sabediah 44

J

JACK, Joshua 23
JACKSON
 Isaac 41
 John 131
 Robert 9
JACOBI
 Francis Lucus 12
 Katharine 42
 W. L. 42
JACOBIE, Francis 51
JACOBY, Daniel 71
JAMES
 Daniel 22, 36, 47,
  81, 125
 Elizabeth (___) 24
 George 22, 47
 Henry 9, 22, 23, 47

JAMES (cont.)
 James 70
 John 11
 Joseph 3, 9, 22, 28,
  36, 47, 48, 67
 Joseph, Jr. 11, 29,
  33, 41, 47
 Mary 36
 Mary (___) 22, 47
JAMESON
 Alvin 114
 D. 103
 David 70, 90, 147
 Eliza T. C. (___) 103
 Enoch 133
 Fanny B. 93
 G. W. 130
 George W. 90, 92, 128
 James 10, 131
 James H. 114
 John 95, 103, 132
 John W. 103
 Lucy Ann 93
 Mary 81
 Mary (___) 147
 Minnie 93
 Philip G. 103
 William C. 90
JANES, Joseph 6
JARREL, Jeremiah 68
JARRELL, James 62
JARVIN, John 14
JECOBY
 Francis 5
 John Daniel 5
JEFFERIES, Thomas 95
JEFFRIES
 Ambrose 107, 132
 Columbia 108
 Enoch 107
 George 106, 107, 108
 George L. 108
 Hill 108
 John 42, 87
 Joseph 87
 Maria 108
 Octavus 106, 107
 Susan 107
 Thomas 122
JENKINS
 Richard 87
 William 32

JENNENS, Frankay 1
JENNINGS
  Augustin 42
  Elizabeth 42
  Hannah 42
  Joshua 52
  Molley (____) 42
JERDAN, Thomas 43
JETT
  Ann (____) 4
  James 4, 19, 20, 28, 43, 66, 74, 81, 82
  John 4, 17, 50, 81, 87
  Matthew 90
  Mildred 19
  Sarah (____) 81
  Stephen 4
  Susanna (____) 20
  William 4, 20
JEWELL, Rachel 24
JIJDGER, Michael 16
JOHNSON
  Allen 87
  Benjamin 134
  George 106
  Polly (____) 116
  Robert 9
  Samuel 102
  William 10, 11, 116
JOHNSTON
  ____ 9
  B. 21
  Benjamin 8, 9, 134
  Betty (____) 68
  Dorothy (____) 21
  George 41
  John 23, 41, 51, 55
  Lucy 68
  Martin 41
  Nathaniel 87
  Polly 113
  Robert 55, 71
  Thomas 51
  Valentine 67
  William 28, 38, 70
JONES
  Agatha 64
  Ambrose 6
  Ann 21
  Anna 58
  Aron 71

JONES (cont.)
  Brooks 13
  Charles 96, 104, 105, 107
  Charles S. 105
  Charles Samuel 96
  E. 96
  E. E. 96
  Edward 22
  Elizabeth 40, 76
  Elizabeth (____) 19, 54
  Epps E. 105
  Frances 84
  Gabriel 11, 21, 33, 34, 53, 76, 84, 121, 148
  Gabriel, Jr. 70
  Jail 34
  Henry B. 105
  James 32, 68, 87
  James Graves 34
  Jane 107
  Jane (____) 96
  Jane F. 105
  John 23, 135
  John Dillard 55
  John T. 96, 105, 107, 109
  Joseph 8, 71
  Joshua 19, 20
  Lucy 58
  Marshall 51
  Martha (____) 21
  Mary 21, 84
  Mary (____) 53
  Mishall 87
  Philip M. 96, 105
  Powhatan E. 105
  Robert 21, 41, 53, 55, 129, 130
  Samuel 51
  Sarah (____) 58
  Susan (____) 130
  Thomas 53, 55
  William 9, 11, 12, 34, 38, 62, 75
  William R. 96, 105, 107
  William W. 154
  Zachariah 76
JORDAN(-EN)
  Eastham 92

JORDAN(-EN) (cont.)
  George 54
  Jenny 78
  Thomas 2, 17, 25, 51, 54
  Effie (____) 78
  Lucy 78
  Thomas 55
JURDEN, Thomas 71

K

KABLER
  Barbery 30
  Christopher 30
  Conwright 24
  Frederick 24, 30, 31
  Nanny 16
  Nicholas 30, 35, 41
  William 18, 24, 30, 35, 37, 41
KELLY
  Anne P. (____) 143
  George 134
  Granville J. 105
  James 134
  John 3
  John P. 92, 93, 98, 101, 105, 109, 143
  Joseph 134
  Mary 134
  Mary Ann 134
  Mary "Polly" (____) 134
  Richard 134
  Susan 134
  Thomas 134
  Thomas, Jr. 134
  Whitfield 134
  Will 31, 32
  William 134
KEMPER, William 128
KENADAY, Salley (____) 64
KENNEDY, John 70
KENNEY, Elizabeth 45
KENNON, William 144
KEY, Robert 49
KEYS, James 90
KIDWALLEDER, John 51
KIDWELL, James 126
KILBEE, Agathy (____) 31

KILBY
  Adam 6
  Ann Catherine 6
  Elizabeth 6
  Elizabeth (___) 6
  Henry 6
  James 6, 65
  John 6
  Michael 6
  Nancey 6
  Susannah 6
  William 6
KINDER, Elizabeth 120
KING
  Joseph 5, 19
  Lydia 42
KINNARD, George 49
KIRK
  Ann (___) 56
  Jeremiah 56
  John 73
  Judah 73
  Margaret (___) 73
  Thomas 73
KIRTLEY
  Anne 34
  Elijah 23, 43, 57, 64, 68, 78
  Jemima (___) 40
  Jeremiah 32, 64
  Margaret 34, 35
  Paulsey 118, 119, 127
  Sarah 64
  Thomas 7, 14, 34, 40, 53, 67, 118, 127
  Thomson 119
  William 7, 14, 20, 32, 34, 68, 71
KLINE, Frederick 78
KLUG
  Mrs. 15
  Ephraim 42
KLUGE, Michael 19
KLUGG
  George Samuel 15
  Samuel 12
KLUGGE, Michael 29
KNAVE, Dr. 70
KNOX
  William 7, 9, 10, 78

KNOX (cont.)
  William A. 129
KUTH, Harriett S. 105

L

LACEY, John 73
LAKEY, Frances (___) 20
LAMB, Molley 80
LANE, Edward H. 90
LANKFORD, John 10
LARUE, Frances H. (___) 155
LATHAM
  F. M. 110, 113
  Fayette M. 93, 94, 97, 100, 107
  Frances 76, 77, 87
  George 74, 76
  J. D. 107
  John 79
  Joseph 2
  Philip 76, 87
  Robert 45, 58, 76, 87
  Robert, Jr. 44, 74
  Thomas 47, 68, 79
  William 7
LAURENCE, Alexander 105, 106, 108, 109
LAWLOR
  ___ 70
  John 19, 33, 39, 41
LAWRENCE
  Alexander 99
  Jean 6
  Mary 108
LEAR
  Elizabeth 44
  Hannah (___) 3
  James 3, 20, 44
  John 44, 47
  Mary 44
  Susanna (___) 44
  William 3, 44
LEATHER, Samuel 32
LEATHERER
  John 60
  Joshua 60
  Margaret 60
  Michael 60
  Nicholas 32, 60

LEATHERER (cont.)
  Paul 32, 60, 64, 68
  Samuel 60
  Susanna 60
LEAVELL
  Edward 48, 49
  John 4, 6
  Joseph 49
  Robert 48
  Sarah 48
LEE
  Frances (___) 80
  John 59
  Richard 80
LEONARD
  Fanny 43
  William 43
LEWIS
  ___ 9
  Alfred B. 105
  Benjamin 87
  Enoch 153
  Fielding 8
  H. 76
  Henry 24, 25, 31, 32, 42, 45, 56, 58, 60, 64, 66, 67, 123
  Henry, Sr. 22, 61
  Henry M. 105
  Jno. 32
  John 108, 133
  Mary (___) 59, 148
  Robert S. 95
  Simeon B. 108
  William 56, 59, 148
  William W. 108
LIGHTFOOT
  Charles E. 95
  F. T. 98
  Francis 125
  Goodrich 10, 24, 25, 74, 81, 82
  Goodrich, Jr. 24
  John 24, 42, 45, 62, 63
  Martha 24
  P. 98, 127
  Philip 24, 93, 95, 101, 130
  Priscilla 24
  Susanna 83
  Susanna (___) 24

LIGHTFOOT (cont.)
  Thomas W. 128
  William 2, 73, 80
LILLARD
  Benjamin 31, 34, 62,
    119, 121, 128
  Gabriel 119
  James 34, 62
  John 22, 31
  Silas B. 113
  Strother 119
  Thomas 62, 87
  William J. 113
LILLIES, ___ 69
LINDSAY, Joshua 39
LINDSLEY, John 32
LINN, William 112
LIPS
  Elonora Sophia
    (___) 69
  George 69
  Henry 69
  John Christian 68,
    71
  John George 69
  Mary (___) 69
LIPSCOMB
  Henry M. 123, 124,
    125
  Jane 124
  Lucy M. (___) 124
  S. C. 126
  Stapleton C. 124
  William 124
LITTLE, William 98
LODSPIKE, William 11
LONG
  Admistead 116
  Benjamin 24, 63
  Betty 24
  Bromfield 24
  Brumfield 10, 66
  Brumfill 27
  Elizabeth (___) 8,
    45
  Gabriel 8, 24, 49,
    51, 62, 73, 77
  George 7
  James 18, 22, 39, 48
  John 23, 24, 25, 39,
    48, 54
  John, Jr. 47

LONG (cont.)
  John, Sr. 63
  Mary 133
  Mary S. 135
  Milly 24
  Nicholas 54
  R. K. 112
  Reuben 6, 8, 24, 32,
    68
  Reuben K. 108
  Robert 63
  Sarah (___) 24
  Thomas 24
  Ware 46
  William 13
  William B. 108, 113,
    135
LORNVEN, George 35
LORVIN, John 14
LOSPIKE, William 5
LOVE, Daniel 77
LOVELL, William 26
LOWEN(-IN)
  Ann 28
  Ben 48, 53
  Benjamin 28, 83
  Betsy 83
  Francis 28
  John 2, 28
  Margaret (___) 28
  Mary (___) 83
LUCAS
  Abraham 92
  Happy W. 92
LUDSPIKE, William 70
LUTSPICK, William 15
LYNCH, Mille (___) 75
LYON, Wm. 70

Mc

McALESTER
  Ann 3
  Elizabeth (___) 3
  Finley 3
  James 3
  John 3
  Mary 3
  Robert 3, 31
  Sarah 3
  William 3
McCALLESTER, Anne 73

McCLANAHAN
  Mary 26
  Thomas 11, 12, 17,
    27, 39, 42, 51
  William 46, 48, 55,
    66, 76
  William, Jr. 79
McCLAYLAND, Daniel 50
McCONCHIE, William A.
  129
McCORMICK,
  Elizabeth (___) 130,
    131
  Stephen 130, 131
McCOY
  B. U. 90
  William 109
McCURDY, Joseph 64
McDANIEL, John 45
McDANNOLD (McDANOLD,
  McDANNALD)
  Alexander 45, 48
  George 45
  John 19, 20, 54
  Nelley 45
  Reubin 45
  Susanna (___) 20
McGRATH, Bryan 18, 41
McGRUDER, Thomas 73
McKELLUP, Hughes 87
McKENNEY, William 87
McKENNY
  John 10, 11
  Margaret 10
  Mary Ann (___) 10
McKENZIE, John 6, 32
McKEY
  Margaret (___) 56
  Robert 56
McKINNY, Ann 12
McNEALE
  Isabella 109
  John 109, 132
  John D. 109
McQUEEN
  Alexander 39, 40, 48,
    77
  Charles 39
  John 39
  William 41

M

MACKCOLESTER, Joshua 127
MADDOX
 Elizabeth 37
 John 59, 61
 Mary (____) 59, 65
 Matthew 65
 Natly 17
 Notley 65, 71
 Samuel 65
 Thomas 65
 Weeden 21
MADISON
 A. 59
 Francis 77, 81
 Mary 59
 William 81, 124, 125
MAGERS, John 45
MAGRATH, Brian 68
MAGRUDER,
 Prissiler (____) 71
 Thomas 17, 65, 71
MAJOR
 Elizabeth T. (____) 155
 John 41, 45
 John C. 103, 134
 Julian N., Sr. 155
 Langdon C. 105
 Richard 35
 Samuel 98
 W. 95
 William 94, 95, 103, 131
 William, Sr. 155
MAKFERCEN, Ellick 17
MALLORY
 Ann 26
 Dorothy 26
 Elisabeth 26
 Mary 26
 Nathan 26
 Roger 26
 William 26, 27, 30, 125
MANIFEE
 Henry 41
 John 5
 Jonas 52
MANK, Matthias 68

MARCOS, John 15, 17, 19
MARKHAM, I. L. 87
MARQUESS, William 79, 84
MARR
 Michael 42
 Thomas 128
MARSDEN, Dr. 51
MARSH
 Jonathan 17
 Joshua 17
 Mary 17
 William 17
MARSHALL
 Agniss H. 132
 Alexander J. 132
 Anne L. 132
 Elizabeth 26, 29
 Elizabeth (____) 26
 Fielding L. 132
 George 26
 George E. 101, 102, 103
 H. 72
 James 51
 John 18, 26, 72, 84, 132
 Lewis 26
 Margaret 132
 Margaret (____) 52
 Markham 26
 Mary 132
 Merryman 9
 Thomas 13, 26, 132
 William 5, 26
MARSTON, Thomas 78
MARTAIN
 Peggy 60
 William 60
MARTIN, Anne 62
MARYE
 J. L., Jr. 98
 James 9
 P. 54
 Peter 87
MASON
 Elizabeth 87
 James 27
 Joel 87
 John 63
 William 37, 58, 117
MASSEY
 John 118, 120, 121, 122, 127, 128

MASSEY (cont.)
 Powhatan 90
MATTHEWS
 Ann 47
 Aquila 47
 Benjamin 47, 107, 109
 Daniel 47
 Elisha 47
 Franky 47
 James 47
 John 47, 87
 Mary 47
 William 47
MAUZY
 F. 97, 111, 130
 Fayette 95, 99, 103, 113
 Henry 78
MAXWELL
 James 62
 Thomas 68
MAY, George 32
MAZE, Richard 5
MEALE, Francis 71
MEDLEY
 Ambrose 40, 42, 45, 55, 74, 82, 83, 84
 Jacob 33, 42, 52
 Ruben 32
MELDRUM
 Mary 27
 William 27
MENEFEE
 Elizabeth (____) 45
 Henry 45
 J. G. 99
 John 54
 Jonas 44
MERCER, Dr. ____ 9
MERRY, Prettyman 68
MERSHALL, William 6
MERSHON
 Andrew 20, 76
 Cornelius 19, 20, 28, 30, 53, 76
MILDRUM
 ____ 11
 Mrs. 11
MILES
 Charles 17, 18
 Elizabeth (____) 17
 Richard 94
 Thomas 98

MILLER
  ___ 9
  Benjamin F. 106
  Elizabeth 92
  Elizabeth (___) 150
  Frances 70
  Henry 50, 55, 69, 71, 78, 106, 150
  John 50, 87, 106
  Margit (___) 50
  William 87
MINOR
  Armistead 26, 68, 78, 84
  Eliott 26, 78
  John 12, 25, 27, 48, 53, 66, 74
  Joseph 14, 26, 78, 84
  Margaret (___) 78
  Mary Allen 78
  O. 61
  Owen 10, 17, 25, 51, 60
MITCHELL
  ___ 9
  Benjamin 21
  Cornelius 4, 18, 26, 27, 71
  E. Y. 112
  Elizabeth 112
  Elizabeth (___) 112
  Fanny 26
  Fisher 21, 87
  Henry H. 112
  J. P. 112
  Jacob 21, 25
  James W. 112
  Jane (___) 26
  John W. 92
  Leah (___) 21
  Margaret 136
  Peggy 21
  Susannah 52
  Susannah (___) 63
  Thomas 52, 62, 63
  William 21, 59, 117
  Willis 63
MOADLEY, Mrs. 15
MOFFETT
  Daniel 150
  H. G. 98, 99

MONCURE, John 133
MONROE
  Mary 37
  Nella 37
MONTEITH
  ___ 55
  Thomas 55
MOORE
  Barnett 117
  Bernard 117, 118
  Harbin 78
  Henry 121
  John 70
  Joseph 87
  Lucy Barbour 148
  Reuben 97, 101, 102, 117, 118, 120, 122, 127, 129, 132
  Reuben, Sr. 103
  Samuel 71
  Thomas L. 101, 102
  William 51
  William H. 91, 97, 101, 102, 103
MORGAN
  Ben 70
  Charles 40, 41, 79
  Francis 19, 63
  John 4, 17
MORRIS(-S)
  Amie 43
  Martha (___) 40
  Martin 43
  Mary (___) 4
  Stephen 55
  Thomas 1, 4, 22
  William 4, 6, 43
MORRISON, Stephen 74
MORSON, Arthur 133
MORTON
  James 78
  Jeremiah 106
  William 76, 77
MOSES, Elizabeth (___) 39
MOUNTAGUE, Peter 79
MOVESOON, Stephen 82
MOYER, Margaret 50
MOZINGO
  Charles 71
  George 41
MURFFIE
  Miles 4

MURFFIE (cont.)
  Richard 4
  William 4
MURPHEY
  Amey (___) 2
  Miles 4
MURREY, James 19
MURRY
  James 17, 87
  Mary 17
  Prettyman 17
  Thomas 17
MURTLE, William 39

N

NALLE
  Ann(-e) 72, 123
  Ann (___) 69
  Clary 72
  Elizabeth M. 150
  Frances 87
  Francis 9, 34, 37, 43, 48, 64
  Isabell (___) 72
  James 34, 43, 71
  Jessee 123
  John 8, 9, 12, 34, 43, 48, 72
  Joseph 90
  Judah (___) 64
  Judith 133
  Larkin G. 133
  Martin 9, 11, 31, 33, 43, 72, 150
  Mary 43
  Mary (___) 43
  Milly 72
  Rachel 72
  Richard 34, 43, 64, 66, 70
  Susanna (___) 43
  Thomas B. 100
  William 43, 72, 120, 155
  Williamson 121
  Winifred (___) 69
  Winny 72
NASH
  Betty 6, 8
  Elijah 6, 8
  Elizabeth (___) 6

NASH (cont.)
  James 8, 15, 16, 21, 22
  John 6, 8, 87
  Leanna 6
  Mary 6
  William 6, 8
NEAL(-E)
  Charles 18, 23
  Esther 23
  Fielding 23
  John 23
  Lucy 23
  Mary 23
  Micajah 18, 23, 67
  Sally 23
NEALL, John 23
NELSON
  Adam 9
  Arthur B. 95, 105
  George 105, 106
  George E. 95
  George Eggborn 105
  James I. 95
  James Jacob 105
  L. P. 92
  Lewis P. 90, 91, 92, 95, 97, 99, 105, 106, 110
NEWALL, Adam 55
NEWBY
  Elizabeth 104
  Ellen 104
  F. Addison 104
  Richard N. 104
  Robert C. 104
  Sarah A. 104
  William P. 104
NEWMAN
  Abner 19, 63
  Alexander 19
  Frances (____) 76
  George 19
  James 19, 20
  Joseph 19
  Reuben 19, 76
  Thomas 19, 20
NEWTON, William 5, 60, 72
NIELSON, Ann (____) 8
NINCE, John 63
NIXON, Robert 33, 41

NOCE
  Basel 62
  Bazil 59
  John 52
NORMAN
  Benjamin 2
  Courtney 1, 3, 4, 10, 17, 22, 25, 46
  Elizabeth 10, 22, 25
  Ezekiel 2, 4, 10, 17, 22, 25
  Fanny 57
  Frances 100
  Isaac 57
  James 57
  John 1, 4, 11, 12, 57, 59, 71
  Joseph 57, 58, 77
  Kisiah 57
  Mary 4, 10, 22, 25
  Mary (____) 1
  Milley 10, 22
  Mimey 57
  Reuben 2, 4
  Sally 57
  Sarah 57
  Sarah (____) 57, 77
  Thomas 57, 100
  William 2, 4, 10, 22, 25, 57
NORRIS
  Elizabeth C. 146
  Richard 95
NORWOOD, Andrew 53

O

O'BANNON, Walter 92, 95, 113
ODELL, Jeremiah 87
ODER (ORDER)
  Elizabeth 118, 120, 127
  Elizabeth (____) 119
OFFER
  John 80
  Mary 80
ONEAL
  John 49
  Sarah (____) 49
ORMO, Thomas 87

OXFORD
  Elizabeth (____) 42
  Thomas 42
OXLEY
  Elizabeth (____) 133
  Thomas 133, 134

P

PAGE, Elizabeth 37
PAINTER
  Isaac 41
  Sarah (____) 39
PANNILL
  George, Jr. 98
  William 17, 76
PARK, Simpson 93
PARKER
  Gressel (____) 43
  Richard 9
PARKS (PARKES)
  Catey 72
  John 8, 9, 64
  Mary (____) 34
  Richard 34, 71, 72
PARROT, A. P. 129
PARSONS (PARSON)
  Elizabeth 88
  George 10, 58
  Jessee 19
PARTLOW
  Benjamin 70
  David 1
PASSONS, George 4, 20, 66
PATTIE
  James 52, 57
  John 57
  Sarah (____) 57
PATTON
  John M. 132
  Robert 117
PAYNE
  Albert W. 114
  Daniel J. 114
  Elizabeth J. (____) 114
  George A. 114
  George S. M. 114
  Mary (____) 138
  Richard 138

PAYTON (See PEYTON)
  Benjamin 4, 55
  Charles 4, 42
  Jemima 42
  Jeremiah 42
  John 4, 41, 44
  Marey 42
  Mary (____) 45
  Nancey 42
  Sarah 67
  Thomas 42, 45, 46
  Ureth 42
  Valentine 67
  William 67
  William Parfield 67
PEACH, Susanna 12
PEARCY, William 55
PECK, Suanah 11
PELHAM
  Fanny 93
  Harriet (____) 93
  John 93
  Samuel 93
PEMBERTON
  John 9
  John S. 90
  Mary (____) 95
PENDLETON
  Benjamin 13
  Catharine 61, 88
  Elizabeth 6
  Henry 3, 4, 5, 6, 7, 10, 11, 19, 22, 27, 28, 56, 66, 69
  James 3, 6, 10, 16, 20, 22, 24, 28, 44, 50, 55, 56, 61, 69, 71, 76, 81, 82, 130
  John 104
  John J. 130
  John S. 98, 130
  N. 2, 6, 16, 18, 26, 28
  Nathaniel 1, 8, 10, 13, 66, 77
  P. 2, 13, 28
  Philip 3, 7, 19
  William 22, 57, 66, 133
PENQUITO
  Jane (____) 134
  William 134

PENROSE, Jessee 83, 84
PEPER, John 68
PERKINS, Margery (____) 56
PERRY
  Ann 88
  Isaiah C. 114, 115
  Pierce 114, 126
  Roderick 13
PETERS, Mary (____) 45
PETTY
  Charles M. 107
  Elizabeth 97, 102
  Elizabeth W. 91
  Georgie 136, 137
  James F. 107
  John 83
  John Abner 107
  John S. 91, 98, 122
  Marshall 97, 102
  Mary D. 108
  Rawleigh 88
  Thomas F. 122
  Thornton F. 101, 102, 103, 123, 124
  William J. 97
  Zachariah 62, 83, 101
  Zachariah S. 105, 107
  Zachary 13, 29
PEYTON (See PAYTON)
  Daniel 41
  William 4, 6, 15
PHILLIPS, William 39
PICKET, John 17
PIERCE, William 39, 47
PILCHER
  Elizabeth 12
  Frances (____) 12
  John 12, 13
  Joshua 11
  Mary 12
  Rachel 12
  Sary 12
PINAR
  John 20
  Margot (____) 20
  Ruth 20
  Thomas 20
PINCKARD
  Charles 103, 121, 122, 128, 129
  John 128

PINEGAR, William 34
PIPER, Thomas 24
PING, ____ 34
PINION, James 41
PINNALL
  John 51
  William 51
PINNEGAR
  Elizabeth 36
  William 36
PINNELL, William 17
PIPER
  David 58
  John 58
  Robert 58
POE
  Jonathan 4
  Samuel 4, 88
POINDEXTER, Lucy (____) 21
POLLARD
  Ann 2
  Elizabeth 2, 3
  Elizabeth (____) 2, 3, 16
  James 29, 131
  John 2
  Lindsay 131
  Milley 2, 3, 16, 26, 29
  Richard 2, 3, 13, 16, 26
  Richard Coleman 2, 3, 29
  Robert 2, 3, 18, 24, 26, 29, 34, 49, 52, 53
  Sarah 2, 3, 16
  William 88
POPE
  Emily 94
  Henry 94
  Jane 94
  Lawrence 94
  Otway Garrett 94
  Sanford 94
  Thomas 39
  Winny (____) 136
POPHAM
  Gerard 129, 130
  Job 9, 11, 36, 39
  John 88, 108

PORTER
  Benjamin 75
  Camp 125
  George 73
  Joseph, Sr. 83
  Nicholas 9
  Samuel 88
  Thomas 3, 6, 15, 38, 41, 42, 69
  William 75, 88
PORTUS, Carter C. 106
POURTER, Thomas 45
POWELL
  ___ 9
  A. 15
  Ambrose 3, 11, 14, 24, 38, 68, 73, 74, 82
  Benjamin 14, 55
  Francis 14
  Hezekiah 129
  Honorias, Jr. 10
  Honorous 14
  James 14, 15, 53
  John 14
  Lucy (___) 129
  Mary (___) 73, 74
  Robert 73, 74, 82
  Sarah (___) 56
  William 14, 56, 73, 74, 79, 82
POWERS
  Ann (___) 79
  Caroline 154
  Jacob 68
PRATT
  John 80
  Jonathan 34, 37
  Thomas 34, 79, 88
PREESONS, John 31
PREST, Jeremiah 41
PRICE
  Arjalon 32-33, 43
  Caty 5
  J. 62
  Kalem 2
  Sarah (___) 76
PRICHARD, Jane 36
PRICHETT
  Jane (___) 13
  William 13
PRILMAN, James 5

PRITCHETT, ___ 14
PROCTOR
  George 75
  John 52
PULLEN, John 58
PULLER
  Ann (___) 151
  John 79, 151
PULLIAM
  B. F. 114
  Ben 38
  Benjamin 11, 12, 23, 55, 75, 113
  Lucy (___) 75
  Thomas 38
PURVIS, William 72

Q

QUARLES, ___ 8
QUINN
  Ben 68
  Elizabeth 38
  Elizabeth (___) 80
  Francis 12
  Frankey 38
  James 38, 43, 44, 45
  Jenny 38
  John 73
  Richard 12, 38, 68, 80
  Thomas 10, 38, 44

R

RAGLAND, Susan A. 113
RAILSBACK, John 7
RAINS, Mary (___) 70
RAKESTRAW, I. 88
RAMSBOTTOM, James 33
RANDOLPH
  Hall 81
  Hutt 31
  James 81
  Jediah 81
RANOLDS, Sarah 23
RANSOM, Lency (___) 45
RASHER, T. 112
RAWLINGS, John 66
RAY, Daniel 34
READ
  ___ 19

READ (cont.)
  Griffin 63
  Hank(-s) 27, 39, 40, 58, 60, 63
  James 13, 84
  John 10, 19, 26, 27, 33, 40, 45, 51, 58, 60, 84
  John, Jr. 151
  Loy (___) 151
  Samuel 88
  Theofelus 19
  Theophilus 10
  Winifred 19
READER, Benjamin, Jr. 41
REASON, George 20
REDD
  Joseph B. 108
  Mordecai 27
REDING
  Isaac 4
  William 4
REDMAN, Katharine 34
REID, Winifred 10
REND
  Elizabeth (___) 24
  Lewis 24
RENDER
  Elizabeth (___) 127
  Joseph 32
  Joshua 32, 45
  Louis 61
  Robert 31, 32
  Susanna (___) 25
RESS
  Ann 45
  William 45
RESTALL
  George 33
  Jane 34
REVELEY, Mary 55
REYNOLDS
  Edward 54
  Jennet (___) 54
  John 57
  John, Sr. 54
  Richard 10, 53
  William 54
RHODIFER, John 67
RICE
  Capt. 31
  Agness 25

RICE (cont.)
  Amon B. 62
  Benajah 32, 35, 68,
    124, 125
  Benajer 20
  Benjamin 20
  Elizabeth 52
  Fisher 31, 38, 41,
    42
  Hannah 32
  Hannah (___) 20, 24
  James Brown 52
  John 32
  Nancy (___) 62
  Richard 32
  Sarah 62
  Sarah (___) 32
  William 32, 42
RICHARDS
  Benjamin F. 130, 131
  Dulcebella (___) 130
  Dulcibella C. (___)
    131
  Eliza. 88
  James 130, 131
  William 62, 84
  Winifred (___) 130,
    131
RICHARDSON
  Daniel 71
  Richard 43
RIDER
  Alex 62
  Archabud 70
  Catharine (___) 35
RIED, William 13
RIGOUR, Jacob 13
RILEY
  Edward 17
  John 41
RINDER
  Elizabeth 119, 122
  Elizabeth (___) 123
  Lewis 123
RINEHART, Matthias 13
RINER
  Abberhart (or Aber-
    hard) 52
  Christian 52
  Daniel 52
  Elizabeth 52
  Elizabeth (___) 52

RINER (cont.)
  John 52
  Mary 52
  Sarah 52
RITENOUR
  Jaqueline C. 114
  Jaqueline C. (___)
    115
  Milton 114
RIXEY
  Charles 137
  Charles W. 103
  Eugene A. 105
  John 96, 98
  John H. 90, 92, 104,
    105, 107
  Jones 96
  Lucinda 105
  Lucinda (___) 137
  Mary F. (___) 96
  Matilda (___) 96
  Penelope (___) 126
  Presley 151
  Presley M. 96, 105,
    107
  Richard III 126
  Richard Hughes 126
  Richard J. 104
  Richard S. 105
  Dr. Samuel Gibbs 126
  Thomas H. 97
  Thomas R. 117
  William 103, 110, 117
ROACH
  Elizabeth (Jett) 4
  George 134
  Sarah (___) 134
ROBB, James 77
ROBBINS, John 11
ROBERSON, Cathoran
    (___) 49
ROBERTS
  ___ 112
  Anne (___) 37
  Ben 71
  Benjamin 4, 8, 11,
    13, 15, 23, 40, 45,
    81
  Benjamin, Jr. 12, 15,
    30, 47
  Boaneges 112
  Boanerges 40

ROBERTS (cont.)
  Elizabeth 40
  Francis A. 112
  George 6, 15, 40, 41
  Helen M. 112
  Hugh 21
  Jemima 40
  John 3, 8, 15, 17,
    40, 41, 42, 70, 71
  Joseph 15, 37, 40,
    41, 50, 67, 72, 78,
    83
  Joseph W. 93, 101,
    111, 112
  Leijah 50
  Lucy (___) 93
  Mary 40
  Meredith H. 112
  P. 93
  Philagathus 98, 111
  Philla Gathous 40
  Sarah 40
  Sarah (___) 40
  Susanner (___) 21,
    93
  William 5, 12, 15,
    17, 26, 35, 48, 70
ROBERTSON
  Ann Piper 144
  H. Anne 92
  Lucy 78
  Mary 8
  Mary (___) 8
  N. 16
  Nathaniel 8
  W. 16, 20
  Walter 90
  William 13, 78, 92,
    129, 144
  William, Jr. 78
ROBINSON
  Israel 55
  James 10, 71
  Joseph 55
  Mary (___) 4
  Sarah (___) 55
  William 4, 5
ROBISON
  James 10
  Samuel B. 94
RODEAVER, John 83

RODEHEAVER
  David 79
  John 79
  Joseph 79
  Sarah (___) 79
RODIFER, Anne 83
ROEBUCK
  ___ 9
  Elisabeth 39
  Lucey 39
  Mary 39
  Mary (___) 39
  Millie 39
  Rawleigh 39
  Robert 39, 67, 84
  William 11, 39, 40
ROGERS
  Ann (___) 64
  Barnard 45
  Barnett 47
  Betty 2
  Elizabeth Todd 80
  Jeremiah 45
  John 45, 54
  Joseph 10, 14, 44, 45, 48
  Tabitha (___) 80, 81
  William 2, 4, 10, 13, 14, 38, 44, 45, 48
ROGGERS, Joseph 55
RONSOW, Sarah (___) 45
ROOTE, Maj. 3
ROSEKRANSE, Mary 2
ROSS
  George 102
  William B. 102
ROSSON
  Benjamin 98
  Daniel 128
  John 36
  Reuben 98, 121, 122
ROUSAU
  Hiram 4
  Sarah (___) 4
ROUTT
  George 136
  John 75
  William Pope 136
ROUZEE, John 68
ROW(-E)
  Edmund 76
  George 3, 31, 42
  Mary (___) 82

ROWELL, Louisa H. D. 100
ROWLES
  George W. 109
  John F. 109
  Judith 109
  Samuel 109
  Susan A. 109
ROWZEE, John 57, 75
RUCKER
  Angus 84
  Augus 78
  Augustin 65, 84
  Elizabeth 30
  Elliott 17, 125
  Ephraim 10, 14, 26, 33, 35, 43, 51, 65, 81
  Esther 29, 58
  Frances 29
  James 57
  Joseph 30, 55
  Katharine (___) 74
  Milley (___) 55
  Peter 10
  Thomas 55
  William 19, 30, 55
  Wisdom 55, 74
RUDASIL
  Alpheus P. 104
  James A. 110
  Louisa (___) 104
RUSH
  James 3, 73, 74
  William 73
RUSSELL
  Col. 8
  Elijah 20
  Elizabeth 20, 24
  Jane 147
  John 20
  Mary (___) 20
  Michael 24
  Michel 20
  Peter 70
  Samuel 91
  William 20, 71
RYAN
  Elisabeth 19
  Elizabeth (___) 5
  John 5, 7, 19
RYMER, Christian 52, 55

RYNOR, Elizabeth (___) 52

S

SACKETT, Barbary (___) 24
SAMPSON
  John 16, 24, 25, 32, 59, 61, 62, 64, 68, 118, 120, 121, 122, 127, 128
  Joseph 24, 25, 119, 121, 122-3, 127
  Mary 120, 121, 122, 123, 127
  Mary (___) 24, 59, 118, 119, 122, 127
  Rhoda 24, 123
  Thomas 24, 57, 67, 119, 120, 122, 123, 128
  William 24, 25, 53, 119, 120, 122
SAMSON, Gavin 10
SAMUEL, Reubin 132
SANDERFER, William 121
SANDERS
  Elizabeth (___) 75
  John 66, 71, 72
  Robert 6
  Winifred (___) 72
SANDES, Benjamin 51
SANFORD
  Joseph 50, 62
  Peirce 75
SATTLER, Sinboysion 11
SAUNDERS
  Ann (___) 8
  Carter A. 113
  Elizabeth (___) 8
  James 8
  John 13, 16
  Lucy R. 113
  Robert 8, 103
  Sally (___) 57
SCHALLGE, Master 69
SCHOOLER, Sarah (___) 13
SCOGIN, Elizabeth (___) 42
SCOTT
  Ambrose 21

SCOTT (cont.)
  George 14, 21, 78
  Hannah 64
  James 21, 68
  John 9, 18, 95, 96, 106
  Johnny 50
  Robert 70
  Thomas 2, 13, 18, 21, 68
SCOTWOOD, Jno. 18
SEALES, John 11
SEAR, John 10
SEBREE, James 45
SEEBREE, Richard 32
SERJANT, John 30
SETTLE
  Benjamin 27
  Benjamin F. 105
  Frances 88
  Isaac 51
  Jesse 140
  John J. 104
  Mary 71
  Merriman 88
  Mrs. Robert 155
SHACKELFORD (SHACKLEFORD)
  B. H. 109
  Benjamin 95, 117
  Benjamin H. 106, 107, 108
  Caleb 99
  Edmond 67
  H. 98
  Henry 102, 107, 108, 131
  James 27, 71, 84
  John 92, 95
  John S. 91, 100
  Richard 57
  William 16, 27
  Zachary 40
SHADRACH, Samuel 101, 109, 112, 115, 122
SHARMAN
  Ann 1, 12
  Elisha 12
  Lucy 1
  Lucy (____) 12
  Robert 1, 12

SHARPE
  Frances (____) 76
  Lynfield 76
SHAVUE, Shadrach 16
SHAW, William 83, 84
SHEARLEY, James 32
SHELTON
  John 10
  Thomas 34
SHEPHERD, Andrew 73, 77
SHERREL (SHERRELL, SHERRIL, SHERRILL)
  James Hoomes 74
  Margaret (____) 56
  William 43, 47, 56, 77
SHIFLET
  John 14
  Stephen 14
SHIP
  Allen 121
  Ambrose 36, 121
  Betsey 121
  Easter 121
  Eleanor "Nelly" (____) 119, 120, 123
  Eleanor (____) 120, 122
  Elinor (____) 118, 127
  Isabel (____) 136
  John 36
  Josiah 36
  Judith 121
  Lucy 36
  Martin 121
  Nancey 36
  Nelley 121
  Nicey 121
  Polley 121
  Rhoda 121
  Richard 36, 41
  Salley 121
  Thomas 36
  Thornton 121
SHIPE, Admisah 113
SHIPHAM, Travis 94
SHIRLEY
  James 83
  Thomas 119, 125
  Zacharias 119
SHORTER, Winnie 21
SHOTWELL
  Anne 60

SHOTWELL (cont.)
  Hannah (____) 60
  Reuben 60
  Robert 22, 37, 60, 61
SHROPSHIRE, Peggy (____) 45
SHUMATE, Joshua 32, 36, 41
SHURLEY, James 31
SIBERT
  Elizabeth J. (____) 114
  James H. 114
SILLS, John 56
SIM, James 117
SIMPSON
  Alexander 18
  Anne 18
  Elizabeth (____) 18
  James 18
  Jane 18, 57
  John 18, 20
  William 18, 53
SIMS (or SIMMS)
  Edward 7, 10, 12, 52, 58
  Elijah 58
  Elizabeth (____) 43, 58
  James 13, 19, 34, 40, 43, 45, 47, 58, 72
  John 5
  Joseph M. 91
  Martha 2
  Martha (Ryan) 5
  Mary (____) 43
  Richard 58
  Sallie M. (____) 91
  Thomas 60
  Thomas, Jr. 16, 58
  Thomas, Sr. 58
  William 2, 21, 23, 58, 67, 106, 109
  William, Jr. 21
  William, Sr. 127
  Zachariah 58
SINGLETON
  Albert R. 118, 126, 127
  Esther 118
  James 88, 118

SINGLETON (cont.)
  Jane 118
  Joshua 118, 126, 127
  Mary 118
  Minor W. 118, 126, 127
  Nancy W. 118
  Nancy W. (___) 127
  Reuben 118
SISK
  Frances 121
  Morgan 121
SISSON
  Elizabeth 83
  Sarah (___) 28
  William 28
SIZESON, William 76
SLAUGHTER
  ___ 83
  B. 25
  Betsy (___) 78
  Cad W. 81
  Cadwallader 18, 35, 44, 82
  Elisabeth (___) 14
  Frances (___) 21
  Francis 5, 18, 71, 75
  George 2, 14, 29, 30
  George Clayton 78
  James 11, 13, 16, 18, 23, 25, 28, 29, 63, 66, 71, 78
  James, Jr. 23, 49, 74, 95
  John 10, 31, 55, 57, 103, 133, 135
  John Field 14
  Lawrence 8, 13, 14, 29, 78
  Maria G. 100
  Martin 98, 109
  Mary 3
  Mary (___) 14
  Milly 14
  P. 49
  Patsey 78
  Phil 18
  Philip 71, 78
  R. 63, 82
  Robert 14, 35, 66, 78, 84

SLAUGHTER (cont.)
  Robert, Jr. 34, 66
  Robert, Sr. 23, 53
  Samuel 120, 121, 122
  Susanna 78
  Susannah (___) 66
  Thomas 13, 35, 41, 71
  William 81
  William, Jr. 118, 120, 122, 123, 127
  William B. 100
SLEMEARD, Joseph 13
SLOAN, Michael 71
SLONE, Michell 32
SMITH
  Andrew 120
  Ann Elizabeth (___) 44
  Anne (___) 16
  Benjamin F. 113
  Mrs. C. H. 136, 137
  Catharine (___) 94
  Dan 7
  Daniel 16
  Darnall 102
  Downing 68
  Edwin 53
  Elizabeth 73
  Frances 14
  Gabriel 121
  Harriet E. (___) 113
  Isaac 9, 31, 32, 67, 71, 127
  Isaac, Jr. 13
  J. 74
  James W. 130
  Jessee 63
  Joel 80
  John 11, 16, 33, 71, 73
  Jonathan 83
  L. P. 88
  Leonard 11, 13
  Mary 16
  Mary (Peyton) 4
  Patty 16
  Presley N. 123
  Robert 12
  Thomas 26, 28
  Weeden 88
  William 16, 63, 71, 83, 125

SMITH (cont.)
  William M. 94
SMOOT
  Benjamin 17
  J. R. 96, 111
  Letha (___) 108
  Theophilus 98, 99
  Walter B. 108
SNEAD, Mrs. ___ 137
SNEED, William 62
SNELL
  Elizabeth 80
  Lewis 67, 80
SNELLING
  Elizabeth 26
  Margaret (___) 26
SNIDER, Adam 65
SNYDER
  Adam 61, 67
  John 64
SOMERVILLE
  James 152
  Mary (___) 152
  Samuel W. 108
SOUTHER
  Henry 53
  Jacob 17, 53
  Michael 17, 53
  Stephen 53
SPALDEN, John 67
SPARKS
  Ann 65
  Elizabeth 36, 52
  Elizabeth (___) 36
  Frankey 65
  Henry 65, 75
  Humphrey 39, 42, 65, 66, 73
  Jasper 36
  John 36, 65
  Lucy 65
  Mary 65
  Mary (___) 65
  Milley 36
  Sary 36
  Thomas 6, 52, 65, 66
  William 13, 36, 38
SPELMAN, Thomas 33
SPENCE, Mary F. 99, 100
SPENCER
  Joseph 118
  Mary J. 92

SPENNY, James 88
SPICER, Levina 70
SPILMAN (SPILLAMAN, SPILLMAN)
  Alice (____) 82
  Ann (____) 56
  B. H. 147
  Benjamin 63
  Catharine (____) 7
  Charles 50, 82
  Edward 98
  Edward M. 99
  Elizabeth 44, 82
  Henry 82
  J. A. 147
  James 4, 7, 63, 81, 83
  John 44, 52, 82
  John R. 147
  Martha 152
  Nathaniel 56, 82
  Peggy 82
  Phillip 82
  Robert 63
  S. E. 147
  Susanah 82
  Thomas 39, 63, 82
  William 82
  Winifred 63
SPINDLE
  R. W. 99
  Robert H. 98
  Thomas 144
SPOLDEN, Thomas 50
SPOLDIN, John 64
SPOTSWOOD
  Alexander 8
  John 8, 57
STALLARD
  Randolph 58
  Samuel 26
  Walter 29
STARKE, William 88
STARR, Merrick 83, 84
STEERS, Joseph 17
STENNETT, Benjamin 32
STEPHENS
  Lewis, Jr. 27
  Mary (____) 27
STEVENS
  Edward 26, 66, 95, 148, 149

STEVENS (cont.)
  Edward, Jr. 149
  Elizabeth 149
  Gilly (____) 149
  Grissell (____) 95
  John 66, 149
  Mary 109
  Micajah 52
STEVENSON, James 60
STEWARD
  James 15
  John 56
  Joseph 22, 56, 60, 79
  William 56, 64
STEWART
  Joanna (____) 37
  Joseph 47
  Joseph O. 105
  Josepha G. 114
  Mary (____) 75
  Robert 81
  William A. G. 105
STIGLER, Samuel 6, 22, 24
STINETT, Jerusha (____) 28
STINNETT, Benjamin 62
STOCKDELL
  John 21, 73
  John, Jr. 21
STOFER, A. J. 90, 97
STOKESBERRY, William 88
STONE
  Agnes B. 130
  Agness B. (____) 131
  Ann (Peyton) 4
  Bryan 4
  John 4
  Simon 40
  William 130, 131
STONSIVER, John 58
STOWERS
  John 14
  William 68
STRINGFELLOW
  Albert L. 114
  Henry 3, 10, 13, 16, 71, 76, 88
  M. S. 112, 113
  Mary 152
  R. S. 112, 113

STRINGFELLOW (cont.)
  Robert 152
  Robert R. 101
  William 92
STRODE, John 74, 76, 84
STROTHER
  Ann 6, 75
  Ann (____) 22, 72
  Anthony 5, 8
  Betsy (____) 139
  Caty 72
  Francis 6, 11, 13, 22
  French 13, 29, 71, 133
  French, Jr. 108
  George 7, 22, 72
  George F. 116
  James F. 98, 99
  Jeremiah 72, 117, 128, 132
  John 7, 9, 10, 11, 12, 17, 22, 25, 39, 41, 45, 47, 51, 72, 80, 88, 132, 139
  John, Jr. 27, 43, 72, 132
  Joseph 22, 45, 68
  Mary 72
  Nancy (____) 75
  Richard 15
  Robert 22, 41, 53
  Samuel 22
  Solomon 51
  William 13, 17
STUARD, Joseph 47
STUART
  Robert 75
  Robert, Jr. 13
STUBBLEFIELD
  Ann(-e) 13, 18
  George 12
  James 8, 12, 18, 22
  John W. 102
  Mary 8, 13
  Thomas 8, 18
SUDDOTH, Benjamin 88
SUDDUTH, Thomas J. 147
SUTHERLAND,
  Frederick 17
  Traves 17
SUTTON
  Betty (____) 28

SUTTON (cont.)
  Christopher 18
  Fanny (___) 73
  John 73, 74
  Mary Bledsoe 73, 74
SWINDEL, Elizabeth
  (___) 77
SWINDLE, Michael 84

T

TALIAFERRO
  Agness (___) 132
  Alexander 132
  Christopher 107
  Elizabeth 44, 107
  Harry 25, 40, 49, 50, 58
  Henry 32, 80
  John 73
  Lawrence 44, 73
  Nicholas 73, 75
TANNAHILL, William 105
TANNER
  Cornelius 122, 129
  Frederick 32
TAPP
  Ann 81
  Ann (___) 66
  Christian (___) 81
  Dicey 90
  Elias 81
  James 81
  John 81
  Lewis 56, 66, 81
  Mary (Jett) 5
  Molly 81
  Molly (___) 81
  Moses 81
  Nimrod 81
  Sally 81
  Sias 81
  Suckey 81
  Vincent 33, 45, 50, 51, 66, 81
  Vinson, Sr. 52
  William 50, 58, 81
TAYLOR
  Benjamin 17
  Charles 17, 56, 61, 73
  James 17

TAYLOR (cont.)
  John 70, 88
  Thomas 17, 22
  Thornton 105, 109
  William 77
  Woodford 105
  Zachary 2
TEBBS
  Ann L. 100
  Betsy 98
  Betsy (___) 99
  Charles B. 100
  Elizabeth P. 100
  Foushee 98, 100
  Foushee C. 100
  John W. 100
  Margaret F. 100
  Sally T. 98
  Samuel J. 98, 99, 100
  Thomas F. 100
  W. W. 98
  Willoughby M. 100
  Willoughby W. 100
TERRILL (TERRELL, TERRIL)
  Ann 55
  Edmund 55, 58
  Elizabeth 55
  Fanny 55
  Herry 82
  James 55
  Jean 55
  John 3, 55, 75, 77, 79, 81
  Lucy 55
  Mary 55
  Nancy 55
  Oliver 79
  Reuben 3, 46
  Robert 1, 24, 55, 68
  Sarah 55
THOM
  Alexander 83
  George S. 116, 133
  John 90, 108
  Reuben T. 108, 133
  William Alexander 108
THOMAS
  ___ 37
  Ann C. 96
  Barbara (___) 37
  Barbara Watts 37

THOMAS (cont.)
  Benjamin 56
  C. M. 97
  Catherine M. 96, 97
  Eliza (___) 96
  Eliza F. 96
  Elizabeth (___) 56
  Esterline V. 96
  George 68, 104
  George S. 96
  George T. 98, 99, 100, 101
  James 25, 28, 42, 64, 75
  James P. 96
  Jesse 31, 32
  Jessey 56
  John 19, 31, 37, 56, 58, 60
  John Catesby 108
  Larkin 37
  Lucy 56
  Mary (___) 28
  Massey 16, 56
  Reuben 31, 33, 56, 74, 96
  Reuben S. 96
  Robert 120, 122
  Robert A. 96
  Robert S. 106
  Sarah E. 96
  William 56
THOMPSON
  Rev. 32
  Elizabeth Fleming 150
  Francis 90
  Francis J. 104, 128, 129
  Garland 129, 132
  George P. 132
  Hugh N. 129
  Jessey 4
  John 8, 57, 90, 102, 123, 129, 130, 150
  Kitty W. 148
  Mary (___) 68
  Mildred 8
  Philip R. 8, 90, 141
  Richard 101, 102
  Sarah 90
  Susannah (___) 141
  William 8, 11, 49

THORN
  Barton 73, 77
  Peregrine 73
THORNHILL
  Bryant 8, 32, 33, 40
  Charles Morgan 40
  Elizabeth (___) 40
  John 32, 53
  Joseph 18, 32, 40, 41
  Leanna (___) 8
  Lucy 36, 55
  Lucy (___) 53
  Morgan 79
  Reuben 32, 40
  Thomas 40
  Thomson (___) 32
  William 32
THORNTON
  Ann (___) 8
  Anthony 25
  Benjamin 76
  Elizabeth 103
  Francis 8, 54
  Jane 103
  John 8, 30, 54, 103
  Luke 27
  Mary 57
  Mary F. 103
  Peter Presley 51
  Philip 142
  William 8, 22, 30
THRELKELD (THRELKHELD, THRELDKILL, THREDKELL)
  Daniel 134
  Elizabeth (___) 134
  Henry 17, 25
  James 88
  John 17, 48
  Mary 17
  Sarah 17
  Stephen 68
  William 79, 80
THRIFT, George N. 106
THROCKMORTON
  Robert 2, 11, 14
  Robert, Jr. 9
THURSTON
  Ann 73
  Lucy Mary 73
  Mary 73

THURSTON (cont.)
  William P. 78
  William Plummer 73
TIBBOO, John 37
TILLERY, Joshaway 7
TINSLEY (TINDSLEY)
  David 39
  Edward 33, 66
  Elizabeth (___) 80
  Henry 124, 125, 126
  John 55
  William 80, 124
  Willis 125
TODD
  Lucy 68
  Samuel 56
TOLES (See TOWLES), Henry 31
TOMLINSON, George 43
TOMPKINS, John 9
TONGUE
  Johuze 129
  Mary G. (___) 146
TOOL, William 37
TOWLES (See TOLES)
  ___ 9
  ___ (___) 37
  Ann 46
  Arthur 102
  Elizabeth 28
  Fanny 59
  Frances 46
  George 101, 102, 103
  Henry 37, 46, 47, 57, 58, 64, 72
  James M. 102
  Jane 46
  John W. 101, 102
  Joseph 3, 46, 102
  Judith 101
  Margary (___) 31
  Mary 46, 88
  Oliver 46
  Robert 46
  Sarah 46
  Sarah H. 101
  Stokaly 31
  William 46, 101, 102
TRASCEY, Samuel 64
TRECLEY, Ann 37
TRIPLETT
  E. 88

TRIPLETT (cont.)
  Frances 23
  George 23
  Hannah 23
  Hannah (___) 23, 34
  Jean 23
  John 23, 41, 57, 78
  Milley 23
  Peter 23
  Robert 90
  Thomas 2, 3, 23, 29, 35, 100
TUCKER
  John 88
  Moses 88
  Reuben 88
TUCKES (?TUCKER), Moses 88
TULLEY, Alexander 11
TUREMAN
  Elener (___) 42
  George 2
  Ignatius 42, 44
  Lucy 42
  Robert 2
  Susanah 42
TURNER
  Benjamin 17
  George 88
  J. G., Jr. 98
  Jeremiah 45, 54
  John 11
  John Bacar 38
  Judith (___) 54
  Mary (___) 45
  Nathan 54
  Rebacah (___) 38
  Richard 46, 54
  Roddy 45
  Zachariah, Jr. 99
  Zepkaniah 133
TURNHAM, John 32, 79
TUTT
  Albert 103
  Ann (___) 75
  Archibald 5, 98, 126
  Benjamin 40, 55, 75
  Betty 5
  Charles 22
  Edward E. 153
  Elizabeth 66
  Gabriel 55, 77

TUTT (cont.)
  Hansford 54, 75
  Isabella (___) 54
  James 5, 16, 39, 55, 58, 75, 76, 89
  James, Jr. 9
  John 11, 12, 48, 66, 72, 88
  Lewis 54, 55, 75, 153
  Mary 5, 75
  Mary Connor 153
  Mildred (___) 153
  Mille 75
  Million 5
  Richard 5, 16, 65, 75, 153
  Richard E. 103
  Richard I. 120
TWYMAN
  Anthony 120
  Frances H. 113
  Frances H. (___) 104
  William 75, 77, 124
  William H. 104, 113

U

UNDERWOOD
  Elizabeth 9
  Ellen (___) 12, 13
  Elonder (___) 8
  Francis 9
  Jael 12
  Jail 13
  Jaley 9
  John 62
  Jonathan 19
  Lot(-t) 9, 13
  Margaret (___) 17
  Mary 9
  Mary (___) 9
  Reuben 26
  William 5, 6, 9, 12, 13, 14
UTTERBACH, Joseph 58
UTZ
  ___ 12
  Adam 59, 77, 84
  Daniel 77, 84
  Ephraim 82
  George 7, 12, 77, 84

UTZ (cont.)
  Michael 35, 77, 78, 84
  Michael, Jr. 84
  Susanna 77

V

VAN VEVER (See BANBEVER)
VAUGHAN
  Albert 129
  Almond Burgess 129
  Eve (___) 129
  Fanny (___) 129
  Frances 129
  Henry 129
  Jacob 13
  Jael (___) 129
  Jane 129
  Jefferson 129
  Jeremiah 129
  Joel 129
  John 98
  Juliett Ann 129
  Mary 129
  Molly (___) 129
  Mordecai 129
  Russell 128
  Sarah 129
  William 58, 89
  William R. 114
VAUGHT, Simon 41
VAWTER
  Bartholomew 21
  Frances 68
  Frankey (___) 83
  Richard 18
  Russell 59, 65
VERNON
  Lussy 39
  Richard 9, 11, 39, 65, 79
  Sarah 39
VINSON, Rufus K. 94
VOSS
  Benjamin F. 89
  Bob B. 89
  Bob S. 89
  Edward 29
  Susan F. 89
  William E. 89

VOUGHT, Christian 17
VOWLES, James 72

W

WADKINS, Edward 16
WAGGONER, Greensby 42
WALDEN
  Eliza A. 114
  Fannie E. 114, 115
  Thomas 103
  Thomas P. 114, 115
WALE, Lawson 89
WALKE, Merry 67
WALKER
  ___ 11
  Ann (___) 17
  Benjamin 16
  Charles 67
  Edward 17, 18
  Elizabeth 16, 17, 109
  Henry 125
  Hugh 77
  Isabel 16
  James 17, 67
  James, Jr. 81
  John 16, 17, 20, 39, 106, 109, 118, 123, 124, 125
  John, Jr. 125
  Lucy W. 109
  Martha E. 109
  Mary 16
  Merry 17, 57
  Thomas 8
  Thomas G. 109
  William 9, 10, 14, 17, 20, 30, 68, 71, 106, 109
WALL
  Andrew Jackson 92
  Ann 63
  Armistead 133
  Isaac 70, 89
  Jacob 81
  William 51, 129
  Zachariah 54, 57, 62, 64, 66
WALLACE
  Dr. ___ 13
  John 5
  Michael 125

WALLACE (cont.)
  William 56
  William, Jr. 129
WALLE
  Ann 81
  Francis 70
  Zachariah 58
WALLER, Ann (___) 21
WALLIS
  John 37
  Mildred Walker 153
  William 153
WALLS, William 12
WARD
  ___ 28
  Anna 79
  Anne 83
  Anne (___) 83
  Caty 19
  Elisabeth 19
  Henry 51, 74
  Jacob 65, 67, 83, 84
  John 83
  Judah 83
  Lucy 19, 43
  Margaret 19, 26
  Margaret (___) 19
  Mitchell 83
  Patty 65
  Reuben G. 103
  Richard 19, 20
  Robert G. 90, 104,
    109, 123, 129
  Sarah (___) 20
  Thomas 65
  William 83
  William H. 92, 96
WARK, Robert G. 106
WARRAN, Robert 17
WASH, Mary 27
WASHBURN (WASHBOURN(-E))
  Eley 26
  Ely 61
  Haney (___) 61
  John 26, 29
  Lewis 26
  Lucy (___) 61
  Reuben 16
  Susannah (___) 26
  Thomas 61, 63, 71
WATERS
  Elias 132

WATERS (cont.)
  George 132, 133
  John 63
WATKINS
  Edward 2, 5, 6, 16,
    26, 28, 29, 33, 51,
    65, 66, 68
  Sarah (___) 66
WATSON
  Benjamin 131
  James G. 131
  Sally (___) 131
  Sarah 91
  William 48
WATTE, William 41
WATTS
  Anne (___) 80
  Barnard 80
  Barnett 48
  Benjamin 80, 81
  Frances (___) 29, 48
  Frederick 30, 37
  Isabel (___) 37
  Jacob 80
  James 80
  Joel 37
  John 48, 80
  Julius 48
  Thomas 43, 80
  Thomas, Jr. 48
  William 13, 16, 33,
    38, 47, 48, 50
WAUGH
  Alexander 33, 39, 61,
    75, 77
  John 55
  Richard 28, 53, 66
WAYLAND
  Adam 10, 12, 20, 38,
    49, 59, 69
  Anney 69
  Elizabeth 38
  Hannah 59, 69
  Henry 53
  James E. 107
  John 18, 38, 49, 69
  John, Jr. 35, 82
  Joshua 69
  Lewis 49, 69
WAYMAN
  Henry 78
  Joseph 61

WEALKEY, John 32
WEATHERALL (WEATHERELL)
  Jane (___) 118, 119
  John 18
  William 118, 119
WEAVER
  Daniel 82
  John 20, 83
  Matthew 83
WEBER, John, Sr. 78
WEEKLEY
  Jacob 4
  John 4
WEEKS
  Ben 62
  Elizabeth 44
WELCH
  Nathaniel 79
  Thomas 98
  Thomas N. 99
WETHERALL (WITHERALL)
  Ann(-e) 28, 37
  George 4, 6, 16, 25,
    28, 31, 36, 37, 42,
    75, 123
  Jane 127
  John 37
  Lenard 119
  Mary 28, 37
  William H. 119
WETMORE
  Octavia T. (___) 113
  Thomas B. 113
WEVER, John 48
WHARTON
  Alexander 131
  Benjamin 128
  John 28, 37, 53, 66,
    83, 84, 109
  John T. M. 106
  Leonard 95
  Lucinda (___) 106
  Susan Walker 106
  Thomas 106
  Thomas W. 130
WHEATLEY
  Garland T. 101
  George J. 106
  James 64
  Lawson 98
  Sarah 106
  Thornton 154

WHIGHTHEAD, James 49
WHITE
  Abbott 5
  Ann (___) 64
  Anne (___) 36
  Armistead 27, 34, 75
  Daniel 4, 64, 80
  George E. 97
  Henry 80
  James 6, 32
  Jeremiah 80
  Jno. 71
  John 53, 64, 80, 81
  John A. 89
  Jonathan 64
  Polly 80
  Presley J. 89
  Presly 5, 27
  Rachel 64
  Samuel 32
  Susannah 64
  William 64
WHITEHEAD
  James 40, 48, 80
  John 79
WHITEN, Ann (___) 28
WHITING, Harriet (___) 93
WHITTEN
  Anne 32
  William 32
WIGINTON (WIGGINTON, WIGGINGTON)
  ___ 19, 66
  Benjamin 92
  Edmonia 92
  Elizabeth (___) 154
  John 15, 16, 20, 21, 43, 44, 47, 51, 56, 60
  John, Sr. 154
  Richard Y. 84
  Richard Young 15, 21, 25, 51
  Sallie 94
  Sally 92
  Susan 92, 94
WIGLESWORTH, John 47
WILAND, Adam 7
WILEY
  Allen 10
  Edward 89

WILEY (cont.)
  Isaac 83
  John 83, 84
  Martha 83
  Thomas 83
  Vincent 83
WILHITE, Mildred (___) 54
WILHOIT(-E)
  Daniel 78
  Edward 89
  Elisabeth 17
  Gabriel 31, 89
  Jacob 9
  Jessee 48
  Joel 48
  John 18, 49, 71, 82, 94
  Lewis 48, 52, 82
  Mary 82
  Mary (___) 49
  Matthias 7, 11
  Moses 49, 94
  N. 89
  Nancy (___) 130
  Nicholas 18, 31, 32, 36, 41
  Samuel 94
  Susannah 94
  Tobias 31, 48
  William 48
WILKERSON, Robert 76
WILLETT, Richard 89
WILLIAMS
  Alice Grimes 153
  Ann 23
  Ann (___) 75
  Clayton 23
  E. 97, 104
  Edward 91
  Elizabeth 38, 80
  James 5, 23, 39, 51, 58, 59, 63, 74, 80, 82, 101, 132
  John 11, 16, 18, 21, 22, 23, 47, 63, 82, 90
  Lucy 23, 39
  Lucy (___) 66
  Mary 51, 63
  Paul 74, 75
  Philip 23, 51, 59

WILLIAMS (cont.)
  Robert 90
  Samuel 23
  Sarah 21, 80
  Sarah (___) 74
  Susanna 51, 63
  Susannah (___) 21
  William 2, 5, 11, 13, 16, 23, 39, 51, 149
  William C. 58, 153
  William Clayton 51
  Zepheniah 90
WILLIAMSON
  Margaret 12
  Margreat (___) 11
  Thomas 10, 11, 12
  William 11
WILLIS
  ___ 9
  Francis 75
  Henry 54
  James 48
  John 55
  Joshua 44, 79
  William 55, 60, 61
WILLSON
  Alexander 63
  Isaac 63
WILLYS, John 36
WILSON
  Edward 17
  James 65
  Maggrater (___) 65
  Sally 65
  Tapley 52
WINE, Daniel 114
WINSTON
  Isaac 103, 108
  James M. T. 108
  Walter C. 103, 108
WISECARVER
  Herman 71
  Tilman 71
WISWELL, Margaret (___) 70
WITHERALL (See WETHERALL)
WITHERS
  Emily (___) 143
  James 59, 65, 76
  Pickett 143
WOOD(-S)
  ___ 9

WOOD(-S) (cont.)
  Alias (____) 44
  Alice 106, 107, 108
  Betty 25
  Edward 60
  Eliza 25
  Elizabeth 2
  Elizabeth (____) 124, 125
  James 11, 15, 25, 77, 123, 124
  James, Jr. 25
  Jane 123, 124
  Jane S. 123, 125, 126
  John 108
  John Scott 25, 33, 34, 63, 77
  Joseph 2, 25, 34, 89, 125
  Joseph, Jr. 25
  Joseph, Sr. 126
  Judith 25, 77
  Latney M. 108
  Lewis 108, 117
  Lucy 124
  Lucy M. 126
  Margaret 73
  Martha 126
  Mary 2, 123
  Mary (____) 25
  Mary C. 126
  Patsey 124, 125
  Peter 26, 60
  Polly 124, 125
  Rebecca (____) 124, 125
  Sally 124
  Samuel 44, 45
  Sarah E. 126
  Thomas 123, 124, 125, 126
  William 126
WOODFORD, Jacob 5
WOODWARD, William 89
WOOLFENBARGO (WOOLFEN-BERGER)
  Catharine 60
  Eliza 60
  Elizabeth (____) 60
  Frederick 60
  George 60, 61, 78

WOOLFENBARGO (cont.)
  Hannah 60
  John 60, 78
  Philip 60
  Sally 60
WRENN, Susan C. (____) 142
WRIGHT
  Alexander 70
  Ann (____) 40
  Ezekiel 49
  Howard 121
  Jno 128
  John 49, 61
  John, Sr. 106
  John T. 106
  Joseph 17
  Milley (____) 57
  Morgan 40
  Polly (____) 124
  Richard 49, 50
  Robert 15, 89
  Sarah (____) 49
  Thomas 10, 16, 21, 22, 40, 48, 49, 66, 71, 79
  Walter 17
  William 17, 41, 49, 124, 125
  Winfield 124

Y

YAGER
  Absolom 36
  Adam 31, 32
  Benjamin 36
  Cornelius 36
  Elijah 36
  Elizabeth 37
  Eve 37
  Frederick 36
  Godfrey 36, 69
  Jessee 36
  John 31, 36, 55
  Michael 31, 32, 58
  Mordecai 122
  Nicholas 36, 41
  Peggy 36
  Rosanna 36
  Sarah 83
  Sarah (____) 83

YAGER (cont.)
  Solomon 36
  Susanna 36
YANCEY
  Ann 154
  Benjamin M. 94
  Birkett Garland 54
  Charles 17, 69, 79, 80, 92, 154
  Charles Major 154
  Co___ 92
  Edward 92
  Eleanor 54
  Eliza 89
  Elizabeth 69
  Elizabeth (____) 79
  George 54
  Henrietta (____) 55
  James 69, 70
  James M. 92
  John 69
  John, Jr. 40
  Judith (____) 15
  Kaleia 154
  Lewis 5, 16, 54, 55, 69
  Lewis, Jr. 47
  Lewis D. 75
  Lewis Davis 69
  Lucy 54
  Major 154
  Nancy 54
  Philemon 69, 74
  Richard 5, 15, 20, 24, 55, 69, 71, 76
  Robert 18, 69, 70
  Sallie 92
  Sarah (Mitchell) 154
  Susan M. 92
  Susan T. 94
  Thomas 54, 80, 154
  William 80, 89, 92, 154
  Willie 92, 94
  Winifred 69
  Winifred (____) 54
YATES
  Benjamin M. 112
  Elizabeth 62
  George 63, 70
  John 70, 71
  Lawrence Catlett 70

YATES (cont.)
  Mary (___) 70, 81
  O. H. 112
  Paul 114
  Richard 89
  Thomas 8, 41
  William 70, 81
YEAGER
  Godfrey 15, 38
  James 79
  Jeriah 28
  Mich 123
YEAMAN, John 13
YOUNG
  Benjamin 147
  Elizabeth (___) 50
  Franklin M. 107
  John 7, 50
  John M. 107
  Mary (___) 15, 147
  Richard 15, 16
YOWELL
  Christopher 22
  David 32, 128
  James 22, 31, 32, 37
  John 3, 31, 32, 38
  Mary (___) 60
  Samuel 31, 32
  Sarah (___) 74

Z

ZACHARY
  Benjamin 40, 57, 79
  John 9, 66
  John, Jr. 57
ZACKARY, William 32,
    57, 67
ZIGLER (ZIGLAR)
  Ann (___) 7
  Christopher 7
  James B. 62
  Leonard 7
  Leond 61
  Sarah Underwood 13
ZIMMERMAN
  Christopher 18, 30,
    33, 35
  F. 62
  Frederick 5, 10, 13,
    30, 49, 50
  Judith (___) 76
  Mary 89
  Michael 32
  Reuben 33, 40, 41,
    49, 73, 77, 80, 89

www.ingramcontent.com/pod-product-compliance
Lightning Source LLC
LaVergne TN
LVHW091546060526
838200LV00036B/719